DOROTHY'S WORLD

DOROTHY'S WORLD

Childhood
in Sabine Bottom
1902-1910

Dorothy Howard

PRENTICE-HALL, INC., Englewood Cliffs, New Jersey

Dorothy's World: Childhood in Sabine Bottom, 1902-1910
by Dorothy Howard

Design: Hal Siegel

Printed in the United States of America

Prentice-Hall International, Inc., London
Prentice-Hall of Australia, Pty. Ltd., Sydney
Prentice-Hall of Canada, Ltd., Toronto
Prentice-Hall of India Private Ltd., New Delhi
Prentice-Hall of Japan, Inc., Tokyo
Prentice-Hall of Southeast Asia Pte. Ltd., Singapore
Whitehall Books Limited, Wellington, New Zealand

10 9 8 7 6 5 4 3 2 1

Library of Congress Cataloging in Publication Data

Howard, Dorothy
  Dorothy's world.

  1. Howard, Dorothy   2. Rains County,
Texas—Social life and customs. 3. Children in Texas.
4. Folklorists—Biography. I. Title.
GR55.H69A33   398.2'092'4 [B]   76-48735
ISBN 0-13-218602-0

Dedicated to
thousands of children in the
United States, Australia,
and Mexico who taught
Dorothy who she was;
and especially to
Ingrid
who, at the age
of three, taught
Sllim Yarg Ythorod
how to write a book.

CONTENTS

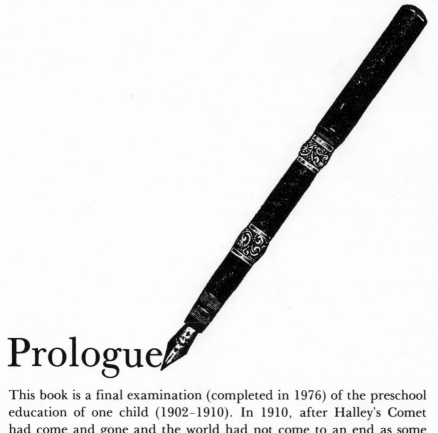

Prologue

This book is a final examination (completed in 1976) of the preschool education of one child (1902-1910). In 1910, after Halley's Comet had come and gone and the world had not come to an end as some people in Sabine Bottom had predicted, the Mills family moved to Lone Oak in Hunt County. There Dorothy's schooldays began when she was eight years old. Yet the most important phase of her education had already happened on a farm in Rains County, five miles south of Point—where the trains stopped—and midway between Woosley Schoolhouse and Flats Schoolhouse just north of Sabine River.

The central purpose of this book is to document the preschool learning of one child: (1) what the child learned, (2) how, (3) where, (4) when, and (5) why or what for, in a way that has not been done before. This is a personal memoir, a social document, and a study in what is now fashionably termed "the cognitive process" but which Dorothy prefers to think of as "reflective aspects of rationality" (Immanuel Kant's term in his *Critique of Practical Reason*).

The central purpose determined the organization. "The Round, Round World" attempts to describe and explain the context or "learning environment" of the lore—not an adult's preconditioned, static view of exteriors but a child's expanding, interior view of an exterior, sensed world related to invisible worlds of the mind created by her responses to language, spoken and written. Each new day necessitated a reordering of her cosmos. Each new day, as she lived it, had to be incorporated into an unending tale.

Among these worlds of the mind are those seen, heard, and felt through the words and songs of Grandma Gray, Uncle Tom, Aunt Lizzie, Mama, Papa, and the neighbors in Sabine Bottom, people whose families had migrated to Texas from the Carolinas, Tennessee, Mississippi, and other states immediately before or after the Civil War, bringing with them traditional language, history, and customs extending backward in time to Colonial America and to European forebears. Those worlds evolved and located themselves on a mosaic mind-map in relation to the real world of Sabine Bottom which happened anew each day when the sun rose.

The "Catalogues" list and describe the content of the preschool curriculum (work and play) of one child in one specific period in history in one specific geographic area and culture, and they suggest a microcosm of child-life in Colonial and rural America.

This book is more than a memoir. But as a memoir, it is an honest one—as honest as a mind can make it.

Dorothy does not vouch for absolute, documentable, objective fact in this book. The relationship between fact and truth can be demonstrated by three stories: the snake story, the marriage ceremony, and Grandma Gray's eunuchs.

Was the snake a big diamondback rattler, a copperhead, or a little ground rattler, coiled under a keg by the sorghum mill that warm, spring Sunday afternoon, unanchored on memory's calendar? Dorothy and her two older sisters agree: (1) there *was* a snake, (2) coiled, (3) under a keg—turned down. They disagree on: (1) the kind of a snake it was, and (2) who moved the keg—Mama or the oldest sister. Dorothy remembers a little ground rattler, his beady eyes rising out of his coiled body pursuing a forked, red tongue quivering forward and upward to strike.

Was it a double wedding or a single wedding (on a rainy April Sunday afternoon) that took place at the front gate while Papa held a black umbrella over the preacher performing the ceremony and Mama and the children stood in the front door watching. The oldest sister (then ten years old) and Little Brother (two) do not remember the wedding. Dorothy and the middle sister *do* remember the wedding and agree on all details except two. The sister remembers (1) a double wedding, (2) with Papa and the preacher standing between two buggies, tops up, each buggy holding a bride and groom sitting side by side. Dorothy remembers (1) one buggy holding one bride and groom, (2) with Papa and the preacher standing between the gate and the buggy. She remembers the red, red rose on the bride's straw sailor hat as she sat in the gloom beside her groom. And she remembers the blue eyes in the thin, pale face of the slender young groom who knocked at the front door to ask for the preacher (Sunday dinner guest). Records in the Rains County Clerk's office in Emory might produce circumstantial evidence to validate Dorothy's memory or her sister's. But documents never can gainsay the inner reality established by memory patterned for seventy years.

Emotional response to a moment caught and held by memory is a thread spun to hold, unbroken, in all future experiences as they are woven into a developing pattern. For example: When Dorothy was seven, she first met the word "eunuch" in the Bible as she read to her Grandma Gray. She asked for a pronunciation and a definition. (Dorothy half-knew about an operation performed on pigs to make meat animals of them. She had heard the pigs squeal in pain and had seen the blood on the men's clothes when they came from the pens.) The words of Grandma's embarrassed answer were soon forgotten. But the embarrassment never. The embarrassment (the emotional response) was woven into what Dorothy half-knew about the process of castration, though not the why. She concluded that a eunuch was a human male operated on and eaten. She knew that most boy calves, boy pigs, and roosters became meat animals. Upon learning that human boys were also operated on and eaten, she felt great compassion for the eunuchs in the Bible and great fear for Little Brother. Coincident with the fear for Little Brother, however, was the comforting knowledge that she was a girl child.

When Dorothy went to college, she learned more about eunuchs from reading about Mardian (in Shakespeare's "Anthony and Cleopatra"), whipped by Cleopatra for bringing bad news. But the accumulation of more factual information, she says, has not broken that old thread of fear and compassion for the human male. Instead, it grows stronger as she grows older, witnessing bigger, more monstrous war machines eat up more and more fattened boy babies. Grandma Gray and Dorothy could not know what was being taught and learned in that initial lesson on eunuchs.

There was a child went forth every day,
And the first object he looked upon, that
object he became,
And that object became part of him for
the day or a certain part of the day,
Or for many years or stretching cycles of
years.

Walt Whitman
(*"There Was a Child Went Forth"*,
written 1855-1871)

DOROTHY'S WORLD

The Round, Round World

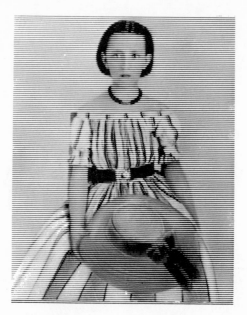

The Thinking Post

The world she was leaving was round. That she knew. That she had known since she was five. Not because the words and pictures in her sisters' geography book told her so—though they had. Not because Papa who taught the Woosley School had told her so—though he had. But because she saw it with her eyes every day, heard it with her ears, and felt it blow from the north, south, east, or west when she sat on the garden corner fence post, on the flat, round top and swiveled in a circle, her buttocks the axis of a round, flat world.

Now, on her eighth birthday, she knew for a fact that she soon would be leaving. Papa and Mama both said so. Mama had bought gingham and made her school dresses. Papa wanted to sell the farm and buy a house in Lone Oak. He had made two trips to Lone Oak and came home to describe the marvels of that wondrous world.

Now, sitting on her Thinking Post at the far corner of the garden, next to the road, she tried to think about Lone Oak—beyond Sabine Bottom, farther than Point or Emory (where she had been), not as far as Dallas (where the aunts and city cousins lived). But her mind refused to leave Sabine Bottom.

The rim of the world was a fringe of trees following Shuffle Creek south, to join Sabine River winding its way westward around Flats

2

Schoolhouse, then northward toward its headwaters. She saw the fringe of trees wander away from the River north of Woosley and bend eastward back to the Lon Hughey house half-hidden in the trees on Shuffle Creek.

Morning wood smoke rose from all the houses in Sabine Bottom. Mrs. Hughey's kitchen stovepipe smoke disappeared in the light of the rising sun. But in the south (from the Malloy and Harlan houses), in the west (from the Driggers', Irwins', and Pollards'), and in the north (from the Calloways' and McKeithens') smoke ribbons curled into a blue sky.

She did not want to leave the people living in those houses, the people who traveled that road to meet in neighborhood gatherings to work, play, worship, and grieve together. From her Thinking Post she had watched those neighbors pass by. On horseback. On foot. In buggies, surreys, and wagons. And she had seen strangers come and go, once some people stopped at the house to water the boiling radiator of a red automobile that had set the cows and horses wild in the pastures.

She had longed to follow those strangers to mysterious worlds she had never seen. But today she clung to the neighbors who came to Woosley to church and Sunday school services and Sunday school picnics in the nearby oak grove, the same people who came to Flats for camp meeting and singing school under a brush arbor, to the River bank south of Flats for fishing and fish-fries, and on Sunday afternoons came walking up and down the road for neighborly visits.

She remembered the winter Papa and Mama and the children, one by one, had smallpox. From a window she watched Mr. Malloy and Mr. Harlan and his boys coming up the road to take care of the stock and farmwork while Papa was sick. And she saw Mrs. Malloy and Polly bringing cooked food which they left on the front gallery because the yellow flag was flying at the front gate. She remembered watching Mama walk down the south road and disappear in the twilight, on her way to sit up all night with Polly Malloy, sick with typhoid.

Again, she saw, in early morning, Mr. Malloy coming carrying his toolbox to help Papa make five coffins for the five little children burned to death in the farmhouse beyond Reader Creek. And the same day, in midmorning, after Mama had washed and ironed two little white dresses, Mama—carrying the dresses—and Mrs. Irwin rode away in the buggy down the Emory road to Mrs. Hughey's house to help bathe and lay out the dead children.

Looking south again, she remembered the cyclone that blew the Malloy house away (while the family was safe in the stormhouse) and set it down in the wheat field. Afterward, all the men in Sabine Bottom came with teams of horses and mules and four ox teams hauling loads of logs. All day she watched the men work. By nightfall the house had been mounted on logs, hitched to a dozen horses and mules, rolled on its log rollers back to its foundations, and put up into place on an inclined plane made of other logs. The next morning smoke rose again from Mrs. Malloy's kitchen stovepipe.

A happy time in her box of memories was threshing season. Like birthdays and Christmas, as soon as it was over, she could retrieve the memory in anticipation of its return next year. On this, her eighth birthday, all threshing seasons rolled into one. Neighbor families — men, women, and children — gathered for the day, and from day to day moved from one farm to another until all the wheat and oats on all the farms had been threshed, the grain all stored in barn bins ready for mill or winter feed for the stock, and the straw stacks piled in mountains in the middle of fields — intended feed for stock and unintended (and dangerous) play place for children.

In the afternoon, when the meal was over and the babies and youngest children were asleep on pallets, the older children took to pastures, woods, and road, led by the oldest, followed by the younger ones, whimpering. Once out of sight of the house and out of hearing from the fields, the older boys and girls decided on the game — always "Hide and Seek" for Threshing Day — and established the rules for the day. The rules were determined by the number, age, and sex of players and the terrain (each farm necessitated specific rules).

On the Mills farm, "home base" was a tree in the woods east of the barn. The boundaries were Shuffle Creek on the east, Point Road on the west, the Emory road on the north, and the Malloy fence line on the south. Safety rules were set to protect the youngest players: (1) no hiding within fifty yards of the pool (the fifty yards were stepped off and lines drawn on the ground); (2) no hiding in the pigpens; (3) no hiding in the cow pasture. In addition, each small child became a charge of an older playmate who taught it to hide and protected it from danger: snakes, thorns, prickly pears, wasps, yellow jackets, kicking and biting horses and mules, cows with sharp horns, and vicious sows. When Dorothy had learned how to hide and run from home base and no longer wanted to be protected, she kicked her sisters on the shins or hit them with sticks and ran away.

The game boundaries on the Mills farm required "It" to count to one million by tens (keeping count by a mark on the ground for every one thousand). By her sixth birthday, Dorothy could count and could shout:

> *Bushel of wheat and bushel of rye*
> *All not hid, holler aye.*

and after a silence:

> *Bushel of wheat and bushel of clover*
> *All not hid, can't hide over.*
> *All within ten feet of my base ARE CAUGHT.*
> *Here I come. Both eyes open.*

An hour could go by before all players were caught or "in free." Meanwhile, players "in" and waiting shouted misleading hints to throw "It" off course. Or they began playing other games to while away the time: "Hull Gull," "William Tremble Toe," or "Club Fist."

On this, her eighth birthday, Dorothy wanted to remember all the games she knew. Some, her sisters had learned at school and had taught her. Others were games Grandma Gray had played as a little girl in Holly Springs, Mississippi, and had taught her. Still others were games she and Little Brother had made up. But always when neighbor families gathered, the men, women, and children separated into three groups and the children played games.

On Sunday afternoon visits the men took walks across the fields and sat together on a log or squatted in a circle to talk about crops, hunting, fishing, road-grading, and politics and to spit tobacco juice between fingers holding whiskers apart. The women sat together on the gallery, fanning themselves and their babies with palmetto and turkey-wing fans while they talked quilt and dress patterns, cures, gardening, canning, and cooking and whispered behind their fans. Dorothy sometimes hid behind Mama's chair or under the gallery steps hoping to hear words emerge from the whispers. And sometimes she followed Papa and the neighbor men, stepping in Papa's footsteps and listening.

Dorothy and her sisters were forbidden to play with dolls or to play games on Sunday. However, they were allowed to take walks in the woods and fields and on the road. And when they were out of sight and hearing of Mama and Papa, they continued play—nameless, and therefore unforbidden. Favorite walks were "up the road" toward Point and "down the road" toward the River (with hopes of seeing strangers from other worlds beyond Sabine Bottom).

Perhaps they would see the gypsies, who came (nobody knew when to expect them) from the east up the Emory road in wooden covered wagons painted in bright colors, drawn by bony horses — dark, fierce men, women, and children wearing earrings, beads, bracelets, and bright-colored, dirty clothes. The men walked beside the wagons in which the women and children rode until they stopped at a farmyard gate. Then the women came to the front door and spoke in a strange voice to sell a wire broom holder or a match-box holder they had made, while the children hid in the orchards or berry patches to steal fruit and while the men robbed the barn for food for their horses and the smokehouses and henhouses for ham, bacon, and chickens. Gypsies stole children too, so it was said. When Dorothy saw gypsies coming, she ran fast to tell Mama and Papa. Nobody knew where they came from and nobody knew where they were going. They vanished across the River bridge into the woods of Van Zandt County.

Dorothy did not think of the Peddler as a stranger. He was the handsome, dark, young man who came every spring, summer, and autumn. He had a name, though he was always called "the Peddler." Mama would say, "It's about time for the Peddler" and make out her list of things to buy and trade: shoelaces, cinnamon, three yards of blue dimity, five of cotton checks, in trade for the old Rhode Island Red rooster, two fryers, two pounds of butter, and two dozen eggs. Each morning after Mama said, "It's about time for the Peddler," Dorothy ran to the Thinking Post to watch for him. He came from Point. Her first glimpse was his red vest, after he had passed the Calloways' and was halfway down the road toward the Driggers'. He walked beside his covered wagon.

She ran to the house to tell Mama, then to the front gate to wait for his coming. And as she waited, she knew exactly what was going to happen — every happy thing. As soon as the Peddler saw her, he called and smiled, his black eyes sparkling and white teeth shining in a dark face. By the time Mama reached the front gate, he had stopped the wagon and was opening all the little doors on either side to reveal his merchandise: on one side, bolts of gingham, calico, cotton checks, lawn, laces (both edging and insertion), ribbons (both velvet and satin — blue, pink, yellow, moss green, and black); on the other side, spices, medicine (for people and animals), axle grease, and candy.

The Peddler stopped smiling as he and Mama traded. But after Dorothy had helped carry the shoelaces and dimity to the house and the butter and eggs back to the Peddler (while Mama carried the old rooster and two fryers by their legs tied together), the Peddler smiled again as he put the chickens in wooden-slatted coops slung under the wagon and the butter and eggs in covered buckets hanging beside the coops. Dorothy waited for him to close all the little trap doors because she knew that the candy door would be the last and that, before he closed it, he would hand her two sticks of striped peppermint candy, one for her and one for Little Brother. She must remember to say — before Mama prompted her — "I'm much obliged."

Sitting on her Thinking Post, she sucked her stick of candy, watched the Peddler's wagon stop at the Malloys', at the Harlans', and disappear before it crossed the River bridge into Van Zandt.

Once a year, from Van Zandt County, hard-riding cattlemen rode by with their spurs jingling, shouting as they drove herds of cattle across the bridge and headed them north toward Point. Those cattlemen were nameless. But the drivers of the ox wagons hauling logs to the sawmill beyond Shuffle Creek had names: Ace, Buck, Doug, Hod; and the oxen had names: Mabel, Spur, Joe, and Beck.

When the mill was running, the empty log wagons rumbled up the Emory road early in the morning and turned south to the River. When Dorothy heard the crack of the driver's blacksnake whip and shouts of "gee" and "haw," she ran to the Thinking Post to be ready to say "Good morning" and to watch the swaying oxen slowly disappear in River woods, the driver walking beside the wagon. Most of the day she waited for the return. By midafternoon the sounds of the whip and driver's shouts could be heard before the wagons came into view. Between the first sound and the first glimpse, she held her breath, then jumped down into the road and ran to the Malloy Branch bridge to wait, hoping the driver would be Hod. Hod always bowed and swept his hat off as he invited her to ride the logs to the McKeithen corner, where he turned east. Sitting high on a log, she was as tall as Hod walking beside her, talking, chewing tobacco, smiling, joking, and winking his eye as he told her to hurry and grow up so she could go dancing with him.

Hired hands had names too: Sid, Orphus, Grit. Loggers and hired hands came to Sabine Bottom, stayed a month, or two or three or four, then went away. Sometimes they came from "outwest" where they had been cattle hands, sometimes from Arkansas. They often rode in, a bundle of clothes tied behind the saddle and a goose-necked guitar slung beside it.

Wagon trains, of three or four covered wagons, came up the Emory road and stopped to camp for three or four days in the hackberry grove across the road from the farm. They brought men, women, and children from Arkansas, Alabama, and Mississippi, on their way "outwest" to settle land claims. The women washed clothes, using Mama's tubs and washpot, and for three or four days all the clothes lines and bushes and grass were covered with drying clothes. The men mended harness and wagons. And the children, warned not to step on drying clothes, played in the hackberry grove and Mr. Calloway's pasture, searching for sheep sorrel and sour dock, playing "Wolf Over the River" in the road or "Mumblepeg" under the wagons.

When clothes were clean, harness and wagons mended, and horses and mules rested after grazing three or four days on the roadsides (hobbled), Papa helped them load the wagons and gave them hams and slabs of bacon from the smokehouse, bags of flour and cornmeal from the barn loft, and oats for their horses and mules.

Dorothy watched the children climb into the wagons, watched the wagons roll westward and out of sight beyond the Driggers and Irwin farms, longed to go with them, but instead played "Going Out West" with Little Brother for weeks and weeks. They made covered wagons of shoe boxes, with spools for wheels, willow fronds for cover staves, and Papa's old, ragged handkerchiefs for covers. In the wagons they stowed acorns and hackberries, clothespin dolls, and toy dishes. Then, pulling two wagons each (by strings), she and Little Brother traveled west — as far as the Driggers' corner.

They sometimes played "Going to Dallas," where the city cousins and aunts lived, and where they would go some day (Papa said) to see the Dallas Fair. Each summer the city cousins and aunts came visiting, wearing fine city clothes. Dorothy begged to wear socks (instead of stockings) and have bobbed hair like her cousin Eva (her own age). But Papa pounded his fist and shouted: "Confound it! My daughters are going to dress and look like girls!" Aunt Della was Eva's mama. But Aunt Eddie, who taught in the Dallas schools, was not married. Papa called her "a lady in waiting."

Dallas was anchored on Dorothy's mind-map on the other side of the Sabine and beyond the woods (on the other side of the Sabine) and beyond Van Zandt County (on the other side of the woods on the other side of the Sabine). Chicago (where Mr. Searsanroebuck lived) was north of Point and north of Red River (which was north of Point, Papa said). The North Pole was north of Chicago (which was north of Red River which was north of Point)—a pitchfork stuck upright in the snow beside an igloo. The locations of Dallas, Chicago, and the North Pole never changed on Dorothy's mind-map, though she sometimes doubted their realities. Full Christmas stockings and a big package from Chicago (in answer to Mama's letters, spring and fall) verified and reverified the reality of those places and the people who lived there. Mr. Searsanroebuck lived in Chicago in a big red brick house (the picture was in the catalogue) full of dolls, gingham, hats, corsets, shoes, horse collars, hame-strings, and kitchen cabinets. Santa Claus lived in the igloo (the picture was in her sisters' geography book) full of oranges, apples, nuts, candy, and toys, and he tied his reindeer to the North Pole.

Each Christmas and each birthday Dorothy added her new toys to her box of "play pritties" kept under her bed. Each day she counted them and sorted them; and each day, all year long, they remained the same, unless Little Brother had stolen something. But her mind was a box of memories mixed with dreams—a box of people, beasts, and places, visible and invisible; and each day she sought tangible evidence of the reality of her dreams. Each day she read the Bible to Grandma and Grimm's Fairy Tales to Little Brother. And the worlds of the Bible and the fairy tales had to be located on her mind-map in relationship to Sabine Bottom, Chicago, Point, and all the places already there in space and time.

Graveyards were worlds beneath the earth where grandfathers, a grandmother, uncles, aunts, and great, great-grandparents lived. She listened to talk about those worlds while sitting, in twilight, on the floor on the back gallery when Great-Aunt Lizzie and Great-Uncle Tom came for a visit. They and Grandma Gray talked about "the War." As she listened, Dorothy saw Mississippi, Tennessee, South Carolina—three vast wastelands covered with tombstones as far as the eye could see, tombstones belonging to: Uncle Frank Craig, killed in the Battle of Peach Tree Creek near Atlanta; Uncle Bob Nelson, shot through the body and dying slowly, slowly, slowly—it took years for him to die; Grandfather Gray dying slowly of Civil War wounds;

Grandfather Mills, dead of war hardships (for four years, as spy and scout for General Forest's army, he never slept under a roof, winter or summer, except when hospitalized with pneumonia, twice; he came home to die of pneumonia).

When Grandma and Aunt Lizzie sang "Tenting on the Old Camp Ground," Dorothy saw the tents pitched on the banks of Sabine River, and the faces of the dying Confederate soldiers were those of her two dead grandfathers in the tintype pictures in the family albums. She saw their oval-framed faces in the light of camp fires reflected in River water.

The picture of the solemn little girl in Grandma's album was Nancy Leannah Nelson, who lived in Holly Springs before Grandpa Gray married her and turned her into mama's mama and later into Grandma Gray. Now when Dorothy thought of the picture of the little girl, sitting primly, dressed in a candy-striped dress, she saw that little girl sitting on the spring seat of a covered wagon leaving Holly Springs on her way to Texas to become Grandma. And at the same time she saw herself as that little girl sitting on the spring seat of a wagon on her way to Lone Oak, leaving Sabine Bottom, leaving the people, pastures, and woods, leaving all the houses sending wood smoke into the sky. Leaving the house north of the garden where Mama and Grandma cooked breakfast, dinner, and supper, where her sisters made beds and swept floors and Little Brother called to her from the window. Leaving the fields where Papa and Orphus or Sid plowed, and the barn where they fed the stock and milked the cows (the barn silhouetted against dawn or disappearing in dusk).

All day long, on her eighth birthday, trying hard to think about Lone Oak, she instead sorted memories. Lone Oak (Papa said) was larger than Point or Emory (both of which she had seen) but smaller than Dallas (about which she had only heard). She tried to think about the big, red brick schoolhouse (like Mr. Searsanroebuck's house) where her sisters would go to school upstairs and she would go to school downstairs (with strange children whose names she did not know), about the red automobile owned by the town doctor (Papa said), and stores and stores and stores of toys, candy, and ice cream.

Instead she thought of Point: the general store and post office with long wooden counters on either side behind which a clerk stood or climbed a ladder to bring down shoe boxes, bolts of calico or gingham, or a chamber pot from shelves reaching to the ceiling; with candy kegs, nail kegs, and cracker barrels in rows in front of the long counters; with the post office in a back corner—a cage to hold packages and letters that came by train from Aunt Eddie and Mr. Searsanroebuck until the mail carrier could bring them to the people in Sabine Bottom.

She had seen the railroad track cutting Point in two; and the roaring locomotives spewing smoke into the sky and excreting flames as the firemen fed their boilers to make them drag long clack-clacking lines of freight cars and—at last—a caboose with a brakeman leaning from a turret window to wave to her.

But her thoughts refused to fly any farther than Point. Time and time again she had tried to fly with the birds to worlds beyond that fringe of trees. Standing on the Post with arms spread, she had jumped with all her might, flapping wild wings. But time after time she hit the ground hard and squatted over stinging feet. This day she sat all morning unmindful of the hawks swooping down on the Harlan henhouse before rising to soar out of sight over Van Zandt.

The sun slowly brought noon (and coconut cake and ice cream, made with ice Papa brought from Point the day before), and slowly brought afternoon, stretching her shadow farther and farther eastward and slowly shrinking the circle of daylight in Sabine Bottom. Her memories were sorted and stowed away safely. But the dream of Lone Oak confused and eluded her.

She scrambled down from the Thinking Post and ran for the house to her box of "play pritties" under her bed. She could take the box with her to Lone Oak: rag dolls, china dolls, tin tea set, doll beds made of match boxes and shoe boxes, buttons for "Hull Gull," five small stones for "Jackstones," pocketknife, cane-joint beanshooter, and doll rags. Again she sorted and arranged them neatly before gathering dark drove her to the kitchen.

The kitchen was a circle of lamplight. She found her place at the supper table in the center of that circle. And sitting on the long bench between her sisters, she saw a circle of lamp-lit faces disappear into bowed heads while Papa said:

HeavenlyFathergiveusthankfulheartsfortheseandallourblessingsamen.

As she lifted her head, she felt the lamplight on her own face and knew that hers was a part of that circle of faces around that table which Papa and Mama would move to Lone Oak. She knew she could keep her box of "play pritties" under the same bed. She could curl into a tight ball under the covers and go to sleep to dream of finding boxes of jewels in Aladdin's cave.

Veil of Early Memory

The world had not always been round. Not until she could shinny up the garden fence post to sit contemplating, day after day, that never-changing circle of trees—periphery of the blue gutta-percha dome above. Until then she had caught glimpses of its roundness when Papa gave her a piggyback or let her ride astride his neck to protect her bare feet from sandburs or let her climb from his shoulders to the first crotch of the hackberry tree where he held her and forbade her to climb further. Until then she saw, in waking hours, the world at her own eye level: globs of moving people and things, shapeless under a shapeless sky.

Heaven was where she had lived before she was born (Grandma said). Being born was floating down through the clouds like little angels (in pictures on Sunday school cards), flapping tiny wings and trailing long, white dresses. Little Brother (when she saw him for the first time, lying beside Mama in bed, crying) had no wings. Was he crying (she asked Grandma later) because he had lost his wings?

She wanted to remember her own birth—floating down through the clouds. Did it hurt when her wings fell off? Often she asked Mama and Grandma why she could not remember when she was born. But Mama always answered, "You are nothing but a question box from morning 'til night." And Grandma said, "When you are older you will understand."

She could not even remember when she was too little to walk. She crawled with Little Brother, when he crawled on the floor, trying to recapture the memory of herself as a baby-child. But Little Brother crawled, in a sitting position, backward on his hands, pushing with his feet (like a crawfish, Grandma said). And she had crawled forward (Grandma said), on her stomach, before she sat up, by pushing her feet, and sideways by rolling over and over. Later, when she could not remember how she looked, she asked Grandma to show her. But Grandma laughed and said her bones were too old ever to crawl again.

The house where she was born she remembered clearly — the outside of the house. She did not remember living there. In her mind she saw the house (a rent house in which the family lived while the home-house was being repaired and improved), looking at it from the home-house into which the family returned in the spring before she was two in July.

She remembered moving: the furniture piled high on the wagon with its sideboards up and the spring seat anchored on top of the sideboards, high in the sky. She sat beside Papa on the spring seat as they rode along. Clearest in her memory was sitting alone on the spring seat when Papa left her to climb down to open the big gate. Clinging to the seat, she looked down at Papa and the ground so far away, too frightened to cry.

The renters who moved into the rent house (in 1904 Papa said) came in early spring — early enough to plant a crop. They stayed only one year and moved early the following spring. Dorothy remembered their "afflicted" child: a boy with a huge head, helpless body, and dangling arms and hands. All day long he lay in a big wicker baby buggy. And on a summer morning his mother wheeled him down the road, into the yard and into the shade of the hackberry tree where the Mills children played "House" with pieces of broken dishes in rooms designated by lines drawn with a stick in the hard dirt. All morning he lay there, his eyes staring, unseeing. Dorothy remembered.

She tried to play with him by giving him a piece of blue broken dish. She tried to fold his fingers around it so that he could hold it. But when she let go, the dish piece fell to the ground and broke into smaller pieces.

Papa and Mama told her of other happenings while the family lived in the rent house. The summer she was born (1902) was the hottest, dryest summer on record; trees lost all their leaves and crops withered in the fields. The night before she was born Papa went to town to get the doctor for Mama, who was sick. No! it was not typhoid fever. Nor malaria. Nor smallpox. All night and all day (Mama said) the doctor sat under the hackberry tree, chewing tobacco, waiting for Dorothy to be born. Then Mama almost died. But Grandma took care of the baby and of Mama, until she got well.

The next winter and the following winter (Papa said) wild animals, short of food, grew bold enough to approach farmhouses, barns, and pigpens. A mountain lion was killed in the woods. And packs of wolves killed sheep, calves, and pigs in their pens.

In the summer of her first birthday (Papa told her) she went for a midnight walk in the moonlight — alone. Mama was away; she had gone to sit up with a sick neighbor up the west road about three-quarters of a mile. Papa, awakening about midnight, found her cradle empty, soon discovered her tracks in the sandy road and ran as fast as he could, thinking of the wild animals. About a half mile up the road he overtook her. Papa liked to tell that story and always ended it by quoting her first attempts to put words together. She called a waxing or waning moon "Biece-a-moon" (piece of a moon).

During her second winter (Papa told her) packs of hungry wolves came at night again and again to the yard fence, and each time, he sprayed the pack with his shotgun to drive them away. All that she could remember of those nights, when Papa drove the wolves away, was an open doorway — a cold, black hole — with Papa standing in the doorway, against the blackness, and a gun blast.

In a fringe of early memories were the sounds of wolves howling, foxes barking, and panthers screaming, like women screaming in the night woods. Awakened at night by those sounds, she called to Papa, and he told her what they were. Clear in early memory was the hoot owl's "Who, who, who are you?" and the "squeech owl's" screech. But clearest of all was the sound of a shotgun blast.

One shotgun blast in clear memory happened on a summer, moonlit night. While the family sat on the back gallery that warm night, she heard a hoot owl and saw the owl sitting on the roof comb of the henhouse silhouetted against a full moon in the eastern sky. She heard a gun blast, saw the owl disappear, and heard the thud of its body on the ground. Papa had shot many owls off many roof combs on moonless nights as well as in full moon (he said), but *that* night and *that* owl he could not directly remember.

Dorothy's first spanking (for spitting in the churn) was a story which Mama liked to tell. Sometime during her second winter (after the family had moved back to the home-house) it happened. Each day, after churning, the churn was washed, scalded, and set on the back gallery in the sunshine and fresh air. One day Mama discovered two blobs of spit in her clean churn, and assuming that Dorothy was the spitter, spanked her. Another day later, while a neighbor woman visited with Mama in the kitchen and her little boy and Dorothy played on the back gallery, Mama saw the little boy spit in the churn and remembered that on the day of the spanking the little boy had been there. Mama always ended the story by saying, "I couldn't unspank you so I gave you a tea cake."

Clear in Dorothy's memory was the morning after Little Brother came. Dorothy awoke as usual with her favorite doll beside her — a small doll with china head, hands, and feet and a cloth body filled with sawdust. Papa told her she had a little brother and led her into the darkened room where she heard him crying before she crawled up on the bed beside Mama and saw his small, red, twisted face.

Shortly before Little Brother was born, Papa had to buy a new cow because both family cows had gone dry at the same time. The man who sold her failed to tell Papa that she hated children and would jump fences or tear them down to attack children. So when Papa discovered her mean temper, he decided to keep her only until one of the other cows had a calf, and he kept her in a far pasture with several fences between her and the house. Every day he warned the children to go no farther than the yard fence, and to run for the house when the cow was anywhere to be seen or heard.

One day Mama sat in a rocking chair on the back gallery, nursing Little Brother at her breast while Dorothy stood behind the chair, one foot on each rocker, hands on the chair back, helping Mama rock the baby. Suddenly a bellow and cow's horns came around the corner of the house. Mama screamed to Dorothy to run into the house. The old cow, horns lowered, reached the steps before Mama could jump up and push the chair between them. She kicked the cow in the nose and pushed the chair over the animal's horns while backing into the house and slamming the door — still holding Little Brother. From a window they watched as the old cow battered the rocking chair against the gallery steps until it fell to pieces in kindling wood.

The next morning Dorothy watched from a window as Papa led the old cow through the gate and down the road, taking her back to her previous owner. Mama said the neighbors would furnish the family milk and butter until a new calf was born.

Dorothy was lonely after Little Brother was born because her sisters were in school, Mama was too busy, Little Brother slept all the time, and she had no one to play with. She wanted to sing and tell stories to Little Brother but if she pinched him to wake him up to listen, he cried instead. Mama scolded and made her sit in a corner alone. When she did not pinch and he did not cry, she sat beside him pretending he was awake and listening, pretending to read from Sunday school cards and singing (softly, Mama warned) a new song her sisters had learned at school:

> My country 'tis of thee
> Sweet land of liver tea.

What *was* liver tea? She asked her sisters, who laughed and called her "silly." Grandma said the word was "liber tea" but that "liber tea" was not a tea. What it was Grandma tried to tell her but she did not understand. She still wondered, for a long time, if it tasted like sassafras tea or cambric tea. Grandma said it had no taste.

Every day, all day long, Dorothy waited for the afternoon, when her sisters would come home from school. Each morning she stood at the window to watch them go, longing to go with them. But she was too little.

When her sisters had turned the McKeithen corner and disappeared, she ran back to the kitchen to help Mama bathe Little Brother. Mama first fed stovewood to the kitchen stove to make the room very warm for Little Brother. While the room was warming up, she laid his clean clothes on a chair beside the kitchen table where she bathed him in a big blue-veined graniteware dishpan. After his bath, she held him on her lap wrapped in a soft blanket and uncovered his body a little at a time to put his clothes on: first, the flannel stomach band; next, the didy; next, the soft ribbed shirt; then the long, flannel underskirt decorated with briarstitching around the hem, neck and armholes; the knitted bootees; the long white dress folded under; and last, the little kimono-sleeved sacque of cream wool embroidered with blue flowers (a present from Aunt Eddie in Dallas). Finally, while he squirmed and cried—with hunger, Mama said— Mama wrapped him in another blanket with only his twisted, red face showing, moved to the armless rocking chair, unbuttoned her dress, gave him his dinner, and rocked him to sleep.

Dorothy knew that once Little Brother was asleep, Mama would wash Dorothy's face and hands and comb her hair. Even though Mama would wet the comb and hold each strand of curly hair with her left hand while she combed with the right, Dorothy knew the pain from untangling each strand. And she knew that, although she whimpered and squirmed with each untangled strand, Mama would not stop until all the straightened curls were braided into two tight pigtail plaits tied at the ends with sewing thread and hanging to her shoulders. So, while Mama rocked Little Brother to sleep, Dorothy tiptoed to some hiding place (behind the stove, under a bed, or under a table) hoping Mama could not find her.

The long, cold winter days inside the house with nobody to play with grew dreary. Every day she asked Mama when Little Brother would be big enough to stay awake and play with her, and Mama answered, "Have patience." Not knowing what patience was, she waited and waited, day after day.

At last Little Brother began to make sounds other than crying. He began to stay awake longer. He smiled, blew bubbles, and reached for her fingers when she said, "Chin chopper chin, chin chopper chin!" When she shook his blue and white rattle (which Santa Claus had put in his stocking), he squealed and kicked. She gave him her rag dolls to hold but he chewed and slobbered on them. And when she snatched the wet dolls away, he cried, and Mama scolded and said: "What did you do to that child? Did you pinch him?" And she sent Dorothy for a load of kindling wood or to beat the plow sweep to call the men to dinner.

She longed for her fourth birthday. Little Brother would then be big enough to walk (Mama said) and play with her. She would then be big enough to go to school—she hoped. Every day she asked Mama if her birthday would come next week? Next month? Spring came, and Mama at last said: "It won't be long now. Have a little more patience."

When warm spring days came, she was allowed to play outside. She could then run away from Little Brother when he cried. She could fill her apron pockets with biscuit crumbs to feed the chickens as they followed their excited hen-mother clucking them to the bread crumbs. She could look for eggs when a hen cackled and jumped off a nest. But she still had to wait for barefoot weather. Grandma stood on the front gallery in the warm, spring afternoon sunshine, said it would soon be time to go barefoot, and let Dorothy run around the yard in stocking feet—promising that the next day she could go barefoot if the weather was warm.

At last a warm next-day came. And, barefoot, she followed the men plowing. She stepped in their tracks and hopped from one track to another. Tired of that, she sat down, stuck a foot deep into the damp, cool earth, packed the earth around and over the foot until she formed a solid mound. Carefully removing her foot from the dirt, she created a little cave into which she herded or pushed bugs, worms, and ants. She then sealed the mouth of the cave with a clod and sat watching the mound for quivers of earth where the prisoners were pushing their way to freedom.

Free in spring afternoon sun, she ran barefooted up the north road to meet her sisters. Running with apron strings untied, she made a breeze to blow her clothes against her stomach and billow the apron into a balloon behind. With arms outstretched, she practiced flying—first taking little hops, hoping to fly like a chicken, and then big and bigger jumps, hoping to be a bird.

If she could learn to fly (she asked Mama) could she fly to her birthday and make it come sooner?

Papa Leonidas, King of Sparta

Papa's first name was Leonidas. His father had named him to honor the brave General and King of Sparta who lived long ago in a far-off land across the ocean. Why? (Dorothy wanted to know).

"Your Grandfather Mills was a great student of history," Papa said, to introduce the story of the Battle of Thermopylae, a pass in the Greek mountains where Leonidas and a small army of Spartans outnumbered and attacked both front and rear, refused to surrender, and held the pass until the last man was dead and the Persians had to climb over the mountains of dead bodies as they fought their way through the pass.

As Dorothy sat on her Thinking Post, thinking about Thermopylae and the Battle of the Alamo (in Mary Lee's history book), the two battles became one. But she saw Papa, not as the dead Leonidas, but as the live General Sam Houston on a white horse, carrying the Lone Star flag, leading his small army to victory.

When she jumped rope, alone, she liked to say, "Le-on-i-das, Ther-mop-y-lae! Le-on-i-das, Ther-mop-y-lae!"

Papa's second name was Menno. His Grandmother Mills ("Your great-grandma," he told Dorothy) was an Anabaptist who did not believe in war. She named him Menno to honor Menno Simons, a famous Anabaptist preacher. Papa did not know any stories about Menno Simons, except he had been dead a long, long time and he had lived on the other side of the Atlantic Ocean.

Papa liked to tell stories when he walked across the fields, when he rode horseback on Old Red or Old Dodson, and when he rode in the buggy. Dorothy, tagging along, or riding behind his saddle, or sitting beside him in the buggy when he was on a surveying trip to survey a school district or a neighbor's farm, begged for favorite stories about Grandfather, John Lockhart Mills, and his two horses, Don Quixote (called Old Don) and Sancho Panza (called Old Sanko).

Papa first hummed a little tune while he thought about the story to be told. And while the story was being told, he stopped for occasional short hums before going on. Dorothy had learned not to interrupt a hum. An interrupted hum could sink in a deep bass note into his stomach and carry the story with it. So, she waited patiently, wiggling her toes and counting the wiggles, until the hum burst into words again and the story continued.

"Your Grandfather Mills was a great reader," Papa said. "He loved literature." When he finished his education in East Tennessee in '58, he bought a horse to ride out to Texas to join his parents, who had moved there the year before. He named the horse—a big, beautiful horse—Don Quixote to honor a man in a book written a long time ago in Spain, a country on the other side of the Atlantic Ocean (but not near Thermopylae, Papa said).

When Papa told stories about his father, he always began at the beginning. And Dorothy listened, waiting for him to get to the horse, Don Quixote. "Your Grandfather, John Lockhart Mills, was born in East Tennessee," the story always began. He was the oldest of six children, but he also had an older half-brother and two older half-sisters. He grew up with two cousins of his own age; all three of them were named John Mills. They came to be known as "Long John" (Grandfather, who grew to be six feet, four inches tall), "Black John" (who had black hair and eyes and dark complexion), and "Little John" or "Johnny" (the smallest in size).

Papa's stories about life in East Tennessee (before "the War") were stories he had heard from his Grandfather Mills (William).

The Mills family owned a flour mill on the Holston River. They ground wheat for all the neighboring farmers and were paid in a share of the flour. When milling season was over, Grandfather

William and his sons built flatboats and rafts to float the flour down the Holston River into the Tennessee, into the Ohio, into the Mississippi to New Orleans. There they sold the flour, tore up the rafts and sold the lumber, bought horses and rode them home, taking three months for the trip. Sometimes they caught a boat back to Natchez and walked overland over the Old Natchez trail—some six hundred miles to their home in the Cumberland Mountains. Since many hands were needed to steer the flatboats, the two oldest sons, James and John, and their two cousins, Black John and Little John, went along on the trips to New Orleans.

"Your great-grandfather was a great story-teller," Papa said. And his favorite stories were about a slave he had owned back in Tennessee: Zeke (Ezekiel), a smart old man who had taught himself to read and write. Zeke and Grandfather William carried on a running battle of words, each trying to top the other with big words—made-up words if necessary. Try as hard as he could, Grandfather William could never top Zeke.

They owned a bull named Old Brin who had the bad habit of breaking out of his pen. And it was Zeke's job to find him and drive or lead him back to his pen. On Sunday morning Grandfather William called Zeke and said: "Zeke, Old Brin broke pen again last night. Go find him and re-empanel him."

Zeke disappeared. Was gone an hour. Then two hours. Grandfather William waiting, imagined Zeke sitting under a tree trying to decide what "re-empanel" meant. When three hours had passed, Grandfather was confident that he had, at last, won the battle of words.

Then he saw Zeke coming up the path alone, mopping his brow. "Well, Zeke, did you re-empanel Old Brin?" Grandfather called. Zeke walked on in silence and waited until he stood before Grandfather to say, "Yes, Masta, I re-empanel Old Brin but Old Brin break the re-empanelment down and scatolofisticated all over the equanimities of the forest."

Papa laughed, said his Grandpa never got the best of Old Zeke, then went on to tell the family history as it had come to him from his Grandfather and Grandmother Mills. Grandfather William was born in 1799 in Western Virginia, the youngest of thirteen children. One brother lived to be 112 years old and one sister, to 118. One brother, Jim, went to California in the Gold Rush and they never heard from him again.

At that point in Papa's story he said, "But we heard about him later, quite by accident." He then jumped ahead of his family history story to the 1880's, when travelers in wagon trains going to West Texas and to the territories beyond the Pecos, to homestead claims, sometimes stopped to camp near his Grandfather William's farm in Collin County. Papa listened to the talk between his Grandfather and the travelers. And once when the talk turned to the subject of gold and copper mining, an old man — an old grandfather in one traveling family — said he had been in California in '49. When told that Grandfather William's brother, Jim Mills, had been there at the same time, the old man said he had known Jim Mills, a confirmed bachelor and a confirmed gambler. The last time he saw him, Jim was backing out of a gambling house with a sack of $50,000 worth of gold bullion in one hand and a gun in the other covering the two men from whom he had taken the gold in a poker game. Nobody ever saw Jim again. And they guessed that he had been waylaid, slain, robbed, and dumped in some canyon.

Returning to family history, Papa said his Grandmother Mills (Martha "Patsy" Routh) was born in 1808 in Tennessee. She told him that her great-grandfather, Lawrence Routh, was born in "Ye Hawes," Yorkshire, England, and that he had come to America in 1688 with his wife Ann Metcalfe (they were married in 1683), first to Maryland and then to Pennsylvania. Both were Quakers.

Papa's Grandfather William moved to East Tennessee with his three children, after the death of his first wife. In East Tennessee he met and married Papa's Grandmother Mills in 1833 and then their six children were born.

From the days of the '49 Gold Rush on, more and more neighbor families were leaving East Tennessee, moving west of the Mississippi — especially to Texas, which had become a state. In 1857 Papa's Grandfather William sold all of their property (including slaves) and moved to Collin County, Texas, where he invested his money in cattle. Papa's father, John Lockhart, stayed on in East Tennessee for another year to finish his education. He attended a private academy owned by a Mr. Gatling, near the town of Gatlinburg — the school that later was moved to Georgia, became Emory College and finally Emory University (Papa said). After his graduation, Grandfather John Lockhart took examinations for a teacher's certificate and taught school for a few months before he bought Don Quixote and rode out to Texas to join his family. Collin County was sparsely settled then and had no school for the children. "When your Grandfather arrived," Papa said, "an educated young man, the people persuaded him to teach a school." They built a schoolhouse at Old Weston (northwest of McKinney, Papa said) and there Grandfather taught a school term of two winter months. In the spring of 1859 he had had enough of the schoolroom, and he saddled Don to ride off to join the Texas Rangers.

From that point on in Papa's story, Grandfather Mills became Don Quixote, on a tall, black horse, sitting high against the sky, spurs jingling, galloping across the Texas plains singing:

> *O bury me not on the Lone prairie*
> *Where the wild coyotes will howl o'er me*
> *Where the north wind sweeps and the grasses wave*
> *Oh bury me not in a prairie grave.*

He rode with the Rangers for two years in the Plains Country, west of the Pecos. In those days the Rangers' business was to keep surveillance of the Comanches, who were required by the United States Government to stay within the boundaries of "Indian Territory." The Comanches insisted on going back to their old hunting grounds west of the Pecos and into southwest Texas. Sometimes the Federal Government granted them permission for such trips and sent along Rangers to patrol them to see that they did not steal cattle and horses. But the Comanches preferred to make their trips without permission and unattended.

In the fall of 1860, eight Rangers, including Grandfather, were out in Pecos country headed east by northeast, following a band of Comanches. Another band had been on a raid in South Texas where they had stolen several hundred head of cattle and horses, and they were headed north trying to reach Red River and Indian Territory. Sul Ross, home on furlough from West Point, had gathered a band of deputized citizens to pursue them. The two bands of Indians came together near Sweetwater and moved northeast. The Rangers and Sul Ross's men joined forces and followed. The Indians decided to make a stand on the banks of the Little Wichita River in Foard County.

That was in December 1860. The white men recaptured stolen cattle and horses, captured some four hundred Indian ponies, and took many prisoners. Among the captured was a squaw, later found to be Cynthia Ann Parker, and her daughter, Prairie Flower. Cynthia

Ann Parker had been stolen in Southwest Texas when she was a baby by the Comanches who had killed all of her family except her father and brother (away from home at the time). She was, when recaptured, the wife of a chief who was said by some to have been killed in the Battle of Little Wichita, leaving the leadership of the tribe to his son Quanah, who continued to battle the white men for years to come.

Cynthia Ann, not allowed to return to her Indian family, lived on with her daughter in Henderson County with Parker relatives. Mourning her dead husband, she lived until after the death of her daughter. Then she too died, of loneliness, and some say she was buried in the Old Fosterville graveyard. Some say her son Quanah later reburied her in Oklahoma and built a monument for her.

When Texas seceded from the Union in 1861, Grandfather joined the Confederate Forces — going in with Sul Ross's Sixth Texas Cavalry — and served four years, most of the time as scout and spy. He served first in Alabama and Mississippi and was in the Battle of Shiloh in April of '62 under General Johnston (Sidney — who was killed in the battle) and General Beauregard, Johnston's second in command. For a time he served with General Forrest's Cavalry (known as "Forrest's Raiders"). He was then transferred to the Virginia Army and served with Lee until Longstreet's Corps was withdrawn and sent to the aid of Joseph E. Johnston at Richmond. He went with Johnston into Tennessee late in '62 and served with Johnston until he was superseded by Hood in '64. He served with Hood in Tennessee and Georgia and was in the Siege of Atlanta. He retreated with Hood into Tennessee in an attempt to draw Sherman's men off from the sea. But the maneuver failed and a second battle was fought, and lost, at Franklin late in '64. Hood's army was cut to pieces and Hood lost his command.

In Hood's army, Grandfather was used as a scout and spy because he knew the Tennessee mountains and valleys where he had grown up. One evening as he rode along a ravine in a heavily wooded area near Federal lines, he heard a horseman approaching along the ridge to the west. He dismounted and got into position to have the light on the horseman coming. As the rider appeared, Grandfather cocked his gun. The horseman heard the click and wheeled his horse. Silhouetted against the sky, Grandfather saw the profile of his cousin, Black John Mills, and called to him to put up his hands. He assured Black John that he would not shoot nor take him prisoner unless he offered fight. Then Grandfather identified himself and the two sat there on their horses and talked for an hour — Black John on the ridge and Grandfather Long John below the ridge out of sight of Federal troops. Grandfather had had no word of the Tennessee relatives since the War began. Black John had been in touch with some members of the family and gave Grandfather the news he knew. But he could tell him nothing of Little John. Somehow Little John had disappeared into the Civil War, whether into the Union Army or Confederate Army, neither knew. And Grandfather never knew.

The two men said good-bye and never saw each other again. Black John rode back to the Federal lines. Grandfather rode back to report to his commanding officer, a Colonel West. He went into the Colonel's tent and told him how he had met his cousin and what had happened. The Colonel listened to the end, then said, "As your superior officer, I order you to forget to put that story into your written report for the day. Some of these West Point officers might not understand it."

The War was over soon after that. News reached Grandfather that his two younger brothers, William and Lafayette, had died in the War. He never knew what happened to his older half-brother, James, who left to join Confederate Forces early in the War and was never heard from again.

Don Quixote and Grandfather had survived, unwounded, four years in the Civil War and two before that in the Texas Rangers. During the six years, Grandfather had not slept under a roof except when he was on furlough and twice during the War when he had been hospitalized with pneumonia. Both times in the hospital he had no food but okra soup.

He surrendered in North Carolina in May of '66 and started his long trip back to Texas, riding old Don. They had reached Hopkins County in East Texas when Old Don fell through a rotten pole bridge, broke a leg, and had to be shot. In nearby Black Jack Grove, an East Texas stockman owned Indian ponies, captured from the Comanches at the Battle of the Little Wichita before the War and sold by the Federal Government to the stockman. Grandfather traded his saddle for one of those little ponies, named him Sancho Panza, and called him Sanko for short. When Grandfather (six feet, four) was mounted on Sanko, bareback, his feet almost touched the ground. Bareback, he rode Old Sanko home, where Sanko lived to be thirty-five years old as best his age could be reckoned. He outlived his master.

"Home from 'the War'" (Papa said) "your Grandfather Mills married your Grandmother Mills (Mary Ann Belew)," whose family had moved to Collin County from West Tennessee in 1859. Papa was the third of four children and the only boy.

Grandfather made a living for his wife and four children by farming, surveying, and teaching school north of Millwood, near Wylie. He also helped his father (Great-Grandfather William), a cattleman whose herds had increased during the War. On surveying trips, he took Papa with him in wagon or buggy. As soon as Papa was old enough to ride behind the saddle, he took Papa on trips to town and about the county, rounding up cattle. And Papa tagged along with him in the fields and went hunting with him in the woods. Whatever the purpose of the trip, the way there and back was full of talk—talk about family history, Civil War history as Grandfather had lived it, Texas history as he had heard and read it, and ancient book-history of lands and people beyond the seas. Sometimes Grandfather's Civil War comrades, traveling through on their way West, stopped for visits. Then talks lasted into the night and Papa—sitting quietly unnoticed on the floor behind his father's chair, out of sight, so he would not be sent to bed—listened.

Papa was eleven years old when his father died of pneumonia, caught in a blizzard when he was on his way to McKinney to serve on a jury. That was 1880. After his father's death, Papa spent more and more time with his Grandfather and Grandmother Mills, who lived nearby. They spoke Holland Dutch to each other and to their grandson "Menno." They called him "Snicklefritz" (meaning "Little Shaver") as a pet name.

The favorite story of Papa's childhood days was the "Polecat Story." Papa was staying with his grandparents one summer night when visitors arrived—a large family. Since there were more people than beds, Papa slept on a quilt pallet on the floor. Doors and windows were all open. The night was hot. Dark. No moon. In the middle of the night Papa awakened looking into two big eyes coming toward him. He rolled off the pallet, grabbed the quilt, threw it over the two eyes, and wrapped it around the animal. Right away he knew he had a polecat and he ran into the backyard with the kicking, stinking cat. The noise awakened the household, and his Grandfather, following him, grabbed a single bit axe as he went by the woodpile. After they killed the cat they examined it, and its foaming mouth indicated that it had hydrophobia. Papa and his Grandfather burned the quilt and their nightshirts. Then his Grandmother Mills made them both take a bath in vinegar in the smokehouse before she would allow them to come into the house again.

Grandfather William Mills died in 1892 at the age of ninety-three and was buried in the Old Millwood Graveyard (near Royce City). At the time, Papa was attending Henry College in Campbell, where his mother and two sisters, Della and Eva, had moved. Though he continued in college, he spent as much time as possible during summers and school vacations helping his Grandmother Mills manage the family business. She died in September of 1895 and his mother died in December.

Papa and his two sisters were the only heirs to their parents' and grandparents' estates. By that time, his older sister, Della, was married. The three children decided to sell all of the property except the homestead in Campbell. Papa (with a partner) used his share of the bequest to build a coeducational college in Garland, Dallas County. The college consisted of one classroom building and two dormitories, and within two years it had an enrollment of almost three hundred students.

Papa had been courting Mama ever since their college days together; and, at last, they were married April 2, 1897. Since Mama's birthday was March 31, Papa liked to tease Mama once a year—at April Fool time—by saying, "Lou, you just missed being a fool twice." To that she would smile and say, "Well, sometimes I'm not so sure I missed the second time."

What happened to the college in Garland? "It burned to the ground soon after your oldest sister was born," Papa said, "and there was no insurance to rebuild it." From Garland, Papa, Mama, and Mary Lee moved to the Mills homestead in Campbell, where Eva Rita was born, and then to the farm.

April
This Side of Jordan

Most distant and most important of Grandma's rivers was the Jordan. It was in the Bible. Her songs about rivers did not always name the rivers but Dorothy knew they were all about the Jordan. Together she and Grandma sang:

> *On Jordan's stormy banks I stand*
> *And cast a wishful eye*
> *To Canaan's fair and happy land*
> *Where my possessions lie.*
>
> *I am bound for the promised land*
> *I am bound for the promised land*
> *Oh, who will come and go with me*
> *I am bound for the promised land.*

Dorothy hoped that among Grandma's "possessions" in Canaan would be the little gold ring (stolen by a Yankee soldier). Grandma had not yet crossed the Jordan but she planned to some day (she said). And when she sang General Stonewall Jackson's song "Let us pass over the river and rest under the shade," Dorothy could see Grandma walking beside the General (being carried on a litter) across the

Sabine bridge—for all rivers looked like the Sabine—into Van Zandt County.

Second in importance of Grandma's rivers was the Mississippi. She had no songs about the Mississippi but she had crossed it three times: first, when she was thirteen years old, with her father, three sisters and three brothers, traveling in a wagon train from Mississippi to Texas (after the death of her Grandma Craig and then the deaths of her mother and Grandpa Craig). That was 1859 (Grandma always said), before "the War." She crossed it the second time when she was fourteen. After the death of her father in 1860, she and her younger sister, Lucinda, went back to Mississippi to live with Uncle Frank and Aunt Ruth Craig. After the War she married Grandfather Gray and they came to Texas in April 1869, to stay, settling in Hopkins County at Reilly Springs.

April was the most important month in all the worlds—Grandma's worlds and Dorothy's. Everything of importance, good and bad, had happened in April.

From the first autumn cold snap Dorothy looked forward to April, when she would be allowed to take off her shoes and stockings, roll up the legs of her long underwear, and run barefoot in new-plowed fields, her clothes blowing against her body, a warm April breeze blowing against her face.

Dorothy learned about Grandma's Aprils listening to stories about when she was a little girl in Holly Springs, Mississippi, before the War. She learned still more when Grandma read and explained old family letters dated 1860, 1861 through 1865, and on to 1883, and when she sang "The Drummer Boy of Shiloh" and "Contraband."

Grandma's most important Aprils were: 1861 (Fort Sumter), 1865 (Appomattox), and April 2, 1899 (when Papa married Mama). She had other important Aprils; when Grandma first came to Texas, General Sam Houston was the governor (she said). That was 1859. In her sister's history book Dorothy read the story of Sam Houston, illustrated with a picture of him leading seven hundred Texans (against Santa Anna and two thousand Mexicans) into the Battle of San Jacinto, shouting "Remember the Alamo! Remember Goliad!" That was April 1836 (the book said).

Still another April was in a poem (in her sister's fifth grade reader, with a picture of a bridge like the Sabine River bridge) which Grandma knew by heart:

By the rude bridge that arched the flood,
Their flag to April's breeze unfurled,
Here once the embattled farmers stood
And fired the shot heard round the world.

When Grandma recited the poem, she told about Great-Great-Great-Grandfather Gray's three sons: two killed in the American Revolution, leaving one to become Great-Great-Grandfather.

The importance of April accumulated from one April to another. The breeze that blew against Dorothy's body and face was the same April breeze that unfurled the thirteen stars and stripes over the rude bridge, fluttered the Confederate flag over Fort Sumter, and carried the Lone Star banner sailing in triumph across the blue dome of Texas.

April was the slowest month arriving. When winter broke with a warm day in February, Dorothy asked if April would come soon. The answer was no, not until March had come and gone. Grandma taught Dorothy to say:

Thirty days hath September,
April, June, and November.
All the rest have thirty-one
Excepting February alone
Which hath but twenty-eight in fine
'Til Leap-year gives it twenty-nine.

Dorothy wanted to know the order of the months; so she borrowed Mama's chill tonic calendar, copied them down, memorized them, and recited them when she jumped rope. On March, May, and June she jumped flat-footed with both feet, and on the other months she jumped with one foot leading the other.

Waiting for April, she jumped the winter months away and listened to Grandma's stories and old family letters. The letters were tied in packets with red, moss-green, and black velvet ribbon and kept in Grandma's little hump-back trunk. Underneath the letters lay her "dress-pattern chart," her autograph album, and photograph album. As Grandma read the letters and autograph album verses, Dorothy liked to hold the photograph album and turn the pages to the oval-framed, tintype pictures of the writers and inscribers—solemn-faced people, looking straight into your eyes: two great-grandfathers, one grandfather, great uncles and aunts, and third, fourth, and fifth cousins.

Dorothy held the album open to the daguerreotype of Grandma when Grandma told stories of her childhood in Holly Springs, Mississippi. The picture was taken when she was thirteen—the summer before the family moved to Texas. She sat, wearing her candy-striped party dress, full gathered skirt to her tiny waist, and puffed, short sleeves dropped off the shoulders. On her lap she held a large leghorn straw hat with velvet bow and streamers hanging. Above a high forehead her black hair was parted in the middle and drawn straight back behind the ears. And her large gray eyes gazed solemnly at Dorothy, listening to Grandma's stories of her happy childhood.

Nancy Leannah Nelson (she explained) was her name until she grew up and married Grandfather, William Gray. She lived with her father and mother, three sisters (one older and two younger), and three brothers (two older and one younger) in Holly Springs. Her Nelson relatives and her Mother's Craig relatives and all the in-laws (Davises, Moores, Montgomerys, Strongs, and Alexanders) lived in the same community. They all belonged to the same Presbyterian church but they differed in Presbyterian beliefs. The Nelsons descended from a very strict sect called Seceders who—a long time ago, in England—seceded from the main church because they thought the church was becoming too worldly. The Seceders wished to adhere to the old ways and practices, in their daily life as well as in their worship: holy fast days were observed; no work was done on Sunday except milking cows ("The ox in the ditch"), and making beds and washing dishes ("cleanliness is next to Godliness"). Other necessary work was done on Saturday: food was cooked, coffee parched and ground, wood and kindling split and brought in (by the boys), and the house and yard cleaned by the girls and Negro Sarah.

Sunday was a day of worship and rest. On Sunday morning the family and slaves attended church. Grandma's father (Daniel Milburn Nelson), a very strict Seceder, believed that the church music should be limited to psalm-singing. But other members preferred newer, more worldly songs. Some leaned as far as the Cumberland Presbyterians' rowdy ways. The Seceders believed that slavery was wrong but that when slaves were inherited, they should be treated well and taught to read and write (which was against the law in some places). Before the War came, the church congregation began to break into factions in such wide disagreements that families moved away to other states and the Shiloh church was abandoned.

"Your Great-Grandfather (Grandma said) held firm to his beliefs, especially about keeping the Sabbath holy." On Sunday afternoon the whole family studied the catechisms: the "Child's Catechism" and the "Shorter Catechism." The children, white and black, and the grown slaves memorized and recited the answers. After catechism, the children and slaves were free to walk in the woods and visit with relatives and friends. Older boys and girls were allowed to ride horseback to the River. Little children, not allowed to play with dolls and toys, had to find ways to play with sticks, stones, and mud puddles on their walks in the woods.

Grandma's father and a partner named Crockett owned a general store, post office, and gin (operated by oxen and capable of ginning several bales a day). The family lived nearby. Slaves and white ginhands helped with the work of the gin. And a young man named Porterwood Wilkins (called Port) was clerk of the store and postmaster. He lived with the family. When ginning season was over, her father took the cotton to New Orleans on a flatboat on the Cold Water River into the Yazoo into the Mississippi (near Vicksburg). In New Orleans he sold the cotton and bought store supplies for the year: a whole cheese, barrels of syrup, kits of mackerel, and other things considered luxuries. On one trip he brought back a sewing machine for his wife—the first in that part of the country.

Food was plentiful. From vegetable garden, orchards, and from wild fruits, nuts, and greens found in woods and fields, the dinner table was always loaded for the family of nine, the store clerk, ginhands, any customers who happened to be in the store or at the gin at mealtime, and for visiting relatives.

The children all helped with the work of the home, store, and gin according to their age, strength, and judgment. Little Grandma helped Black Sarah in the kitchen. But Sarah said she sometimes helped her backwards. Once, after churning, Little Grandma decided to take up the butter but the butter paddle slipped and the butter dropped into the slop bucket. Sarah had to fish it out and wash it again and again before it could be put on the dinner table. Another time, when Little Grandma spilled hot grease on her foot, Sarah sent her to the spring to soak her foot in cold water; and there she stayed all afternoon forgetting about her kitchen chores.

Of all the slaves, Sarah was the favorite. She had a little son, Andy, and a daughter, Anne, who also helped in the kitchen. When there were no kitchen chores, Anne, Andy, and Little Grandma played together in the backyard. Sarah's husband belonged to another man, who refused to sell him and refused to buy Sarah and her children because Sarah was afflicted by short sleepy spells.

Of all the errands that Little Grandma liked, best of all was going to Grandpappy Craig's house on the other side of the grove. She and her younger sister Lucinda followed a path through the woods to Grandpappy's blacksmith shop and the house beyond, where he and Grandma Craig lived. Sometimes, when work was light, they were allowed to visit for a whole day. Little Grandma helped her Grandma Craig knead and bake bread and churn. Grandpappy liked buttermilk better than anything in the world, and when he called from his shop, "Leannah! Little Poosy! Buttermilk!" Grandma Craig gave Little Grandma a small pitcher to carry to the springhouse, fill with cold buttermilk and carry very carefully, so as not to spill it, down the path to Grandpappy sitting in the shade outside his shop. When the pitcher was empty, Grandpappy went back to work and Little Grandma stood in the door to watch the forge fire burn the metal to bright red and to hear the hot metal hiss as it dipped into the wooden water vat.

When Grandpappy had no work on hand, he told stories about when he was a little boy in Pennsylvania where he was born and named James Dickey Craig, and about how as a young man he had gone to North Carolina and there met and married Grandma Craig (Agnes Nancy Greer), and finally, how he and Grandma Craig had moved to Oxford, Mississippi. Grandpappy's father and mother were born and married in Ireland and, because of the persecution of Presbyterians there, had migrated to Pennsylvania before the American Revolution.

Grandpappy had other stories. A favorite was about the laziest man in Lafayette County. This man was so lazy he wouldn't work his crops, and his wife and children would have starved to death if the neighbors hadn't fed them. This went on year after year until, finally, the neighbors got tired of it and two of the neighbor men decided to take the lazy man to the graveyard and bury him. So they hitched up the wagon and went to his house. Found him lying on the back gallery fast asleep, loaded him on the wagon, and started for the graveyard. Along came another neighbor man on horseback. They all stopped to pass the time of day and the horseman asked where they were going. They told him and why. Said the man was too lazy to live. Said if the neighbors had to feed his family, they might as well have one less mouth to feed. "Give him one more chance," the horseman said. "No more chances. He's better off dead." "I'll tell you what I'll do," the horseman said; "if you'll give him one more chance, I'll give him a sack of feed corn to plant a crop." Before they could say anything, the laziest man in Lafayette County raised his head about two inches off the wagon bed and, without opening an eye, said, "Is it shelled?"

When Grandpappy Craig grew tired of telling stories, he sent Little Grandma back to the house, saying, "Ask your Grandma to tell you some." If Grandma Craig was not busy, she sat in her rocking chair on the back gallery and told about her father (James Greer) who was born in Ireland, came to Pennsylvania first, then to Mechlenberg County, North Carolina, where he met and married her mother (Margaret Moore). They then moved to South Carolina where he became a rich weaver.

Grandma Craig's favorite story—usually told while the children helped her wash the dishes—was about an old woman who lived alone with her little dog named Soap-and-Water. When visitors came to dinner and offered to help with washing dishes afterward, the little old woman said, "No, thank you. Soap-and-Water will wash them." Whereupon she placed all the table dishes on the floor and the little dog licked them clean.

The walks through the woods to Grandpappy Craig's house and home again were adventures. Little Grandma, four years older than Lucinda, was always told to look after her little sister to see that she did not get hurt. But Lucinda would not always do as she was told. And sometimes she caused trouble as a little tattletale. Once when they were going home from Grandpappy Craig's house, they met a man riding a mule. Little Grandma picked up a piece of bark and hit the mule on the flank. The mule pitched and bucked until he threw the man off. When the girls reached home, Lucinda told the story to their brothers and sisters, who teased Little Grandma until she crawled under the bed into the trundle bed to escape them. There she fell asleep and slept until bedtime and was discovered when the trundle bed was rolled out for the night.

Grandma liked to tell happy stories of her childhood. But her happy childhood was over when she was eleven. First, her Grandma Craig died. Two years later her own mother died of consumption, and a month after that Grandpappy Craig died. The three were buried side by side in the Shiloh graveyard.

For two or three years before her mother died (Grandma said) her father had talked of selling out and moving to Texas, because of her mother's health. Also the dissension in the church congregation was growing more and more bitter—over politics as well as church practices. Her father (she said) was a spiritual man, less worldly than most of the Shiloh congregation.

When her mother died, her father had already sold the gin and store in preparation for leaving Mississippi. Letters from neighbors who had moved to Texas told of fertile, cheap land, and a good climate. Two neighbor families by the names of Coffee and Bramlett were ready to leave for Texas and urged the Nelsons to join them. Although the home was yet to be sold and business transactions completed (many debts to the store and gin were uncollected), her father decided to leave with the Coffee and Bramlett families since traveling in a wagon train was necessary for safety.

Immediately after Grandpa Craig's burial in early November the wagon train set out. The household goods were hauled in ox wagons but the families rode in covered hacks drawn by mules. The Nelson slaves rode in one of the ox wagons but Mr. Coffee made his slaves walk most of the way. The Coffee girls and Nelson girls often rode the extra horses and had a good time riding ahead of the wagons.

The good times soon ended, however. For, within two days' journey from Holly Springs, an early, bitter winter set in. Heavy snowstorms and blizzards hit them. At night the men raked places in the snow, put up tents facing in to a circle, and spread fodder on the tent floors for beds. In the circle a fire was built of huge logs dragged in by oxen and the men took turns feeding the fire all night. So, in spite of the cold, they slept warm.

They arrived in Hopkins County at Christmas time (1859), and there friends took them in and housed them until they could buy land and build homes of their own. The Nelsons soon bought a farm some three miles southeast of Sulphur Springs and, with the help of neighbors, built a log house of two large rooms with an open hallway between, where a ladder led to a long loft room above. A fireplace at each end of the house kept the house warm in winter; and the open hallway was a cool, shady place in the hot summer.

Aunt Lizzie (Grandma's oldest sister, then twenty-two) took charge as mistress of the house and she and Sarah took care of the younger children including Sarah's son and daughter. By March the family was settled and content in their new home. The children worried, however, about the health of their father and oldest brother Calvin. The two had caught bad colds on the hard trip from Mississippi and the colds grew worse instead of better.

The earliest letter in Grandma's packets of old letters was dated March 21, 1860, written by her father to his brother Robert in Mississippi. And her story-telling from that point on was a combination of letter-reading and explaining. That letter first discussed details of unfinished business transactions (which his brother was looking after for him) and then went on to current events in Texas:

> Some of our boys left a few days since for somewhere beyond
> the Rio Grande. The emigration is teeming into Mexico
> from all the Southern States. I find the excitement is general
> and has been conducted on the secret plan. The object is
> to assist the Liberal or Republican party in the subjugation
> of Mexico with an eye to annexation to the United States as
> Southern Slave territory and I would not be surprised if the
> trick wins, for Mexico cannot exist as a government any
> longer but must fall into the hands of some other power and
> of course that ought to be the U.S.

Grandma explained that "some other power" meant England, France, and Spain; the three were threatening to interfere in Mexican politics.

That letter (the only one written by Grandma's father, who died in June) ended: "I wish you would come and see us this summer. I think you would like our country...."

Before their father's death Lizzie had met and married John Wells, and after their father's death Uncle John and Aunt Lizzie came to live on the Nelson farm and look after the family.

In early autumn, before winter could set in, Uncle Frank Craig (their mother's brother) came to Texas to take Grandma and her sister Lucinda back to Mississippi to live with him and Aunt Ruth. The other children stayed with Aunt Lizzie and Uncle John: Calvin, twenty years old (and sick), Bob, sixteen (and able to help Uncle John with the farm), Adelaide, twelve (with weak lungs), and Willie, five years old.

Uncle Frank and Aunt Ruth took good care of Lucinda and

Little Grandma. Uncle Frank gave Grandma a little gold ring made from a nugget which he had brought back from California in Gold Rush days. And although the two sisters were back in the land of their happy childhood and although they loved Uncle Frank and Aunt Ruth, the happy world of their childhood was gone: Grandpappy Craig's house and blacksmith shop belonged to strangers; their own home, store, and gin belonged to somebody else; cousins, uncles, and aunts had moved away; their own father and mother were dead; and their sisters and brothers were a month's journey away in Texas.

Mr. Lincoln (Grandma always called him "Mr. Lincoln") had been elected President and Uncle Frank talked of a coming war. Before the year was out, South Carolina had seceded from the Union, followed by Mississippi in January and later by Florida, Alabama, Georgia, Louisiana, and Texas. By the end of April the Confederacy was formed and Fort Sumter was held by the Confederacy. Uncle Frank hoped that war could be avoided because Mr. Lincoln had made speeches saying states had a legal right to secede.

Meanwhile, in Mississippi and in Texas local and state militia were being formed and readied for war — if war came. Grandma and Lucinda received a letter from their sister Lizzie, bringing news of the death of their brother Calvin, in March, and of the enlistment of her husband and her brother Bob in the local cavalry in Hopkins County, for one year.

In Holly Springs, in Lafayette County, and in all of Mississippi, the boys and young men were leaving daily. In July Grandma's favorite cousin, Richard Craig, then nineteen years old, joined the local militia at Oxford under a Captain Falkner, and in August he joined the Confederate Forces in the 22nd Regiment of Mississippi Infantry "for the duration."

"The duration" was expected to be a few months. But before the year was out, news came from Texas that brother Bob and John Wells had enlisted in Ector's Texas Cavalry Brigade and been ordered to join Confederate Forces in other states.

Early in '62 Uncle Frank joined his nephew Richard in the 22nd Regiment of Mississippi Infantry. And Aunt Ruth was left with the care of her own children, the two nieces, and the Negro slaves. Grandma, the oldest of all the children (she was then sixteen) helped Aunt Ruth as much as she could. One of her tasks was to teach the children, including her own sister, the Craig children, and the slave children, together in one class.

The War was not soon over. It dragged on and on. Postal systems ceased to exist. Letters were carried by travelers maneuvering on roundabout routes to evade capture by moving enemy forces. And as the fighting shifted, as men were moved from one battle area to another and sometimes from one command to another, their contacts with homefolks were lost.

At home, women and children worked and waited for letters to find their way through battle lines. But letters grew fewer, were longer delayed, and brought sadder and sadder news of the wounded, captured, and dead. Before the seige of Vicksburg, Mr. Lincoln had proclaimed the Emancipation Act setting the slaves free. The Craig Negroes stayed on with the family. But as the War continued and food grew more and more scarce, more and more hungry "freedmen" roamed the countryside stealing food to survive.

Before the Siege of Vicksburg, heavy fighting took place in northern Mississippi around Oxford, Caswell, and Holly Springs, which was used as a supply depot by both Federal and Confederate Forces. Again and again the Yankees and the Rebels fought—taking, losing, and retaking the town. When news spread that the Yankees were coming, all hands of all ages, black and white, scurried to prepare for their arrival. Livestock were driven to heavily wooded bottomland for hiding; silverware, dishes, and all household treasures were buried or hidden. Grandma's little gold-nugget ring, her greatest treasure, was always tucked in a small box and hidden in a rotten stump far from the house. That done, they waited, listening for guns and cannon shot followed by the appearance of the soldiers in blue.

Time and time again the Yankees came searching the house, smokehouse, barn, land, taking all the food they could find (one time, dumping a tub of butter into the best linen tablecloth, which they tied by the corners to carry). Each time they left, Grandma ran to the old stump and each time found her ring safe—until after their last raid (that was just before the Siege of Vicksburg). The ring was gone. On that same raid they burned her Uncle John Craig's house and barns and confiscated his livestock.

Providing food for the family and slaves became more and more difficult with each raid and with the increasing number of hungry freedmen stealing. ("Mr. Lincoln did the best he knew," Grandma would say, "but he didn't know enough.")

After Vicksburg fell to the Yankees, fighting shifted to other states. Daily life grew more calm but each day brought sadder news.

Letters sent by travelers were exchanged between relatives in Texas and Mississippi but many letters were lost and those that arrived were delayed—sometimes for months. Finally a letter arrived in August telling of Uncle Frank's death in July—that was '64—at Peach Tree Creek near Atlanta. Cousin Richard had been with him when he died.

In September a letter came from Grandma's brother Bob from a hospital in Forsyth, Georgia, saying:

> *Dear Sister, I received a very severe wound on the third of September, the ball striking me near the backbone and ranging across coming out below my ribs. I have suffered a good deal from it. It was thought by many at first to be mortal but it is now doing well...*

It was not doing well, however. In November a friend, Mr. H. E. Spencer, wrote a letter to Grandma saying her brother Bob was "rather weak now" and "exceedingly nervous." The letter went on to say:

> *He has written several times but is doubtful whether you have received his letters.... You must feel comforted.... The ladies here visit the Hospital frequently and your Brother has one friend who pays him much attention, Mrs. Dews. He thinks he will be able to get a furlough and come to see you about Christmas....*

The furlough did not come and a letter from Bob, dated January 5, 1865, from Ocmulgee Hospital, Macon, Georgia, read:

> *Dear Sisters, I write a few lines to inform you of my whereabouts. My wound has very near healed up but I am very weak. I have sat up some today, walked on my crutches to the fire...I will try and visit you if I can get a furlough. There are no enemy near this place at this time but they passed near here about one month ago but did not coil....*

Bob wrote again from Ocmulgee Hospital on January 17 (his last War letter), saying:

> *...I don't think you need fool away your time looking for me to visit you for there is no chance for me to get a furlough for the doctors at this place have refused me on account of my living on the other side of the Miss. River. They are afraid I*

will go home.... I think I will be able for service again
soon.... I have been going on crutches...but am not near well
yet.... I am very weak in my back.... I learned that General
Hood will pass through this place with a portion of his army
in a few days. If so I hope to see my command as I have not
heard from them in four months. Neither have I heard from
home.... I have not heard from you since Uncle's death.
Have spent many uneasy hours about you all since I was
wounded for I have nothing else to do but lie and study....

From January '65 (Grandma said) Confederate men, convinced that the War was lost, were deserting and going home to families and crops or heading west to gold and copper mines or for the Rio Grande, hoping to reorganize south of the border and continue the War. An exchange of Confederate and Federal prisoners was under way and the War seemed to be drawing to a close. Word finally came that Bob had received a furlough and had gone home to Texas.

By the end of April news had come of Lee's surrender at Appomattox and of President Lincoln's death. From then on, Confederate soldiers—the ones who had survived—were returning home, one by one from day to day. Many were sick or wounded. All were disheartened and restless. By summertime, however, most of the surviving local boys and men in Lafayette County had reached home and crops were in.

Though the War was over, the South was far from peaceful. Because of the disfranchisement of returned Confederate soldiers, "the Radicals" in office, and hungry freedmen roaming the land, the country was still in turmoil. Travelers traveled in groups for safety. Letters still had to be sent by travelers.

Aunt Ruth, her children, and Grandma and her sister Cinda talked more and more about moving to Texas to join their Craig and Nelson relatives. But women could not travel alone and they continued to wait for a brother, uncle, or cousin to come for them.

Meanwhile, in Texas, Bob was trying to farm the Nelson farm. Because of his poor health, however, he began to think about giving up farming. And in the late spring of 1867 he and his cousin Richard Craig joined other restless young men of the community and set out for Mexico to join Confederate comrades assembling below the Rio Grande. The Mexican Emperor Maximilian (they had heard) had agreed to help them continue the Civil War. When they reached San

Antonio and learned that Maximilian had been overthrown and killed, the two cousins joined a cattle drive going north to Abilene, Kansas.

Back in Mississippi, soldiers from Virginia, the Carolinas, Georgia, and Tennessee, on their way westward, sometimes stopped in Oxford, Holly Springs, and Caswell. William Gray (from Flat Rock, South Carolina) was one who had stopped to visit a Confederate comrade before heading west again. At a party one night he met Grandma and decided to stay on in Lafayette County awhile. (At that point in her story, Grandma always said, "That was your Grandfather Gray.") And she described him as he looked that night at the party: he was twenty-five years old, tall, lank, with gray eyes that twinkled ("like your Uncle Robert's," she would say). He asked if he could call on her the following Sunday afternoon, and when he came, she invited him to write in her album. He took from his pocket a paper from which he copied a poem he had composed for her:

> *To Miss N. L. Nelson*
> *Thine is a mind of maiden artlessness*
> *Unstained, undarkened by the drop of earth*
> *A soul that through thine eyes bright beams express*
> *Thy nature e'en as noble as thy birth.*

He continued to call on her every Sunday afternoon and at least one night during each week. He was a builder by trade (as his father and all Gray men had been ever since and before his great-grandfather, William Gray, had come from England to Newbern, South Carolina, long before the American Revolution; they were builders of gristmills). He hoped to stay in Lafayette County and earn a living by building gristmills. Meanwhile he found work helping rebuild houses and barns in the war-torn countryside.

On Sunday afternoon visits the two took walks in the woods and fields; and on midweek night visits, they sat in Aunt Ruth's parlor. (And what did they do? Dorothy asked.) They talked. (And what did they talk about?) They talked about his home and family in Flat Rock: four brothers and three sisters (all younger than he), his father, Levi Rogers Gray (still living), and his mother, Camilla Jane Shields (dead). His grandfather, William Edward Gray (he had been told), when he was a lad of fifteen, had been present at the signing of the Mechlenburg Declaration of Independence. The story had come from his Grandmother Gray, Margaret Elizabeth Rogers (who was still living and 105 years old). She had told him that most of the signers of the Declaration were Presbyterians—good Presbyterians who did not believe in slavery—and that the Declaration included an anti-slavery clause. She also told him that she was a cousin of John Randolph and a descendent of Pocahontas.

Camilla Jane Shields' grandfather, John Shields—and his wife, Rebecca Oliver—came from County Antrim in Ireland before the American Revolution. The Shields family (he had been told) were a family of giants; the Shields men (all seven and eight feet tall and long-legged) could leap over fences and small trees and could outrun deer and rabbits. Camilla Jane Shields's mother was a McClure and her Grandfather McClure's wife, Nancy McMillan, came from Scotland.

After he had told her all about his family and she had told him about hers, he asked permission to copy another verse, which he had composed, in her album; and he wrote:

> I think of thee at morn when glisten
> The tearful dewdrops on the grass
> I think of thee at eve and listen
> When the low whispering breezes pass.
> W.G.

Soon after that they were married at Aunt Ruth Craig's house (October 28, 1867). Soon after the wedding, Aunt Ruth, her children, and Cinda, Grandma's sister, set out for Texas, traveling with a neighbor family. Grandma and Grandfather stayed on in Mississippi, where he hoped to follow his trade.

By mid-December, Aunt Ruth and her children were settled in Hunt County, Texas, with Craig relatives. And Cinda was living with her sister Lizzie, near Bright Star (in Hopkins County). Grandma received a letter from Aunt Ruth, saying Richard Craig and Bob Nelson (after their cattle drive to Abilene) had returned home: Dick was with his family in Hunt County and Bob had returned to the Nelson farm near Sulphur Springs.

In the spring (1868) Grandma received a letter from her sister Cinda (then eighteen years old) from Bright Star:

> ...Lee, I want you to move to Texas next fall. You can get land much cheaper than you can there....
> Lizzie is going to sell our place [the Nelson farm] next fall if she can get the value of it. They say they won't take

*less than six hundred dollars in "hard iron" for it. If they do
sell Lizzie says she is going to send your part of the money to
you the first opportunity. Then she is going to invest hers and
Willie's in land and that I may go to school on mine or marry
just as I like best about that. I believe I will choose the latter
and then when my money is gone I will have some one to
take care of me. I have four or five beaux that call on me
frequently. I guess they will be telling their business sometime
soon and if they do I will just politely tell one of them yes
and a chicken to boot....*

*I have just got through scouring. Tomorrow I am to
receive a call from one of my chicken eaters and you ought
to see me fixing up the house, cleaning off the yard and
ironing my Sabbath suit to put on.... As a certain lady in
Mississippi said about this time last year I can stretch my
neck enough at best but put me to talking to a certain chap
and I stretch it about ten foot longer than ever.*

*I went to church last Sunday a week with a young man
that had a pistol buckled around him. I thought of what I
said before I left Mississippi that if a young man had to go
to church with firearms he could not go with me. But in such
a place as that I think they are perfectly justified in carrying
them. He knew his life was in danger....*

*Bob got into a scrap about some hogs that I fear will
terminate in a serious manner. He and Charlie Frost were
hunting hogs and came up on a pack of scamps in the act
of killing a hog that belonged to Ben McGill.*

*They gave the alarm and Thom and Mob Mc who were
at work closeby joined them. They killed all the dogs [which
belonged to the scamps] and if the men had not got out of
the way some of them would have found themselves full of
lead but they all ran while the boys were killing the dogs.
They got on their horses and pursued them but could not
find any of them and they have never seen them since but
have heard that they are going to waylay and murder them.
The boys go armed all the time and if they ever get near one
of those demons they will kill their next hogs in the lower
worlds....*

Bob was farming the Nelson farm. And Lizzie and John Wells
were living on the Wells farm near Bright Star. On August 15, 1868,
while visiting his sister Lizzie, Bob wrote to Grandma:

Times are rather excitable with us now. There has been a good deal of murdering going on among us lately. A man named Flowers was called out of his house and shot to death not long since. We live about five miles from the men who killed him—claimed to be following some horses that had got away from them and wanted directions to Reilly Springs. As it was very dark he walked out to show them the road near his house. After showing the road to them they killed him and went their way. The next day a man named Stroud was killed and Jesse Star's little boy and Star badly wounded. They were fired on from the brush as they were going home.... The next day Luke Star and a man named Jackson were killed at home and Jesse Star's house burned to ashes. Lee, I expect you remember the characters of the Stars. They have done a great deal of mischief here since the War.

There is a good deal of excitement here now about the Presidential election. There is to be a big Democratic speaking in town today, also a barbecue. I am afraid we will have some troublesome times in our country before long. We will have a yanky garrison of about sixty men in our town. And the number of Ku Klux around here is not known. They and the Yanks can't agree but there has been no disturbance here this year. One hundred and fifty K. K. marched through the town last Saturday night but never interfered with anything and nothing bothered them....

Mississippi continued to be slow in rebuilding after the War. The situation was not better than in Flat Rock, South Carolina, when Grandfather left. So, after urging from Craig and Nelson kin in Texas, Grandma and Grandfather left Mississippi and arrived in Hopkins County in early spring of 1869. By that time Brother Bob, having become involved in the troublesome times (particularly with the Star family), was ready to turn the Nelson farm over to his sister and her husband and leave that part of the country. He and Cousin Richard finally settled down to farming in Hunt County. Bob married a Miss Ida Stribling (who then became Aunt Ida). After the birth of their daughter Lucy, he died of his old War wounds. Then Aunt Ida married Cousin Richard Craig; and their children (John, Minnie, Ruth, and Dick) were cousins with whom Mama grew up.

Grandma's first child was born May 9, 1869, soon after she and Grandfather arrived in Texas. The baby was named Eddie Camilla (for her dead great-grandfather, William Edward Gray—whose wife, Margaret Elizabeth Rogers, was still living and 108 years old—and for her dead Grandmother Gray, Camilla Jane Shields).

The next two babies were girls: Mary Adelaide and Lou Florence (Mama). The fourth and last baby was William Robert (Uncle Robert), who was born in 1876.

When the first baby was three months old, she weighed less than when she was born because Grandma's small breasts (though they provided enough milk) could not hold the milk (it leaked out). No wet nurses were available and the baby was starving to death. There were no bottles for babies in those days (Grandma explained). In spite of warnings from neighbor women that she would kill her baby, Grandma began to spoonfeed the child: canned fruit juice, pot liquor from turnip greens, and cow's milk, diluted. The baby began to gain weight and grew into a healthy child and grew up to be Aunt Eddie. Grandma was able to nurse the other three babies. Grandfather found plenty of work to do in Hopkins County, building cotton gins and presses and cultivating his farm. But his health was not improving. He still suffered from a war-wounded leg that would not heal.

Hopkins County gradually became more peaceful. "The Radicals" had been voted out of office. The Military Government was ended and Texas was readmitted to the Union. Grandfather was appointed Deputy Sheriff by J. A. Weaver, the County Sheriff, and two years later was elected Justice of the Peace in Precinct No. Three. The Commission to be Justice of the Peace was signed by "Richard Coke, Governor of the State of Texas." In the oath of office to be Deputy Sheriff (dated January 5, 1874) Grandfather swore:

> ...I being a citizen of this State have not fought a duel with deadly weapons nor committed an assault with deadly weapons upon any person either within this State or out of it; nor have I sent or accepted a challenge to fight a duel with deadly weapons or acted as second in carrying a challenge or aided or assisted any person thus offending and further that I am not disqualified from holding office by the Fourteenth Amendment of the Constitution of the United States and am a qualified elector of this State. So help me God.

Grandfather's health was poor however. On March 12, 1878, he wrote to his cousin Henry C. Gray at Blanco, Texas:

*We are having fine weather now and the farmers are going
ahead with their planting. The prospects are very favorable
so far. Wheat and oats are looking fine. The general health
of the country is good.... My health is not good and has not
been since December. I have done no work in two months.
I have something growing on the underside of my jawbone.
At first it had the appearance of a tumor or wen but it has
changed and looks more like a large rising of some sort but
has never run any except a little bloody water. It is a puzzle
to the doctors.... Give my best respects to your Father's
family. Lee and the children join in love to you. Write soon
to your Cousin Wm. Gray*

The doctor could do nothing to relieve Grandfather's pain so
Grandma made hot poultices of roots and leaves gathered in the
woods and changed them night and day. Grandfather died June 19,
1878, and was buried in the graveyard at Reilly Springs. One month
later little Mary Adelaide, age six, died of typhoid fever and was
buried beside her father.

With the money from Grandfather's life insurance policy Grandma paid their debts, placed tombstones at her husband's and
daughter's graves in the Reilly Springs graveyard, and bought a farm
in Hunt County, near Lone Oak, in a country community known as
"The Hall." "The Hall" had a good private school for the children to
attend. Her youngest brother (Uncle Willie), then twenty-three and
unmarried, came to live with her and help her farm the land.

The move to Hunt County brought Grandma closer to her Craig
cousins in Campbell and to Aunt Ida (Stribling) Nelson, who had
married Cousin Richard Craig. After Uncle Willie courted and
married Miss Laura Cowan, Grandma and her three children were
alone again. The farm at The Hall was a lonely place at times. A
railroad, being built, passed near the farm; and tramps following the
tracks often came to the kitchen door asking for a handout or stole
chickens and other food. Bruno, the family dog, kept watch over the
family at night and herded the cattle by day. One night in the
middle of the night the family were awakened by Bruno's snarling
and barking, and the next morning they found a man's big shoes
under a window and a torn piece of a man's pants on the gate.

As a cattle herder, Bruno could distinguish the Gray cattle from
neighbor's cattle that sometimes jumped fences into the Gray's grain
fields. Bruno herded the Gray cattle back to their pasturelands or

lots where they belonged. But neighbor cattle were not treated gently. He chased a neighbor's cow, caught her tail, and popped it off before he drove her to jump the fence into her owner's property.

The family lived at The Hall about seven years. To help make a living Grandma sold chickens, eggs, vegetables, and fruit in Lone Oak and taught pattern-making by the chart. For her trips to Lone Oak and about the countryside to teach pattern-making, she bought a horse, "White" (named for the man from whom she bought him). White was a beautiful saddle horse and worked equally well hitched to a buggy, wagon, or plow.

Grandma rode sidesaddle, wearing a long full, black skirt that billowed behind her in the wind as she rode about the country, stopping at farmhouses where she had pupils. Young ladies who were about to be married depended on Grandma to cut their wedding dresses of gray silk poplin, made with hoops and worn over a bustle.

Grandma's oldest daughter (Aunt Eddie) completed all the grades at The Hall and then attended high school in Lone Oak. Eventually, Grandma, wanting her fifteen-year-old daughter to get a good education so that she could become a teacher (and afraid that she might decide to marry one of the country boys instead), decided to sell the farm and move to Campbell to a good high school and college (Henry College).

When Grandma sold the farm, she traded old White to a lumberman in East Texas for enough lumber to build a house near Campbell. Months went by; the lumber did not arrive. So Uncle Willie made a trip to East Texas to look into the matter. He found the lumberman had gone out of business and the horse had been sold. Unable to retrieve the horse, he took a surrey instead. Then he took the surrey to another sawmill, traded it for lumber, and shipped the lumber to Campbell.

Grandma traded a cow to a carpenter to build the house. Uncle Willie and the Craig boys helped with building (the Craig cousins shingled the roof). The house had two large rooms with an open hallway between and a loft above with ladder stairway. A brick fireplace and chimney were built for the kitchen room at one gable end of the house. A wide front gallery extended the length of the house. Later a shed-room-kitchen and back gallery were added as well as another brick chimney at the other gable end of the house and a brick flue for the kitchen stove in the shed-room-kitchen.

Grandma continued to earn a living by teaching dress-pattern cutting "by the chart" and she traded lessons for another saddle horse. When Uncle Willie's wife died, he came again to live with Grandma bringing his baby son and daughter, Ernest and Grace, for Grandma to take care of until he married Aunt Mandy.

Grandma's two daughters, Eddie Camilla and Mama, graduated from the Campbell Public School and from Henry College (where Mama met Papa), and both became teachers. Her son Robert married Bertha Smith and became a businessman in Campbell. Camilla went to Dallas to teach and Mama married Papa, April 2, 1897.

Dorothy never tired of hearing the letters read and reread nor the stories told and retold. Grandma's life story — full of Aprils — unfolded and accumulated from day to day as she went about her work pursued by four grandchildren, each begging for a favorite story or letter and quarreling over who should hold and turn the pages of the old photograph album (very, very carefully) while Grandma talked or read.

It was in the dusk of evening or in dim lamplight that Grandma sang her river songs. She sat in her rocking chair, her hands folded in her lap. And Dorothy sat on the floor beside her, joining in:

> *On the other side of Jordan*
> *In the sweet field of Eden*
> *Where the tree of life is blooming*
> *There is rest for me,*
> *There is rest for the weary*
> *There is rest for me.*

General Stonewall Jackson's song was an April song (Grandma said) for it was April when General Jackson lay wounded on the battlefield listening to his men sing:

> *Though the dark waves roll high*
> *Let us be undismayed*
> *Let us pass over the river*
> *And rest under the shade*
> *Rest under the shade of the tree.*

All sad Aprils rolled into one in that song. General Jackson, dead Grandfather Gray, dead Grandfather Mills, dead Uncle Frank, and dead Uncle Bob all became one, and April was their month. Listening, Dorothy saw "the dark waves roll high" over the Sabine River bridge, separating Grandma from all her April-War dead. And, listening, Dorothy sat, safe and secure beside Grandma who had survived all her sad Aprils, "undismayed."

Aunt Lizzie  and Uncle Tom

Uncle Tom was dead Grandma Mills' brother. Uncle Tom came for long visits in winter and in summer, arriving, unexpected, in the middle of the night.

Aunt Lizzie was Grandma Gray's oldest sister. Aunt Lizzie, Uncle John and Cousin Lutie lived on a farm near Emory; and Cousin Mamie, Cousin Ada, and Cousin Louis lived nearby. Visits to Aunt Lizzie's were planned. "When the crops are in," Papa would say, "we'll go see your Aunt Lizzie." When each visit was over, Uncle John patted Dorothy on the head and said, "Do you want to stay and be my little girl?" Dorothy wanted to say yes and no; but she always said no. And on the homeward trip she fell asleep thinking about the next visit to Aunt Lizzie's.

On a summer visit the family started before dawn, traveled by wagon over the deep sandy road, northeast, over the bridge on Shuffle Creek, past the Ace Hughey's, the graveyard, and crawled through the night woods on both sides of the road until the team, struggling through the deep sand, pulled the family into the bright sunrise with Emory in clear view ahead and the turnoff to the right leading to Aunt Lizzie and Uncle John's house. Two miles brought

50

the house into view—long, low-slung, gray, boxed and stripped, wooden, chimneyed at both ends and at the back, with a wide gallery extending the length of the front and a shed-room the length of the back—sitting on a knoll beyond a branch crossed on a wooden bridge; beyond the persimmon tree to be climbed and a fig bush to be searched for figs; beyond strawberry, watermelon, and cantaloupe patches and the garden with gourd vines and Kentucky Wonder beans climbing and running over the fence; beyond the green mound of the storm house, dark and cool inside, where Aunt Lizzie would send the children to bring jars of pickles, chow chow, brandied peaches lifted from wooden shelves that climbed three log walls to the timbered ceiling through which a joint of stovepipe let the blue sky in.

The noisy ducks and guineas scattered on both sides of the road before the oncoming wagon. Aunt Lizzie appeared in the doorway to start the hand-waving welcome, "Light and hitch! Light and hitch!" And the children tumbled from the tailgate before the wagon stopped, before Aunt Lizzie reached the big wagon gate to open it. They rushed through the paling yard gate to meet Cousin Mamie coming from the garden, her caught-up cook apron full of vegetables; to see Cousin Lutie coming from the kitchen wiping her flour-caked hands on her apron; and to glimpse Cousin Ada coming around the corner of the house with her weed yard-broom in her hand—all coming to hug and kiss, one by one, in order, beginning with Little Brother. Aunt Lizzie snatched him up, kissed him, held him up, looked at him, and said, "What a big little booger you are getting to be," and passed him along to Cousin Lutie to Cousin Mamie to Cousin Ada.

After the hugging and kissing, the children waited politely for the welcome talk to be over, the welcome circle to break up, to return to the noontime dinner underway in the summer kitchen. On its cool, dirt floor, swept and sprinkled, Cousin Lutie, Cousin Mamie, and Mama walked about, lifting pot lids on the black iron range, seasoning the food with a pinch of this, a dash of that, fetching the dough tray hanging by a leather thong on the wall, dumping the pea shells in the slop bucket behind the stove, laughing and talking, forgetting the children.

Aunt Lizzie, saying, "Too many cooks in the kitchen spoil the broth," took Grandma Gray with her to sit in the shade of the grape arbor in the back yard; and Papa went walking over the fields to find

Uncle John and lend him a hand. Ada gave each child a drink of cold water from a gourd dipper dipped into a cedar bucket that had just come dripping up from the brick-lined well, then raced them to the persimmon tree and on to the branch, to wade, scolding and cautioning them to step carefully and look for quicksand which they soon found, got mired in, and were pulled out of just in time. Washed off (feet, hands, faces) in branch water, they were arranged in a neat row to listen to stories of all the little children who had disappeared forever in quicksand, who had sunk so far that the moles couldn't find them, who had sunk maybe all the way to China where the children sang, "Durn upe tink wah chee."

When the dinner bell rang, Ada straightened the up-tucked skirts and pants legs and shooed the children up the path to the house, where Papa and Uncle John, their shirts wet with sweat, were splashing their faces with water in the tin washpan on the shelf inside the summer kitchen and combing their wet hair as they looked into the tiny mirror above the comb tray.

The long dinner table with benches on either side was covered with a table cover to keep the flies off. The table cover made a broad low tent coming to a peak held up by the spoon holder in the center of the table. Ada carefully removed the cover and turned up the plates while Cousin Lutie, Cousin Mamie, and Mama brought the food to the table. Uncle John sat down at the head of the table and bounced Little Brother on his knee and patted the girls on the head while the food was brought to the table. First came the platter of hot, fried ham slices with a bowl of brown ham gravy; then fried chicken piled high on a platter with a pulley bone for every child and a big bowl of chicken gravy; and fresh light bread and hot corn bread, cooked in an iron skillet and cut in wedges, and hot buttermilk biscuits; creamed squash, black-peppered on top; okra dipped in cornmeal and fried; red-ripe tomatoes, sliced; shallots; green black-eyed peas, snapped and shelled and cooked in ham broth; cold buttermilk from the springhouse; and coconut cake and peach cobbler right out of the oven.

Aunt Lizzie and Grandma Gray sat in chairs at the other end of the table. Papa sat next to Uncle John with the four children lined up beside him on a bench; and on the other side of the table, Mama, Cousin Mamie, and Cousin Lutie sat while Ada waited on the table. Papa, invited to say the blessing, spoke more slowly that when at home: "Heavenly Father, Give us thankful hearts for these and all thy blessings. Amen." Uncle John shouted, "Help yourselves! Help yourselves!"

As the bowls and platters passed up and down and around the table, the food piled higher and higher on the plates until Uncle John, fork in left hand and knife in the right, called, "Pitch in! Eat hearty!" All forks and knives clicked and the talk stopped. When mounds of food disappeared, leaving little vacant spaces on the plates, Ada brought hot biscuits from the oven to fill them. The butter was passed around again, the women began talking recipes, and Papa said, "That gravy is good; it tastes like more" as he took another helping.

At last the children began to say, "No, thank you. No, thank you" to Ada. They were saving room for Aunt Lizzie's peach cobbler eaten with spoons to the last sweet drop of juice, leaving plates clean.

With dinner over, with the men returned to the field, with Grandma, Aunt Lizzie, Cousin Mamie, and Cousin Lutie gone to sit on the shady front gallery, Ada brought out the chunk of lye soap, put it in the big tin dishpan, and poured boiling water over it from the black iron teakettle. She washed the dishes while the children dried them and set the table again: knife and fork placed to the right of each plate; plate turned face down to protect it from dust; spoons in the spoon holder (handles down) in the center of the table with the pepper sauce bottle. The table, reset, was covered with a thin cloth table cover tent to keep away the flies.

The long, hot, lazy afternoon followed. Aunt Lizzie and Grandma rocked in their rocking chairs on the shady front gallery. Cousin Lutie, Cousin Mamie, Cousin Ada, and Mama sat in chairs (with rawhide bottoms) in a group at the other end of the gallery. The children sat cross-legged on the floor or lay on quilt pallets listening first to Aunt Lizzie and Grandma talk mysteriously about old times, then to Cousin Mamie tell about the man who took to drink. He lived in Emory. He had a little wife about as big as a minute and he was a big mule of a man. Every night he took to coming home later and later and drunker and drunker and meaner and meaner, beating her up oftener and oftener.

She got tired of it and decided to cure him. So she bought plenty of heavy cotton-sacking and sewed the strips together to make two big sheets; then she put the sheets on the bed and sewed them together across the bottom and down one side. That night he came home drunker than ever, beat her up, and crawled in bed and went to sleep. When he began to snore, she took her needle and thread and thimble and sewed those sheets together top and side, with him inside. And she took an axe handle and started to work on him. He woke up yelling and rolling around like a bag of snakes off the bed and onto the floor, trying to get away from the axe handle. She kept right on whaling him. He got to the door and wriggled through onto the gallery, then off the gallery onto the ground, but she kept beating him every step of the way. Mama and Cousin Lutie laughed and laughed. But Dorothy sat still for fear Cousin Mamie would stop and say, "Little pitchers have big ears."

By the time he hit the ground, he was about half sobered up and he thought the Bad Man had hold of him and was taking him to the Bad Place. So he started praying: "Oh Lord! Save me! Save me! Save me and I'll quit my drink! I'll stay sober the rest of my life!"

He kept on praying and she kept on whaling him until he finally said, "Good-bye, Lord, Old Toffet's got me." Then he lay still.

Directly the little wife took her scissors and cut the stitches and opened up the cotton-sacking sheets. But he was so petered out he just lay there with his eyes shut, in the yard, the rest of the night. When he opened his eyes next morning and remembered the night before, he thought it was resurrection morn and the Lord had saved him. So he never took another drink after that. He was good to his wife and he never knew she was the one that cured him.

When the talking and laughing stopped, the rocking chairs kept rocking in rhythm with the heat waves shimmering along the sandy road, hovering above the sweet corn tassels beyond the garden until, at last, the children felt permitted to speak, to ask Aunt Lizzie to tell them stories about when she and Grandma were little girls living in Holly Springs, Mississippi.

Aunt Lizzie, older than Grandma, knew things Grandma didn't know. The Nelsons were English; the Craigs were Scotch and Irish. Both the Craigs and the Nelsons were Presbyterians and had been persecuted in England, Scotland, and Ireland for their religion.

There were afternoon naps, then supper, and, in the cool of the evening, more talk. Uncle John and Papa sat at one end of the front gallery, propped back in their straight chairs, talking politics and crops, and at the other end of the gallery the women sat. The children played in the yard, pushing sand into little caves and piles with their bare feet and when tired of that begged Aunt Lizzie for more stories. But Aunt Lizzie, talked out, sent them to Uncle John.

"Go ask your Uncle John to tell you about when he fought the Yankees," she said. But Uncle John said, "I let Lizzie do the talking for the family. I just listen. Go ask your Aunt Lizzie if she is descended from Lord Nelson."

Back the children went to Aunt Lizzie with the question. "It's a fact that the Nelsons are English," she said. "They came to this country before the Revolution. We may be descended from Lord Nelson's family. But if it should ever prove to be true, we'll hate to admit it because we don't approve of his private behavior."

"What's his private behavior?" Dorothy asked. Uncle John slapped his leg and laughed. Everybody laughed (the children too). But Dorothy got no answer and when she later asked her sisters, she still got no answer.

There was nothing now for the children to do but to sit quietly (all but Little Brother) in the growing dark, listening to grown-up talk. Little Brother told Papa that he ate a green persimmon that day. Uncle John and Papa laughed and Uncle John told Papa a joke about Mike and Pat, two Irishmen just arrived in this country. Never had seen a persimmon tree. Mike climbed the tree, picked a persimmon, ate it, called down to Pat. Said, "Pat, if you want to ask me anything about the auld country, ask me quick because I'm closing up for good."

Sometimes the visit to Aunt Lizzie's included spending the night and part of the next day, if Papa had business to attend to at the courthouse. But usually, after supper and conversation, Papa hitched Old Red and Old Dodson to the wagon and made a quilt pallet on the wagon bed for the sleepy children. The good-bye voices mingled with the rumble of the wagon wheels and turned to dreams of trees talking and herds of cattle thundering over the Sabine bridge.

There were no visits to Uncle Tom's house. He had no home, Mama said. His wife was dead and he traveled around visiting his children, nieces and nephews and taking long trips to discover lost relatives.

Like Santa Claus, he came in the night. But unlike Santa Claus, who always came at the same time each year, on tiptoe, Uncle Tom might arrive any night, shouting, "Hello! Menno!" His deep voice rumbled like thunder in the blackness. Awakened, the children heard Papa's voice and Uncle Tom's recede toward the barn, then return to the kitchen. Sitting up in bed, they listened to the talk until Uncle Tom dropped one boot, then the other behind the kitchen stove before he thumped up the kitchen stairs in his sock feet.

The children were too excited to sleep. They tiptoed from bed to bed, whispered, agreed that the first one awake in the morning would awaken the others. They hoped to be up before Uncle Tom came thumping down—to help him pull on his warm boots (two children to a boot), to make his spurs jingle, and to hear his very first words emerge with coffee drops from his longhorn mustache.

Uncle Tom was a news-bringer, bringing news of cousins, uncles, and aunts (all living) and legends of the dead. The children knew that he would stay for a long visit to help Papa with the farm work and to tell long tales by evening lamplight in the kitchen, or on the back gallery in shadows that lengthened as a south breeze blew the limbs of the hackberry tree before a new high moon. On a Sunday afternoon as he and Papa walked about the fields with the children tagging along, they talked as they walked. And when they sat down on a log to rest in the shade, the children sat down nearby to play silent games so they could listen to the talk.

When the children begged for stories, Uncle Tom told them about his father, Zacharias Belew, who was born in North Carolina, then moved to West Tennessee. "That was your great-grandpa," Uncle Tom said. Uncle Tom, his two brothers, and three sisters were all born in West Tennessee. The family moved to Texas before the War, to Collin County, to a community called Millwood.

"Your Grandma Mills was my youngest sister, Mary Anne Belew," Uncle Tom said. "When the War was over, she met and married your grandpa, John Lockhart Mills."

Uncle Tom's Grandfather Belew, named Zacharias Calvin, had told him that the Belews were French Huguenots who came to the Florida coast long before "The Revolution." Two, or maybe three brothers, they spelled their name a French way: "Belleau" or "Bealleau" or something like that. The brothers pioneered westward, one toward Oklahoma and California and one northward until he reached South Carolina "Where your great-great-grandpa, Zacharias Calvin, was born," Uncle Tom said.

"What's a Huguenot?" the children wanted to know. Uncle Tom always roared with laughter before he replied, "The Belew Huguenots turned into Methodists and Cumberland Presbyterians."

That was the extent of Uncle Tom's family history stories when

Mama was within hearing. She did not want the children to hear his stories about long-lost relatives he had discovered on trips to Oklahoma, Arkansas, and other parts of Texas; about Belew uncles who had been sheriffs in the early days and who notched their guns for every outlaw killed. On one long trip into "Indian Territory" Uncle Tom had discovered Belew relatives who were part Indian. One of Great-Grandpa Zacharias's brothers had gone to Oklahoma and had taken a squaw-wife. When Uncle Tom mentioned "Indian cousins," Mama shushed him, so the children had to wait for Sunday afternoon walks with Papa to ask for those stories.

"Do the Indian cousins live in wigwams and talk in Indian language?" the children wanted to know. Uncle Tom roared with laughter and slapped his knee before saying no.

"If we have Indian cousins, are we part Indian? Mama says we are not." Dorothy waiting for his answer hoped he would say yes.

"Maybe so, maybe not," was his gentle answer that followed a chuckle through his tobacco-brown whiskers.

On one long trip into "Indian Territory" Uncle Tom bought a pony from a Choctaw Indian chief who had put his brand on the horse's flank. On Uncle Tom's next trip to the farm, he brought the pony and sold him to Papa, who named him "Old Dodson."

He was good for nothing but eating, Papa said. When he was hitched to a wagon or to a turning plow, he ambled along in slack harness making the other horse do all the work for the team. But, stabled with another horse for feeding, he ate fast and fought for the other horse's share. So Papa had to stable him alone.

Old Dodson's fat back and rump made him a favorite with the children. All four could sit comfortably on his bare back. They mounted, one at a time, beginning with Little Brother, who sat in front. The child mounting grabbed Old Dodson's mane with the left hand, placed the left bare foot on the horse's knee, and with a heave from the next rider, was hoisted up. Mary Lee, the tallest, could mount, unaided except for a hand-up from Eva Rita — already mounted. They dismounted by sliding off his rump. (He was too lazy to kick.)

Old Dodson was not skittish. He did not shy at shadows nor sudden sights or sounds. Seldom could he be urged into a trot or gallop. Papa considered him safe for the children to ride alone as far as the Flats Schoolhouse and back.

Sometimes when Old Dodson was not in the mood to let the children ride, he would not let them mount. As a child grabbed his mane, he turned his head, seized the child's clothes in his teeth, and no amount of coaxing could entice him to let go. Once when Eva Rita was mounting, he stepped on her right foot. She screamed, but Old Dodson would not budge even when Mary Lee kicked him as hard as she could. Dorothy and Little Brother, already mounted, slid off his rump to push him while Mary Lee kicked. Then Dorothy ran to the barn for an ear of corn, which Little Brother held three feet before his nose while Mary Lee and Dorothy pushed on his flanks. Still he would not move, so Dorothy ran to the house for Mama, who picked up a stick of stovewood on her way down the barn path. Telling the children to stand back, Mama whacked Old Dodson on the flank with all her might and snatched Rita as he jumped, kicked up his heels, and galloped off across the pasture. Mary Lee and Mama made a pack saddle to carry Eva Rita to the back gallery to sit with her foot in a pan of coal oil while Dorothy ran to the field to tell Papa to come. He came running, felt of her foot, had her stand on it, walk on it, felt it again carefully, and said no bones were broken.

When Aunt Della and the Dallas cousins came for the summer visit, the children, paired by age, took turns riding Old Dodson to the Flats Schoolhouse and back: Mary Lee and Irma (the oldest), Eva Rita and Pearce, and Dorothy and Eva (who had first turn because they were youngest). Mary Lee and Irma—not playing fair—once rode on past the schoolhouse, over the bridge, into Van Zandt County before they turned homeward. The four, waiting their turns, grew impatient, and when Old Dodson emerged over the rise north of the Harlan farm, they armed themselves for revenge. With branches of willow fronds they waited at the Malloy bridge for the attack—two on either side of the road. On Pearce's signal, they tickled Old Dodson on the flanks, stomach, behind the ears, and over the nose and eyes. Startled, he lunged forward into a lope pursued by the four, shouting. On past the farm, past the McKeithen's, past the Calloway's, and on to the Woosley Schoolhouse, two miles north, he loped with Mary Lee and Irma screaming and bouncing. Mama and Aunt Della ran to the front gate when they heard the screams and shouting. The whole family was assembled to meet them when Old Dodson arrived, and Mary Lee and Irma slid off his rump. The children were all scolded—two for not playing fair and four for taking dangerous revenge. That night at the supper table Papa, told of the afternoon, was amazed to hear how fast and far Old Dodson had run.

Old Red was getting old and would soon be put out to pasture. So Papa sold Dodson to Mr. McKeithen and bought a sorrel to be a better teammate for Old Red. To the children, Old Dodson, grazing in Mr. McKeithen's pasture, remained a link with Indian cousins they whispered about under the bedcovers at night as they talked about Uncle Tom who had ridden away in a cloud of dust on a sunny morning but would surely come riding in again some night. Each night they went to sleep hoping to be awakened by the thunder of his "Hello! Menno!" and his jingling spurs.

Four,
Going On Five

Dorothy was the artist in the family. Papa said so. When she sat on her Thinking Post looking across the garden at the house, she could see through the walls—every corner, every shelf, and every member of the family at work and play. That was the picture she liked best to draw: the gabled house without the end-wall, upstairs and down. Then the people: Papa on the back gallery on his way to the barn with lantern and milk bucket; Little Brother sitting on the kitchen floor beside Grandma, who was churning; Eva Rita curled up in a chair in the front room, reading; and Mama chasing Mary Lee, who ran through the house to escape having her kinky hair combed.

Papa's favorite picture was the one she drew of Mama dressed in her Sunday clothes. When a neighbor farmer stopped by to sit on the front gallery and "pass the time of day," Papa told Mary Lee or Eva Rita to lend Dorothy a pencil and give her a piece of tablet paper so that she could draw a picture of Mama to show to Mr. Calloway or Mr. Malloy or Mr. McKeithen or Mr. Hughey. In that picture the house (with walls) was small and Mama was big. She walked from the house to the buggy hitched at the front gate. Her body was drawn in profile showing the shape of her little bustle under a sweeping skirt, her tiny waist and her balloon bosom that narrowed to a high neck edged in ruching under her chin. Mama's head was drawn full face (as if she were looking sideways) and was topped with a plumed hat tilted to show part of her pompadour. One arm stretched forward holding a ruffled parasol (closed in winter; open in summer), and from the outstretched wrist a little sealskin pocketbook dangled. Papa thought the picture was very funny but Mama did not like it. She liked the house-without-a-wall best.

Sometimes Dorothy added to her pictures: fences, the garden, north orchard, and flower beds in the yard; and colored the flowers with polkberry juice (purple), strawberry juice (red), bluing, and brick-bat-dust mixed with spit to make brown. And sometimes beneath a picture, she wrote, explaining as she wrote:

tmmllllooopppttt

copying letters as she had seen her sisters write.

Carrying a book, Dorothy followed her sisters about the house, saying, "Show me the 'A's; show me the 'B's," until her sisters grew tired and refused to answer. They had taught her to say the "A.B.C's." She wanted to read them. And when they refused to teach her she sought Grandma Gray, who opened her Bible and pointed out the letters and words (with emphasis on "God" and "good").

In the beginning God created the heaven and the earth.... And God said, Let there be light.... And God saw that it was good.

When Dorothy wanted to print the letters, Grandma found a piece of brown wrapping paper and a cedar pencil which she sharpened with a small, pearl-handled pocketknife, holding the lead point down in the palm of her left hand. Dorothy sat on the floor beside Grandma's chair, the Bible open on the floor, and with Grandma's help, located the capital letters, printed them in order, then located and printed the lower case letters.

As soon as she could print the letters, she found that saying the alphabet backward made a rhyme for skipping and jumping rope:

Z, Y, X double-ya V
U, T, S, R, Q, P,
O, N, M, L, K, J,
I, H, G, F, E, D,
C, B, A

By her fourth birthday Dorothy could skip, both long skips and short skips, high skips and low skips. But she could still not jump rope though she had often tried, using her sisters' ropes while they were in school. At first she held the rope still while she jumped over it, flat-footed, as it rested on the ground. Later, after watching her sisters and trying again and again, she could jump flat-footed over the turning rope. Still later, she could say (while she jumped flat-footed):

Shadrach
Meshach
And
Abed-nego

as her sisters did. Finally she learned to jump on one foot then the other and say:

Nebuchadnezzar
The King of the Jews
Traded his wife
For a new pair of shoes

In the middle of Grandma's Bible she found a page full of names. Among them were hers and Little Brother's, Grandma said, pointing to the bottom line and reading: "Robert Lockhart Mills, September 2, 1905," then to the line above: "Dorothy Gray Mills, July 8, 1902."

It would be better to learn to print her name first, Grandma said, when Dorothy wanted to write it. So they turned again to the first page of Genesis. Grandma helped her find and copy a capital "D," small "o," "r," "t," "h," and "y"; a capital "M," small "i," two small "l"s, and "s." All day long she practiced until both sides of the brown paper were covered and she could print her name by heart. Proudly, she showed the paper to Mama, to her sisters when they came home from school, and to Papa at suppertime.

Mama called her "Dorothy Gray Mills" when she scolded. Papa called her "Dot" whether she was good or bad. And when she asked why, he always said, "Because when you were born, you were no bigger than a fly-speck."

Papa had two pet names for all four children: "Horsefly" and "Snicklefritz." "When I sit down to rest," he said, "you climb all over me and cling like horseflies, I can't shake you off." He played a game of "Horsefly" when he was not too tired, bucking around the back yard with a child clinging to his back. Papa said "Snicklefritz" was the pet name his Holland-Dutch grandfather and grandmother had given him. It meant "Little Shaver."

Aunt Eddie, who had named Dorothy, insisted that she be called "Dor-o-thy"—with every syllable pronounced correctly. Mary Lee and Eva Rita called her "Dorothy Gray Mule" when she was "stubborn as a mule," they said. At first she cried. Later she kicked them, making them run away calling "Dorothy Gray Mule." One day she decided to hide instead of chasing them. And while hiding, she decided to change her name by writing it backward. Grandma found a piece of brown paper for her and soon she had printed "Sllim Yarg Ythorod." After that, when her sisters called her "Old Gray Mule" she told them she had changed her name to a new name which was a secret between her and Grandma, who told them, "I don't tell secrets. And I don't tease your little sister."

At night after supper dishes were done and her sisters sat at the kitchen table with their books, school tablets, and pencils, studying their lessons, Dorothy longed to sit with them. She longed for tablet paper like theirs to write her name on in straight, ruled lines. But neither would give her a sheet and Mama said to her, "Stop bothering your sisters."

One day when Dorothy asked to learn to print Little Brother's name, Grandma brought out an old Sears, Roebuck catalogue which she gave to Dorothy to use instead of Genesis, which was getting dirty, Grandma said.

Dorothy wanted to know if Genesis was a man or woman. Grandma explained that Genesis meant "creation" and then went to the kitchen to help Mama. Dorothy listened to their talk "...Genesis... Dorothy...woman." She heard them laugh and knew that she had said something important. She then heard Grandma tell Mama that she had given the old catalogue to Dorothy, and heard Mama reply, "We really need that old catalogue for the closet. But I guess we'll have to use corncobs until Dorothy learns to write." They laughed again and Dorothy ran into the kitchen to join in the laughter, feeling more important still. But the laughter died to smiles when she appeared. She was told "little pitchers have big ears" but she did not know how she was a little pitcher.

Using a stick for a bookmark in the old catalogue, Dorothy marked the pages of toys. The doll pages were her favorites. "Dorothy" and "Doll" both started with "D" and "o"; and the double "l" in "Doll" was like the double "l" in "Mills." When leaves came loose, as the toy pages soon did, she folded them and carried them in her apron pockets. Following her sisters about the house, she pulled the pages from her pockets, asked them to tell her words, and as soon as she knew a new word, she wrote it down; dolls, doll dishes, doll buggies. Grandma saved brown paper for her and when there was none, gave her ruled paper from her own writing tablet kept in her little hump-back trunk. Dorothy wrote very slowly and carefully in straight lines on the ruled paper to make it last as long as possible. But on the brown wrapping paper, she wrote fast to use it up as soon as possible.

In the spring before Dorothy's fifth birthday in July, Grandma made a new gingham cover for the primer, out of leftovers from Dorothy's red plaid dress. After sewing the cover on securely with neat little stitches inside, Grandma wrote Dorothy's name on the fly-leaf beneath Eva Rita's name, which was below Mary Lee's. Now the book belonged to Dorothy.

Every day she carried the book with her, walked around the house twice, pretending to go to school, and sat on the bottom front gallery step, using the top step for a desk to study her lessons. On cold or rainy days she sat at the kitchen table after walking through the house and through the house again. After studying her lessons, she recited: first, saying the alphabet; second, spelling her name; and third, pretending to read from the primer.

The first pages were easy: cat, rat, mat, sat. "The cat sat on the mat." When she did not know a word, she carried the book to Mama or Grandma; and when she had mastered a whole page, she was ready to recite her lesson to Grandma, who put down her darning or knitting to listen to Dorothy, sitting on a stool by her chair. When Dorothy had read half through the book, Grandma made a gingham school satchel to match the primer—a bag with a strap to go over the shoulder.

Each morning Dorothy walked twice around the house, her book satchel over her shoulder, holding her primer, catalogue pages, Sunday school cards, and later, an Indian head tablet and cedar pencil.

Some days Grandma could find no brown wrapping paper for Dorothy and needed her tablet paper to write letters to Aunt Eddie. On those days Dorothy begged for an Indian head tablet like her sisters'. But, having none, she had to write with a stick, marking on the ground—until one rainy day when she could not go outside to play, she discovered the blank flyleaves in the books in the bookcase. There were books and books that looked alike ("Shakespeare's books," her sisters called them); and another lot that looked alike ("Dickens' novels," they said). Each day she sneaked a book out, took it to a hiding place, covered both sides of the flyleaves with her name and Little Brother's, then sneaked the book into the bookcase again. She had used up all of the Shakespeare books and most of Dickens, when Papa went to the bookcase to get his leather money pouch which he kept hidden behind Shakespeare.

"Confound it!" he roared, "Where's Dot? Come here this minute!" He forgot about his money purse. Silently, one by one, he opened all the books — as she stood watching, watching, watching. And without a word, he turned her over his knee, turned up her dress, and spanked her drawers-covered bottom. Smack! Smack! Smack! Smack! Smack! He told her to sit on the chair until she stopped crying and left for the barn to saddle a horse to ride to town. When he came back to get his money purse, Grandma came into the room, handed him a quarter, and told him to buy four Indian head tablets and five cedar pencils. Papa looked at Dorothy still sitting in the chair, still whimpering, and told her she could go play.

All day she thought about those four tablets. Were they for her sisters? Grandma smiled when she asked and said, "Wait and we'll see." At suppertime Papa returned from Point and handed a package to Grandma. She opened it to let four Indian head tablets and five cedar pencils tumble out on the supper table. Nobody said a word. Grandma looked at Dorothy, handed her a tablet, then a pencil. Dorothy must write on both sides of every page she said, and when the tablet was completely used up, she must bring it to Grandma to exchange for a new one

As soon as she had ruled paper, Dorothy wanted to write her name the way it was written in the Bible. She practiced making lines of "t"s and "r"s across the page — whole pages of them — until Grandma wrote her name and helped her copy it. Soon she could write as well as print all of her names including "Dot" and the secret one.

Dorothy wanted to teach Little Brother to print and write his name. But Grandma said no. He was too little. He was only one. Sometimes he listened when Dorothy told a story from her Sunday school cards. His favorites were Daniel in the Lion's Den and David and Goliath because she made the lion and Goliath roar and he could roar with her although he had not learned to say words. He refused to listen to Dorothy's favorites: Jonah and the Whale, Noah and the Ark, and the Jesus stories (Jesus raising Lazarus from the dead and Jesus and the loaves and fishes). Jesus was magic like Aladdin in the fairy tale book. He could create something of nothing: dolls, doll clothes, dishes, silk dresses, ruby beads. She sometimes wondered as she sat on her Thinking Post if Jesus and Aladdin produced the toys for Santa Claus's pack, and the kitchen cabinet, corsets, shoes, gingham, and horse collars for Mr. Searsanroebuck to send from Chicago. If Jesus could walk on water (as he did in the Sunday school picture), he probably could walk on clouds. On windy days when a south wind blew white clouds across the sky, Dorothy lay on her back in the grass for a long time watching for Jesus to come stepping from cloud to cloud on his way north to Chicago.

How far away from Chicago did Jesus and Santa Claus live? Her sisters laughed and would not answer. Mama and Grandma said when she was older she would understand.

She felt time. Space she could understand when she saw it. The barn was one hundred yards from the house, Papa said, and the Malloy house was two hundred yards to the south. The Calloways lived one mile away, by the road, and Flats Schoolhouse was two miles south as the crow flies. Papa measured space in yards, miles and axe handles. One day when he returned from Point, he told Mama he had seen a fat woman who was "about two axe handles across the caboose." Dorothy asked Papa what the woman's caboose was, but Papa laughed and said, "Ask your Mama." And Mama said, "Your Papa ought to be ashamed of himself."

When Dorothy could see an entire distance at one time, she learned to reckon distances with her eyes, by comparison with the spaces she knew (to the barn or to the Malloys). But distances to places she could not see (Point, where she ate ice cream sitting at the little round table in Mr. Peeple's drugstore) she had to reckon in a timed landscape through which the buggy slowly carried her, its wheels throwing up sand sprays to fan edges of the buggy shadow crawling behind horse-shadow sprays from his lifted hoofs. Five miles from Point was a long, long way to watch lengthening afternoon shadows when the was going home tired, sticky-dirty, and sleepy.

Distances beyond Point, Emory, and Sabine Bottom (Dallas and "Out West" where Cousin Grace lived beyond the Pecos); distances to worlds of the dead (Mississippi, England, Spain, Thermopylae); to storybook worlds ("Briar Rose," "Jack and the Beanstalk"); to the worlds where Lord Ullin's daughter and Barbara Allen lived in Mama's songs: those places existed in fluctuating time and space somewhere beneath or beyond the constant heavens above the earth and the waters under the earth (all belonging to God, Grandma said; all except Hell, her sisters told her).

The far-away worlds she had never seen existed like changing dreams in sleep. "Do I dream with my eyes open?" she asked her sisters. "I can see in my dreams." But they said no, called her silly, and laughed.

What was real and unreal? She thought about those dreams sitting on her Thinking Post in early daylight. As the sun rose, she stood up to make her shadow reach the fence on the far side of the road. Though she stood for a long time, her shadow never changed; yet if she went away and returned at midmorning, the shadow reached the middle of the road and at noontime diminished to a round spot beneath her. Did time control her shadow?

When Papa rode home from Point with a bag of striped peppermint candy for her, she took a bite, chewed it to make a mouthful of sweet spit, then held her breath as long as possible trying to make it last forever. Waiting for the horses to be hitched to the buggy to take the family to Point, or to the wagon to take the family to Sabine for a fish-fry, she tried to make time go fast by running around the house until she was out of breath.

She could not control time nor understand its duration. The day before (Christmas and her birthday) were longer than a week. All day—that day before—she raced down the road to the Malloy's gate and back; to the barn and back; to the Driggers' corner and back; running, running, running all day long to make tomorrow come faster. By nightfall, time had whipped her to exhaustion and she climbed into bed early in tearful despair.

A minute could be an hour. An hour could be a day, a week, a month. And a month could be a year. Her birthday lasted an hour. But every minute lasted an hour when she sat on a chair for punishment. Sitting on the chair, she tried to make time go faster by thinking of Aladdin, Jesus, and Mr. Searsanroebuck and naming on her fingers all the things they might bring her: "sleepy doll, sky-blue silk dress, lace-trimmed handkerchief, ruby beads, and a turquoise ring."

The day after (Christmas and her birthday), when Mama told her she could not have another birthday or Christmas for a whole year, was a long, sad day. A year was like forever, and forever was how long dead people were gone—never to return, Grandma said.

In her dreams she could see dead grandfathers, grandmothers, uncles, and cousins; but never did she see them walking the roads and fields in Sabine Bottom. Were dead people real? Was Mississippi real? Was the Little Lame Prince real?

Her sisters said no. Papa said no. Mama and Grandma said no. And when she asked why, they said, "When you are older, you will understand." She wanted to know how long it would be before she could be older. A day? A week? A year? But nobody would answer that question.

Sitting on the flat top of the garden corner fence post, she waited to be older. With her eyes shut, she pretended to be asleep so she could dream that she was older: that she went to school everyday with her sisters, that she could read all the books in the world (as they could), and that she could know—at last—what was real and what unreal so that her sisters would never call her silly again.

Five, Going On Six

That was the year of the smallpox which was over in early April when the county health officer took down the yellow flag that had been flying at the front gate for three long months. On her memory calendar, everything that year took place before or after the smallpox. In the autumn, after her fifth birthday, she had, for the first time, driven a wagon team and had cooked a complete meal. In December she had, for the first time, witnessed a funeral procession go by: five little coffins (covered in cedar boughs and mistletoe) resting on the flatbed of a wagon on its way to the Woosley graveyard.

In autumn, winter, and early spring when her sisters were in school, Dorothy carried water to the men working in the fields. And when they worked in bottom land along Shuffle Creek, plowing or pulling stumps, she stayed to wander and wait for the men to quit work at noon or evening so that she could ride a horse back to the barn. As they gathered crops in the wagon, she sat on the spring seat beside the driver watching every move of his hands and reins: to the right, to the left, the pull to stop, the jerk and smack to go. Sometimes Orphus let her hold the reins; but she longed to drive the wagon, sitting alone on the spring seat.

At last, one day when he and Sid were pulling corn to feed and fatten the hogs for market, Orphus said yes. And while she drove the wagon and guided the team down the rows, the two men, one on either side, gathered the ears and threw them into the wagon bed. Once the team shied at a rabbit and lurched forward; Orphus and Sid sprang for the bridles and held the horses until they were quiet again. And when the wagon bed was full and could hold no more, the men climbed to the spring seat, one on each side of her, and she drove the wagon to the pigpens where they threw the corn to the hogs.

Indoors on rainy days Mama had always said, "We'll wait and see" when Dorothy had asked if — when she was five — she would be old enough to cook. She had been five for a long, long time and Mama was still waiting to see when, one morning, she was playing with Little Brother on the back gallery and heard Mama call from the front room. She ran to find Mama sick in bed (she had fainted, she said). Dorothy ran to get smelling salts and a wet rag to bathe Mama's face. But Mama still could not get up.

The three were all alone. Grandma was away, visiting Aunt Lizzie. Papa was away (he was teaching the Woosley School that year). Her sisters were in school. And Orphus and Sid were working in bottom land pulling stumps. Mama told Dorothy to mind Little Brother, to see that he did not leave the back gallery. Later she asked if Dorothy could build up the fire in the kitchen stove and fill the big pot of water to boil.

While Dorothy cooked dinner, Mama kept Little Brother in the room with her. Back and forth from the front room to the kitchen Dorothy ran, getting instructions and carrying them out. Standing on a chair, she lifted off a stove cap, slanted three sticks of stovewood into the firebox, one at a time, and put the cap back on. When the fire was hot, she removed a back cap, set the three-legged iron pot over the open flame and filled it half full of water. After carefully dropping the hambone into the water, she put the lid on to let it boil.

Next, she moved the chair over to the kitchen cabinet, stood on it, and washed the turnip greens which Mama had gathered earlier. She soused the greens up and down in the dishpan to wash off the dirt and picked each leaf on both sides to be sure she cooked no worms with the greens. Mama called when the hambone had cooked one hour and told her to put the greens in the pot to cook for another hour. The chair was again moved to the stove and the dishpan full of clean greens to the stove hearth, after which Dorothy removed the pot lid and dropped handfuls of greens into the pot liquor, punching each handful down with a long-handled wooden spoon (as she had seen Mama do). Again, the chair was moved to the kitchen cabinet.

Dorothy made the corn bread while the greens cooked. In a graniteware bowl she mixed soda, salt (three pinches each), two eggs, and three cups of cornmeal in buttermilk. She added more buttermilk as she stirred, until the batter was just right to pour. Next, she placed the iron skillet on the front cap of the stove and dished lard (the size of an egg) into the skillet. Waiting for the lard to melt and smoke, she moved the chair back to the stove. And carefully carrying the bowl, she set it on a corner of the chair while she climbed up to pour the mixture into the skillet. Hopping to the floor, she grabbed two big potholders; and after opening the oven door (carefully, Mama cautioned her, so that the hot door would not fly shut and hit her), she used both hands to lift the heavy skillet, lower it, and slide it into the oven. Then she slammed the door.

A little later, Mama called to say Little Brother could beat the dinner sweep to bring Orphus and Sid from the bottom. Dorothy had to lift him to stand on a keg and hold him while he banged with the hammer. He refused to stop; she took the hammer away from him and he fell off the keg and cried. But this time Mama did not scold her; she scolded Little Brother.

Orphus and Sid were surprised to find a new cook in the kitchen. Sid lifted the hot skillet from the oven and cut the corn bread into wedges before sliding it onto a plate for the table. Orphus dished the turnip greens from the pot into a bowl. And Dorothy filled the milk pitcher and placed the butter, pear preserves, and molasses pitcher on the table.

As the men ate, they said — over and over again — that the turnip greens were the best turnip greens they had ever eaten. Both told her she was a very smart girl, for five years old, to be able to drive a wagon team and cook a meal. And both said they wanted to marry her when she grew up.

All afternoon she waited for her sisters and Papa to come home from school so that she could tell them how important she was. Mama told them too, how Dorothy had cooked dinner and had taken care of her and Little Brother all day. At the supper table Orphus and Sid praised her cooking again and laughed and argued about which one would marry her until Papa pounded the table and shouted, "Confound it, that's no way to tease a child."

Nobody said a word for a long time. Orphus then said he would whittle a new top for her; and Sid said he would make her a new whistle — if that was all right with Papa.

After Christmas the children in Woosley School began to get sick one after the other. When Mary Lee got sick, Papa went for the doctor, who came and said she had typhoid fever. Two days later he came again with the county health officer to say she had smallpox; and they nailed a yellow flag on the front gatepost. One by one, Eva Rita, Papa and Mama had smallpox. Dorothy and Little Brother were last.

All day and all night for three months smallpox filled the house with cold fear, creeping under the doors. In March she lay in bed hot with fever and heard Little Brother cry in his sleep all night long and, all day long, watched him walk in circles around the room, his eyes shut, crying tearlessly — with one big pox on the end of his nose (and no others that Mama could find).

March blew the smallpox away. And on a cold morning in early April, the county health officer rode up to the front gate in his buggy, tore the yellow flag from the front gate, and rode away.

On one Sunday in late April she lost her first baby tooth; witnessed, for the first time, a marriage ceremony; and, most joyous of all, she awakened that morning to find Little Brother alive — after a night of fear that he would die and be buried with the five little children in the Woosley graveyard. Through that night of fear she awakened again and again to hear Little Brother screaming with pain from a "rising" on his temple (which, the doctor had said, was not ready for lancing).

Each time she awoke, she sat up and tried to stay awake (if she could stay awake, she could keep Little Brother alive). Shivering in the cold night, she remembered the cold December night the five little children had burned to death in the farmhouse beyond Reader Creek. She saw, again, the flames leap into the eastern sky above the black trees as she had seen them that night — standing on the back gallery with Grandma, Mama, her sisters, and Little Brother — while Papa ran to the barn, bridled a horse, and galloped, bareback, through the gate, kicking the horse in the ribs.

They watched and watched. The flames dashed higher and

higher and suddenly faded into a glow and died in the black night. The children wanted to stay up until Papa came home but Mama sent them to bed. Dorothy tried to stay awake to listen for Papa's voice. She was afraid he had burned up. Her fingers grew tired trying to hold her eyelids open and she fell asleep.

In the morning she awoke to hear Papa's voice. Jumping out of bed, she grabbed her clothes and ran to dress in the warm kitchen and hear what Papa was saying. The five little children (he said) were alone in the house while their parents were at the barn milking and feeding the stock. A coal oil lamp had exploded.

All day long that day, Dorothy thought about the exploding lamp. She had seen a lamp explode early one morning when Papa was at the barn and Mama was cooking breakfast. The light suddenly grew dim; Mama looked to see the flame burning down into the oil bowl, snatched the lamp from the table, ran to the kitchen door, and flung it as far as she could into the back yard, where it exploded in the air, shooting hundreds of flames into a big circle in the sky. The flames fell to the ground and burned out one by one.

After breakfast that day Papa and Mr. Malloy left for the sawmill beyond Shuffle Creek, to work all day with neighbor men, making five small coffins. Mama washed and ironed Little Brother's baby dress and a white dimity (Dorothy had outgrown) to take with her to Mrs. Hughey's, where she, Mrs. Hughey, and Mrs. Irwin were to wash and dress the five little children for their coffins.

All day Dorothy sat on her Thinking Post thinking about the exploding lamp and waiting for Papa and Mama to come home. At the supper table all ate in silence — even Little Brother.

The next morning Papa dressed up and, alone, drove off in the buggy to the funeral. Mama and the children stood on the front gallery to watch the procession go by. Following the wagon with the coffins, surreys and buggies carried the parents and neighbors, all covering their eyes with white handkerchiefs (both men and women).

The white handkerchiefs fluttered in her dreams that Saturday night in late April when Little Brother cried with pain all night — the white handkerchiefs, the flames from the burning farmhouse, and the exploding lamp. The flames from the lamp fell to earth and died, one by one, as Little Brother's screams died one by one. And she crawled deep under the covers.

Awakening slowly that Sunday morning to a silent house, she suddenly remembered the screaming night and ran to the kitchen.

There sat Mama holding Little Brother in her arms, a bandage around his head, his eyes shut. Her heart stood still (he was dead). But Mama smiled (he was asleep). The rising had opened (Mama said) when he accidentally rubbed his temple on an open didy pin in her dress. The pus drained out; the pain went away; and he slept. He slept all day. And all day, whenever she remembered his screaming night, Dorothy ran to see if Little Brother was breathing.

After breakfast that morning, Papa felt of her loose tooth again and said it was ready to be pulled. He sent her to Mama's sewing basket for the largest spool of white thread, and, breaking off a long piece, tied one end around her tooth and the other end to the doorknob of an open door. He then told her to slam the door. She did. The tooth flew out of her mouth and dangled there on the string. Papa took her to the back gallery for water to wash her mouth and gave her the tooth to keep in her apron pocket (because she was a brave girl, he told Mama, and she did not cry).

Papa and her sisters dressed up in their Sunday clothes and went to Sunday school and church. But she stayed at home with Mama and Little Brother and her tooth. In the quiet house Mama was busy all morning baking pies, frying chickens, and mixing biscuits. (Brother Dement, the preacher, was coming to dinner, she said.)

The smell of vanilla and frying chicken filled the house. She sniffed the fragrance, standing at the front window watching for Papa, the preacher, and her sisters through the rain. Waiting, she touched her nose to the windowpane and when a raindrop hit that spot, her nose raced it to the bottom of the pane.

At last the buggy stopped at the front gate, and one by one, two black umbrellas ballooned to the ground, raced through the gate and on to the front gallery. Through the window she looked up into the faces of Brother Dement and her sisters under the tent umbrellas, which were left open and resting on the gallery floor before the three stomped into the house.

Mama came from the kitchen to shake hands with the preacher, then excuse herself to return to the kitchen, leaving the three sisters to sit with the preacher in the front room waiting for Papa to come from the barn after he had unharnessed the horse and put him to pasture. Dorothy sat on a chair, knees stiff, legs straight before her and said, "Yes sir," to the preacher's questions, wishing Papa would hurry.

As soon as she heard his stomp on the back steps, she ran to the kitchen to help Mama. Soon the food was on the table and the family seated with Brother Dement at the head praying to Almighty God. On and on he prayed: "sin...sinners...sin...sinners." Dorothy's eyes did not want to stay shut nor her head stay bowed but, if she opened her eyes, the preacher might see her (then she would be a sinner). She tried to think of words to go with "sin" and "sinner." She thought of "pins" (the didy pin that opened Little Brother's rising); "bin" (where Papa fed the horses); "gin." "Didy pin and horse's bin and Mr. Williams' cotton gin." For "sinner," the only word she could think of was "dinner."

Brother Dement, at last, said "Amen." Papa passed the platter of chicken down the table, past the children, to the preacher and asked what piece he preferred. Holding his fork, prongs up, he said, "Brother Mills, I always take the rump." Papa laughed but Mama frowned, and later told Papa that was no way for a preacher to talk, especially before children. Papa laughed again and she told him he should be ashamed of himself.

After dinner, Papa and Brother Dement sat in the front room. Mama and the children washed dishes, then joined Papa and the preacher for afternoon Bible-reading and more prayer—this time kneeling, elbows resting on chairs.

Footsteps on the front gallery and a faint knock at the front door interrupted the prayer; and Brother Dement said "Amen" so Papa could answer the door. A young man stood in the opened door, a dripping hat in hand. Dorothy saw his frightened, blue eyes (as he asked for the preacher and motioned to the front gate where a buggy was hitched), and she heard the word "marry." Brother Dement nodded his head. Papa picked up one of the umbrellas and, holding it over Brother Dement and himself, the two followed the young man to the front gate where he climbed into the buggy to sit beside a young woman wearing a white dress and a leghorn sailor hat with a red rose on top. Mama and the children, standing in the doorway, could not hear, but they could see that the preacher was holding a book in his hand and talking; and the young couple in the buggy were holding hands.

In a few minutes the buggy drove away and Papa and Brother Dement came back into the house talking. Dorothy heard Papa ask something about "her old man" and the preacher reply "mad as an old wet hen." Papa shut the door and the preacher ordered the family to their knees again to finish the interrupted prayer which began with an explanation to God of the interruption—something about saving the souls of the young couple and removing them from temptation. Suddenly Dorothy heard a galloping horse, then heavy footsteps on the front gallery and pounding on the door. The preacher stopped praying. The door flew open. And standing there in the doorway was a bearded man demanding to see the preacher, who got up from his knees to face the angry face. The bearded man shook his fist at the preacher, and his heavy, black beard poured out shouts and curses while the preacher stood silent before him. He stopped, suddenly, and said quietly, "Which way did they go?"

Brother Dement nodded his head toward the west road. The man turned, walked back to the gate, and rode away at a trot up the west road. From the door and windows, the family watched him go. Brother Dement laughed; said he knew her Pa; said the old man would never catch them because he would stop in Point to get drunk, and before he sobered up the couple would be on the other side of Red River.

From the window Dorothy watched the rain pouring down and was glad the young couple were headed for Red River and not the Sabine because the Sabine (Papa said) was rising. She remembered when it rose over its banks, when the bridge went down carrying hundreds of cattle to drown and rot and be eaten by buzzards until their bones were left to bleach in tree limbs or lie half-buried in mud.

Six,
Going On Seven

In early summer before her sixth birthday, Dorothy learned about death from typhoid fever. Beautiful Grace Harlan (sixteen years old, Mama said) lay in a coffin surrounded with red roses and white cape jasmine. The organ played "Nearer, My God to Thee," the neighbors sang, and Grace's father and grown brothers wept aloud. Papa helped to carry the coffin from the Harlan house to the wagon on which it rode to Woosley graveyard. Sitting on her Thinking Post, Dorothy thought about Grace Harlan lying still in her grave; Grace and Barbara Allen became one ("Out of her grave grew a red, red rose/And out of his, a briar").

Before she was six, Dorothy had learned about death by fire, (the five little children), by drowning (the cattle in Sabine River), from smallpox, and from typhoid fever. She had heard about death by war—the War Grandma told about where her Uncle Frank Craig was killed in the Battle of Peach Tree Creek. She knew that wind could kill. Time after time Papa and Mama had watched the sky all day and all night, and when the air grew still and sultry, had herded the children into the old stormhouse when a twister appeared on the southwestern horizon. She had heard Aunt Lizzie tell about the "cyclone" that blew Emory away: that blew houses to kindling wood; oak trees to splinters; killed children; picked up a cow, carried her six miles and set her down, unharmed, to graze in somebody else's pasture. But she knew that people could not be carried safely anywhere by a cyclone.

On her sixth birthday, Aunt Eddie sent her *The Wizard of Oz*, a book with pictures about another little girl named Dorothy who lived in Kansas and who was carried to the land of Oz in the eye of a "cyclone." Dorothy could not read the book, so her sisters read it to her. After the first reading she insisted that they skip the first pages about the trip to Oz. Her sisters called her "silly" because nothing in a book was real, they said. Kansas *was* real, they said, but Oz was *not*.

Dorothy tried to read *The Wizard of Oz* by herself, and all the big books with big words her sisters could read, to find the secret of what was real and what unreal. She was tired of being silly. She worked hard to read strange words, spelling and sounding them out before she asked for help—sometimes with success, sometimes not. In reading from *Grimm's Fairy Tales* to Little Brother, one day, she pronounced "giant" with a "g" as in "go" and created in her mind a new creature different from the "Jiant" she knew in Jack the Giant Killer and the Jiant that David slew with a slingshot. She was coming to the end of the story when Mary Lee walked by, heard her, and ran laughing through the house to tell everybody about her silly mistake. She decided never again to ask for help from her sister nor to read to Little Brother where she could be heard and laughed at. Little Brother did not care how she pronounced words.

Dorothy tried to read the primer to Little Brother. She knew every word perfectly. But he was not interested in "The cat sat on the mat." He wanted "The Three Little Pigs" with "I'll huff and I'll puff and I'll blow your house in"; and "Red Riding Hood" with "What BIG teeth you have, Grandmother." "The better to EAT you with, my dear." He huffed and puffed with Dorothy and shouted, "Eat! Eat! Eat!"

Dorothy told the stories in the big books with big words as she turned the pages. And gradually, as she sounded out new words and received help from Mama and Grandma, she began to read along with telling. She wanted to teach Little Brother to read. She wrote his name beneath hers on the flyleaf of the primer and asked Grandma to recover it with a scrap left over from his blue rompers. Then the book could be his own. But Grandma said no. He was too little. He was only three.

She longed to go to school, and when school started in the fall after her sixth birthday in July, she began begging, every day, to go with her sister. Mama said no. School was too far. The weather, too cold. Wait until next year when she would be older. Mary Lee and Eva Rita begged Mama to allow Dorothy to go for a visit—just one day. Finally, Mama promised. Some Friday, she said. And Grandma taught her a recitation to say for the Friday afternoon program:

> *Is it rainy, little flower?*
> *Be glad of rain,*
> *Too much sun would wither thee,*
> *'Twill shine again.*

But Fridays went by and Christmas went by and still Mama had not kept her promise. Meanwhile, waiting, she continued to read and tell stories to Little Brother.

He demanded two stories again and again: "Chicken Little" and "Epaminondas"—stories told them by Aunt Eddie and Cousin Grace when they came to visit. Both were teachers. Both wore their hair in high pompadours, high-necked, white waists trimmed in lace, and sweeping swishing dark skirts on Sunday as well as every day. Aunt Eddie lived in Dallas and taught children with strange names like Peter Lopiccalo and Angelina Moriali; and Cousin Grace taught "outwest" beyond the Pecos.

When their visits were over, Little Brother cried for the stories, which Dorothy did not like because of their endings: In "Chicken Little," Fox Lox trapped Hen Pen, Duck Luck, Goose Loose, Turkey Lurkey, and Chicken Little in a cave and ate them one by one. In "Epaminondas" his Mama spanked him for making tracks in her pies. Dorothy refused to tell the stories until Little Brother agreed that she could change the endings. And, in time, he came to prefer her endings, especially the one where Epaminondas threw up pumpkin pie all over himself and all over the bed and it ran down all over the floor.

Little Brother laughed while the pumpkin pie ran through the kitchen, over the back gallery, and down the steps into the back yard. Sometimes Dorothy let the river of pumpkin pie run down the path to the barn and into Shuffle Creek.

Little Brother liked songs too, the ones Dorothy had learned from Grandma, Mama and Papa. Sitting under the hackberry tree with him, she sang Grandma's song "The Feast of Belshazzar":

> At the feast of Belshazzar
> And the gathering of his hordes
> As they drank from golden vessels
> So the Book of God records.
> In the night as they reveled
> In that golden, palace hall
> They were filled with consternation
> At the writing on the wall.
> 'Twas the hand of God on the wall. . . .

When she came to "the hand of God on the wall," Little Brother joined in. And while they sang the chorus she wrote "God" on the ground with her finger or a stick. Little Brother scribbled—thinking he was writing "God" too.

God was the reason Grandma decided the time had come for Dorothy to study the catechism. She wrote a letter to Mr. Converse, editor of *The Christian Observer*, to order a *Child's Catechism*. Dorothy carried the letter across the road to the mailbox, put up the flag, then sat on the front step watching the north road, waiting for the mail carrier until she saw him drop the letter safely in his leather mailbag. Thereafter, each morning she sat on the front step waiting for the mail carrier, saying to Grandma, "Is this the day it will come?" Each day, Grandma said no until, one day, she said maybe. But many maybes went by before the package finally arrived. Grandma let her open it and find the little black book with gold letters on the cover. When she opened to the first page, to her joy and amazement, she could read it:

> Question: *Who made you?*
> Answer: *God.*
> Question: *What is God?*
> Answer: *God is good.*

As she turned the pages, however, more and more strange words sent her to Grandma for help. She wrote her name on the flyleaf, put the catechism in her schoolbag with the primer, Sunday school cards, tablet, pencil, and torn catalogue pages. Each day she memorized a new page and, before the day was done, recited the answer to Grandma along with the preceding pages. The process, she found was like the game of "Club Fist."

> *What you got way down in there?*
> *Bread and cheese/ Where's my share?*
> *Rat gnawed it/ Where's the rat?*
> *Cat caught it/ Where's the cat?*
> *Hammer killed it/ Where's the hammer?*
> *Hidden behind the old church door*
> *and the first one who smiles or shows his teeth*
> *gets a hair pull, pinch and a slap.*

Sometimes she memorized two pages in one day, until, at last, she could recite the whole book perfectly. Grandma then wrote a letter to Mr. Converse, who sent Dorothy a prize: *The New Testament* — another black book with gold letters.

She found, upon opening the book, the list of the books in the New Testament, beginning with Matthew, Mark, Luke, and John, followed by a long list of unpronounceable words. She knew how to say "Matthew, Mark, Luke, John" in a rhyme used for skipping and for jumping rope.

> *Matthew, Mark, Luke, John*
> *Saddle the cow and I'll get on*
> *Open the gate and I'll be gone.*

Papa had taught her the rhyme and had given her a piece of "calf rope" (he called it), about five feet of half-inch hemp with a knot tied in each end to prevent raveling. The knots also made hand-holds to keep the rope from slipping through the hands.

After she had memorized and could recite the books of the New Testament in order, Grandma wrote a letter to Mr. Converse, who sent Dorothy a little gold pin for a prize. Grandma told her how to pronounce the big words; and while she was learning to say them, she found that she could jump rope or skip or hop while reciting them. Some (like Acts, James, Jude and Mark, Luke and John) were better for hopping; others (like Galatians, Ephesians, Philippians, Colossians) were good for skipping; and some (like first Thessalonians, second Thessalonians) were best for jumping rope.

Little Brother liked Colossians. And when they made a loblolly, patting the quivering mud with bare feet, they said, "Colossians, Colossians, Colossians" until the mud quivered no more and firmed into dough to be shaped into mud pies, mud dishes, mud tombstones (for little chickens' graves), and mud people (for God to breathe the breath of life into—though he never did and they always returned to find the mud people cracked open and crumbling to dirt again).

After Dorothy taught Little Brother how to make the S's whistle in "Thessalonians," they played a game with the chickens by creeping up on a rooster or hen and shouting in duet, "Thes-s-s-alonians," making the chicken jump into the air, flap his wings, cackle angrily, and hop-fly away.

When she wanted to learn the books of the Old Testament, Grandma copied them on paper for her from the Bible. Dorothy found that they were better than the New Testament for jumping rope and skipping, but not very good for hopping: "Genesis, Exodus, Leviticus, Numbers, Deuteronomy, Joshua, Judges, Ruth, first and second Samuel, first and second Kings, first and second Chronicles, Ezra, Nehemiah, Esther, Job, Psalms, Proverbs, Ecclesiastes, Song of Solomon, Isaiah, Jeremiah, Lamentations, Ezekiel, Daniel, Hosea, Joel, Amos...." When she was tired, she stopped on Obadiah and said a rhyme Papa had taught her:

> Obadiah jumped in the fire
> Fire was hot, he jumped in the pot
> The pot was black, he jumped in a crack
> The crack was wide, he jumped outside.

When she was not tired, she continued jumping through the Old Testament. "Jonah, Micah, Nahum, Habakkuk, Zephaniah, Haggai, Zachariah, Malachi," and on through the New Testament.

After memorizing the books of the Old Testament, she received another prize from Mr. Converse: a bigger, gold pin. Then she wanted to read the New Testament, which began with the begats: Abraham begat Isaac... Jesse begat David, David begat Solomon... Jacob begat Joseph... Joseph married Mary, mother of Jesus Christ, Son of God. She did not memorize the begats in order but chose the ones which were best for skipping and jumping rope. When she practiced "hot pepper" and "high water," she repeated the word "begat! begat! begat!" over and over again. And when she was teaching Little Brother by holding the rope still for him to jump over, they both chanted, "begat! begat! begat!"

Dorothy could jump her handrope forward and backward (turning it herself) and both "high water" and "hot pepper." However, when her sisters threw the big rope, she could not yet run in the "front door" nor "back door" nor "catch flies" properly. Neither could she jump "high water" nor "hot pepper," though she *could* jump "low water" to one hundred and "salt" to two hundred.

She was also beginning to understand time by the clock. When she asked permission to go to play with Polly Malloy (to escape from Little Brother), Mama told her, pointing to the clock, "When the little hand is on four and the long hand is on twelve, you come straight home."

She could not *feel* clock time, however. Playing with Polly she forgot about the clock on Mrs. Malloy's mantel until she heard the angry clang of the dinner sweep telling her that Mama stood with a peach tree switch in one hand as she beat the sweep with the other. She ran all the way home dreading the whipping from which there was no escape and knowing that she would not be allowed to play with Polly for a long, long time.

She could count to five hundred by ones and tens for "Hide and Seek." And she knew her "two-times" and "three-times" of the multiplication table. Still, Mama only said maybe when she asked if she could go to school with her sisters the coming Friday. Maybe! Maybe! Maybe would never come.

When April came and Mary Lee and Eva Rita begged Mama to let Dorothy go to school with them, she said, "Pretty soon." That was more encouraging than "maybe." So Dorothy practiced her speech, "Is it rainy, little flower?" and waited. Every afternoon she waited at the front gate searching the north road for the cloud of dust from the buggy bringing her sisters from school. The first faint dust sign sent her out the gate and up the road running. When they saw her, her sisters stopped the buggy and waited until she climbed the spokes of a back buggy wheel, stood—out of breath—on the buggy floor behind the seat, and leaned over, her head between theirs, to listen and tell. And while they talked about school, she saw it all in her mind, saw herself there too, and hoped Mama would say tomorrow was the day.

Each morning she watched Mama pack her sisters' lunch buckets and hoped there would be a third bucket for her with a cold biscuit left from breakfast, sausage, and a baked sweet potato. And each morning, saw her sisters drive the buggy out the gate and away without her. Then back to the kitchen she ran to ask Mama if tomorrow was Friday and to hear Mama say no. "You are the biggest question box I ever saw."

Little Brother was now three. He could talk plainly and begged for Dorothy's pencil and tablet to scribble on. She tried to teach him to write his name by showing him the "R" and "O" in "Roebuck" in the Sears and Roebuck catalogue pages and then a "B" and "E" and a "T." But he would not pay attention and ran away with her tablet. Dorothy found him in the smokehouse sitting on the floor with her tablet on the washboard, copying letters from the advertisement above the soap rack, and she took her tablet and pencil away from him. He ran crying to the kitchen, dragging the washboard behind him and Grandma gave him another pencil and a piece of brown wrapping paper, which he placed on the washboard on the kitchen floor and continued copying the advertisement — the name of the manufacturer, "Winchester." The ridges on the board made his letters wiggle. Dorothy asked Mama to make him place the paper on the floor and to make him allow her to teach him to write. But Mama said no; he was too little. Little Brother copied the large, fancy "W" in Winchester again and again, making them overlap and slant downward into a scribbled mass of wriggling curves. Dorothy ran away.

She drew a bucket of water and carried it to Orphus plowing in the field, and stayed the rest of the morning to follow his foot tracks in the upturned soil. Orphus glanced up at the sun several times before he decided it was time to unhitch for dinner and let her ride the horse to the barn. They heard the clanging plow sweep as they went together to the house to wash their faces and hands at the wash shelf on the back gallery.

"Wash your face and hands," Mama called to Little Brother as he ran to the back gallery.

"What?" he asked. Mama repeated more slowly, a little louder, "Wash your face and hands."

"What?" he repeated. "For the last time," Mama said, "wash your face and hands."

"What?" said Little Brother.

Dorothy explained to Mama that he really meant "Why?" when he said "What?" Mama laughed. Dorothy felt important. And Mama told Little Brother, "Because no boy with hands and face as dirty as yours can come to my dinner table." She then told Dorothy to pour the water into the washpan for Little Brother and to help him. Little Brother stood on a wooden stool to reach the washpan, dipped his fingertips into the water, and raked them from forehead to chin, creating running dirt streaks. Then he grabbed the towel.

Dorothy stepped onto the stool behind him and snatched the towel. Reaching around him, she held his wrists and plunged his hands into the water. He screamed, kicked backward, and upset the washpan, drenching himself.

"Stop teasing your brother," Mama called.

Dorothy left him — to sit on the steps. Wet and dripping Little Brother came to sit beside her. She jumped up and ran around the house — with Little Brother following — running barely fast enough to keep out of sight. He began to cry and then to scream. As Dorothy ran past the kitchen door, Mama called, "Dorothy Gray Mills, I told you to stop teasing your Little Brother."

Dorothy stopped and sat down on the top step again before she answered, "I'm just sitting here, Mama. I'm not teasing him. He's in the front yard."

Mama appeared in the kitchen door with a washrag in her hand, hurried down the steps and around the house to return pulling Little Brother by the hand, his wet front covered with dirt and his grimy face streaked by tears and nose blubbers. She brushed him off and stood him on the stool by the wash shelf, sniveling, scrubbed one hand and the other before holding him by one shoulder to wash his face. Trying to wriggle out of her grasp, he screamed, "Quit it" but Mama held him screaming, soaped the rag, waited for him to open his mouth again to say "Quit it!" and thrust her soapy, rag-covered finger between his teeth. He gagged and whimpered as she circled her finger in his mouth, and continued to whimper, standing still while she washed his face, legs, and feet and dressed him in clean, dry rompers which she sent Dorothy to bring.

Mama told both to behave themselves before she hurried back to the kitchen. In silence the two sat together on the top step, the silence broken only by an occasional sniffle. Dorothy did not run away again. She thought about "What." Mama always said:

"What on earth made you do that?"

"What on earth will you do next?"

"What *are* you up to?"

"What made you do that?"

"What made you do such a thing?"

"What *are* you doing?"

"What *will* you think of next?"

"What did you let Little Brother do *that* for?"

Mama never smiled or laughed when she asked "What questions." "What" named all the things Little Brother should not do but did.

He should not go past the front gate alone.

He should not go into the pasture with the cows.

He should not go into the woods alone.

He should not wade in the pool.

He should not talk back to Papa, Mama or Grandma.

He should not get his Sunday clothes dirty.

He should not play with his toys on Sunday.

He should not tell a story (lie).

He should not sing at the table.

He should not say "privy," "golly," "darn," "durn," "pee,"
    "hocky" (all words learned from the Driggers boys).

Little Brother refused to learn to print "what" and "why" when Dorothy tried to teach him. He preferred the fancy "W" in "Winchester." And while he was busy covering his brown paper with scribbled "W"s, Dorothy walked around the house and around the house carrying her gingham school satchel holding the old primer, Sunday school cards, *Child's Catechism, New Testament,* and *The Wizard of Oz,* practicing to be ready to go to school with her sisters some day.

At last a morning finally came when Mama said she could really go to school "tomorrow." While Grandma churned, Dorothy stood before her practicing "Is it rainy, little flower?" Mama said she must not put her fingers in her mouth, but must place her hands by her sides and keep them there. She must not stand on one foot but must stand firmly on both feet. Mama had studied elocution and she asked if Grandma thought Dorothy should make hand gestures. Grandma said no; she should speak "loud and clear."

Practice was interrupted by the sounds of men shouting and cattle bellowing. Mama, Grandma, and Dorothy ran to the front door and Dorothy ran to climb the support post of the barbed wire fence beside the front gate for a better view down the south road. Leaning far over to see better, she felt a barb pierce her stomach just as she saw cattle charging across the Malloy branch bridge with a hard-riding horseman racing before them to head them off at the corner. In fright, she jerked away and jumped down. The barb ripped a gash in her stomach and she ran to the house with blood gushing over her torn apron.

To prevent lockjaw from the rusty barbed wire, she had to lie on the floor of the back gallery all morning with clean, coal-oil-soaked bandages across her stomach. After dinner she vomited and was put to bed with a headache. While Grandma bathed her forehead with a cool cloth, she went to sleep and awakened at suppertime to find Grandma had made cambric tea for her instead of supper. Mama said no, she could not go to school tomorrow; next week, maybe.

The long, long week finally went by and again Mama said "to-morrow." All that long day she tried to sit quietly so that no accident could happen. When bedtime came, the new gingham dress was hanging over the back of a chair; clean Sunday drawers, suspenders, and underskirt lay on the chair beside clean stockings and patent leather one-strap shoes; and she wanted to go to sleep as fast as possible to make tomorrow come sooner. She shut her eyes tight and held her breath; but excitement would not let her go to sleep until Mama had let her get two drinks of water and Grandma sang to her: "Let us pass over the river and rest under the shade of the trees."

Miss Ella was the teacher. Until morning recess, Dorothy sat between Mary Lee and her deskmate, hardly able to see Miss Ella's big, white bosom above her sister's desk with an inkwell in the middle. Mary Lee let her look at the pictures in the history book and geography book, and let her copy numbers from the arithmetic book and draw pictures. But she slapped Dorothy's hands when she wanted to write her name in ink with Mary Lee's pen lying in the pen trough.

She grew tired sitting still while Miss Ella lined the children up in front of her and listened to them read. She grew so tired that she tried to stick her head in the desk to take a nap. But her head would not go in. And Mary Lee pinched her to make her sit still.

At recess time two big girls made a packsaddle to carry her to the girls' closet, which had four holes of different sizes and a blind (so the boys could not see girls going in). Dorothy wanted to use the largest hole but Mary Lee made her use the little hole because, she said, "If you fall in, nobody will pull you out. You will have to stay there the rest of your life."

After recess she sat on the other side of the room with Eva Rita and her deskmate. As the morning wore on, noontime grew further and further away. Weary of sitting still, she saw children raise their hands (holding up one finger or two), ask to be excused, and leave the room. She whispered "why" and Eva Rita whispered back that they were going to the closet. Dorothy decided to raise her hand, thinking that if she could go alone, she could use the big hole. When

Miss Ella nodded, answering her raised hand, she said, "Miss Ella, may I go make a branch?" The children giggled; Miss Ella smiled before she frowned around the room to stop the giggling and then told Eva Rita to go with Dorothy.

At noontime the big girls played "Crack the Whip" and let her ride tail. And in the afternoon Miss Ella let her sit on the steps in the sunshine and play "Jackstones" until time for the Friday afternoon program. When Miss Ella called her name, Eva Rita told her to go stand on the teacher's platform and say her speech, and gave her a little shove. For the first time she said in public, "Is it rainy, little flower?" The children clapped their hands and she stepped down from the platform feeling very important.

Going home from school that afternoon was a long, long journey. Her weariness was mixed with shame, for all the way home her sisters scolded her for having said, "I want to make a branch"—out loud. They were going to tell Mama on her, they said. And they would never take her to school again.

Seven, Going On Eight

Slowly, slowly the months crept by. Over and over she said, "Thirty days hath September, April, June, and November," and turned the pages of the Raleigh calendar hanging on the kitchen wall until Mama said, "Dorothy, I declare. You are going to wear that calendar out." When Mama tore August off the calendar, Dorothy used the back of the page to draw a picture of the big, brick schoolhouse Papa had told her about, in Lone Oak. She drew it to look like Mr. Searsanroebuck's house in Chicago, on the catalogue cover. All morning she carefully drew bricks, one by one, after which Mama gave her some beet juice to color them with a rag swab on a stick. When August was gone, she could count on her fingers the months until her eighth birthday.

After her birthday Papa was going to sell the farm. The family would move to Lone Oak and she would go to school with Mary Lee and Eva Rita in the big red schoolhouse. They would go to school upstairs and she, downstairs, they told her. Ever since she was five, she had wanted to go to school. But Papa had said she was too young; she would ruin her eyes reading and have to wear glasses like Eva Rita. When Dorothy was six, Mama had said no; it was too far for her to ride in the buggy in the cold, winter weather with hot bricks at her feet under the lap robe; she must wait another year when they would move to town. She waited. But when her seventh birthday came, they had not moved to town. Papa had been to Lone Oak and had told all the neighbors that he wanted to sell the farm.

By November Wes Driggers had told Papa that nobody would buy land because Halley's Comet was coming (the Almanac said so) and the world was coming to an end (the preacher said so). There was talk of holding a meeting at Flats Schoolhouse early in March instead of in August — after the crops were laid by so that sinners could be saved before Halley's Comet burned the world up.

Dorothy knew what the world would look like when it burned, remembering the burning brush arbor at Flats Schoolhouse last summer. Maybe her next birthday would never come; the family would never move to Lone Oak; she would never go to school. Papa and Mama both laughed and said the world was not coming to an end. But the Driggers boys said their Pop knew and could tell what was going to happen; and he had quit drinking whiskey so he could be saved and not burned up by Halley's Comet. They said when the world burned up, all the good people would fly on angel wings out of the flames, up to heaven; but the bad people would burn and burn and burn to live coals that would never go out. Grandma Gray said her Grandpappy Craig had told her about seeing Halley's Comet when it came before she was born; and nothing bad had happened. Grandma was not afraid.

Sitting on her Thinking Post thinking about Halley's Comet, she saw again the flickering pine knot torches at camp meeting last summer and heard again the singing: "Are you ready? Are you ready? Are you ready for the judgment day.... When the saints and the sinners will be parted right and left...."

The saints and sinners, all seated together on long wooden benches, sang and listened to the bald-headed preacher who mopped his sweating brow and waved his handkerchief at the people as he described the fires of Hell on judgment day: "On that great and glorious day God will wind up the lightning and set the thunder behind his throne."

Papa, Mama, Mary Lee, and Eva Rita sat on a bench at the edge of the arbor. Beside them on a quilt pallet Little Brother was asleep and Dorothy sat, wide awake, watching the pine knot torch above her flicker in a gentle breeze.

The roof of the arbor, made three weeks before of green boughs, was parched and dry from summer sun. The arbor was fringed with pine knot torches fastened by leather thongs to arbor posts and slanted outward away from the roof.

As Dorothy watched the fringe of torch lights flickering in a south breeze off Sabine River in the blackness outside that circle of light, suddenly the wind rose. The torches flared upward. The roof flashed into a giant flame. The people shouted and ran. Papa snatched Little Brother; Mama snatched Dorothy by the hand and ran, shooing Mary Lee and Eva Rita ahead of her. Huddled together in the buggy, they watched Papa run to join the men who had found a ladder, buckets, and a washtub to bring water from the River. Men climbed the ladder to pour water on the schoolhouse roof. Others found tow sacks to beat out the flames in dry grass around the arbor and schoolhouse; and others stamped out sparks with their feet. The flames leaped higher and higher into the black sky. The frightened horses and mules, hobbled and grazing around the schoolhouse grounds, snorted, reared, fell, regained their legs, and hobbled off into the darkness.

As suddenly as the wind had risen it sank again to a gentle breeze. The flames had burned the square arbor roof into a dull, red lace of embers framed by the pine knot torches hanging from smoldering posts and lying on the ground.

Little Brother's screams sank to whimpers and he fell asleep in Mama's arms before Papa came—his white Sunday shirt blackened, torn, and wet with sweat—to say Mr. Harlan and his boys would keep watch on the fire for the rest of the night.

The shouting died as the fire died and the men disappeared into the darkness to round up the horses and mules. Papa found Old Red, hitched him to the buggy, and headed him toward home. Dorothy, sitting between Papa and Mama (holding Little Brother on her lap) tried to stay awake in hopes Papa would say something important about the fire. Just before she drifted off to sleep, she heard Papa say the sinners were no better than the saved at stomping out the fire. Mama said, "Shame on you, Menno."

That was last summer. That was before the Almanac and the *Rains County Leader* told about Halley's Comet. Papa said the Comet would look like a giant falling star with a long, long tail. It would come near enough to be seen but would go away without hitting the earth. Dorothy had seen shooting stars many times; and Polly Malloy had said if you make a wish on a falling star, it would come true.

Papa was not afraid the Comet would burn up the world. But Papa had been mistaken about the cyclone. He had said the cyclone would hit Grand Saline. But it didn't. It hit Emory. Afterwards, when they went to visit Aunt Lizzie and Uncle John near Emory, she had seen all along on either side of the road, giant oak trees, fallen and splintered; she had seen straws driven through oak tree trunks — by the force of the wind, Papa said. She had heard Aunt Lizzie tell about the little orphan baby whose father, mother, brothers, and sisters were blown away and killed by the cyclone while the baby slept, protected and safe under a caved-in oak bedstead. A miracle, Aunt Lizzie called it. Uncle John told of how the cyclone had lifted cows out of pastures, carried them five miles through the air — unharmed — and set them down to graze in somebody else's pasture; and of churches blown away and good and bad people killed.

That was the same cyclone that had passed south of Woosley and Flats, moving along the River, then veering northeast toward Emory. Dorothy remembered that sultry day. The air was still and cyclone weather, Mama called it. All day she had watched the sky for signs of a funnel cloud. At midafternoon she called the children and herded them into the roofless stormhouse northwest of the house — roofless because Papa was in the process of building a new roof and had torn the old one away. Papa came running from the field as the funnel cloud appeared in the southwest between the Driggers' house to the west and the Harlans' to the south.

Papa held Dorothy in his arms and Mama held Little Brother as they stood in silence watching the weaving cloud. Suddenly, from the west, across the still air, came shouts, curses, and doors slamming. Wes Driggers ran from their back door, slamming it behind him, and headed for the barn. The door opened again and Mrs. Driggers ran out, shouting and waving a broom, following Wess. As she gained on him and swung at him, he turned and grabbed one end of the broom. The two went round and round in a whirling "stiff starch," shouting and cursing. The Driggers boys ran from the house and from the barn to dance around their whirling parents. The Driggers girl stood in the kitchen door watching.

Papa laughed but Mama did not. She took Little Brother and Dorothy by the hand and shooing Mary Lee and Eva Rita ahead of her, rushed the children into the house and slammed the door so that they could not hear the curse words. Papa followed, shouting, "Confound it, Lou! Have you lost your mind?" But Mama did not answer. She slammed the door again while he kept shouting, "Confound it!"

He was still shouting, "Confound it!" when the wind struck. The door flew open. The chairs banged about the room. Glass from broken windows tinkled on the floor. The counterpane from the bed billowed into a white cloud against the ceiling as Papa pushed Dorothy and Little Brother to the floor and knelt over them. Peeping out, Dorothy saw her sisters crawl under the bed but she could not see Mama anywhere. From the roof came a bump, bump, bump, bump and then a crashing on the front door. Billowing counterpane, quilts, and sheets came down on Papa. And, underneath Papa, it was dark—and, suddenly, quiet.

Papa threw off the bedclothes and stood up. The wind was gone. The chinaberry tree in the front yard, blown up by the roots, had climbed the steps and wedged itself in the front door. Her sisters crawled from under the bed. And there stood Mama, safe and sound. Together they went to the back gallery and saw chicken coops scattered about the yard, upside down; broken limbs on the hackberry trees; and bricks scattered about—the bricks that had gone bump, bump, bump on the roof. Papa pointed to the funnel cloud moving southeast toward Grand Saline, and walked about the yard and around the house. When he came back, he said the storm had not touched the Driggers' place. Mama said, "Well! I'll declare!"

Wes Driggers, Papa said, was not afraid of cyclones: but Halley's Comet was sending him to church sober. On his way home from church he always stopped by to sit on the front gallery and give an account of the sermon. Away back in Bible times—Wes said the preacher said—the people of Jerusalem were so sinful that God sent Halley's Comet to warn them to repent; but they paid no heed so God destroyed Jerusalem. Ever since that day God sent the Comet once in a while to warn sinful people somewhere. But this time he was planning to send it to burn up the whole world full of sinful people everywhere.

Mama did not talk much about the Comet. She said the Almanac said it would be brightest in April—Dorothy's most important month except for July (her birthday) and December (Christmas). Because Mama was not afraid the world would end, she sent an extra large order to Mr. Searsanroebuck in March: extra material for school clothes for Dorothy and her sisters (gingham, nansook, bleached and unbleached domestic, thread, sewing machine needles, lace, braid, and ribbons); romper cloth for Little Brother's rompers; cotton flannel for winter nightgowns and winter underskirts and bloomers; and unbleached sheeting for new sheets and pillowslips.

All winter the quilting frames had been up, and Mama, Grandma, and neighbor women had quilted quilt after quilt, which Grandma had pieced and kept in her little trunk until needed. Grandma had given Dorothy a little thimble for her middle finger and had taught her how to quilt. By April Fools' Day the new quilts were all quilted, folded, and stored away in old pillowslips (to protect them from dust), and the quilting frames stored away in the smokehouse.

Each morning after April Fools' Day Papa got up very early to milk the cows, hoping to see the Comet. Dorothy tried again and again to awaken early too but she never could. Papa told her to wait until May, when the Comet would appear in the evening, trailing its long, long tail halfway across the sky. Then, Papa said, the children could all stay up late to see it. But when May came, try as hard as she could to prop her eyes open with her fingers, she always fell asleep and awakened next morning to hear Mama and Papa describe the Comet as they ate breakfast. By the end of May the Comet was fading away, Papa said.

Mama and Papa talked more and more about moving. Papa wanted to move "outwest" beyond the Pecos. Uncle Willie (Grandma Gray's brother) had gone west, had settled claims on land, section after section, and had a big ranch in Pecos County. Papa, Mr. Malloy, Mr. Lon Hughey, and Mr. Calloway talked about cattle country and settling claims on land. But Mama wanted to move to Lone Oak.

Mama and Papa agreed that the family must move because Mary Lee was thirteen years old and each day becoming more and more interested in boys and less and less interested in books. They did not want her to run away and marry some country boy the way some of the girls in the community had done—at fourteen or fifteen. They wanted their children to get a good education and agreed that the family should move to a place where there was a good high school. Papa wanted his daughters to be teachers of Latin and trigonometry; and Mama wanted them to study elocution.

When the quilting frames were stored away, the sewing machine

was opened, threaded, and going as Grandma cut garment after garment (usually by the chart) and Mama pedaled the machine. Dresses,
underskirts, and drawers for Mary Lee, Eva Rita, and (last) Dorothy
were completed and hung behind the corner curtain, ready for
school days in Lone Oak. Dorothy's new school drawers and underskirts were trimmed in Grandma's knitted lace and insertion with
rows of tucks between the insertions—all except the cotton flannel
underskirts and bloomers—for cold, winter weather. After the school
clothes were finished, flannel nightgowns for all the family and
rompers for Little Brother were made and stored away in dresser
drawers. Finally, after the new sheets and pillowcases were hemmed,
the machine was closed, rolled into place under the west window,
and the embroidered linen doily replaced on top with the gold-lipped
vase sitting in the middle.

In March Papa had plowed the garden. Dorothy and her sisters
helped Papa plant the vegetables (a larger crop than usual because
Mama wanted to can a large supply to take to Lone Oak). By the
end of May, with the sewing done and the garden planted and
weeded, Mama and Grandma could take afternoon rests on the back
gallery—waiting for vegetable and fruit canning time. Except for
dishwashing, and bringing in water and stovewood, Dorothy and her
sisters were free to play, hindered only by Little Brother tagging
along.

With time to sit on her Thinking Post on lazy June days—the
blue skies of God's firmament stretching from horizon to horizon and
a gentle breeze blowing from the southwest—Dorothy forgot Halley's
Comet and dreamed of her coming birthday and of school days in
Lone Oak to follow. In her apron pocket, the folded pages from the
Sears and Roebuck catalogue pictured the birthday presents she
dreamed of: a sleepy doll as big as Little Brother to hold in her arms;
store-bought paper dolls with little flaps to bend to make the clothes
stay on; a big, store-bought doll house with upstairs and downstairs
full of store-bought furniture. And, looking at the sky, she longed for
a sky-blue silk dress with little white polka dot stars on it.

Dreaming of school days in Lone Oak: She wore her new, red
plaid, long-waisted dress with pleated skirt, and her new red hair
ribbon bow on her hair, which was parted on the side and hanging in
curls. She sat at a desk with another little girl (whose face she could
not see). Her own books, pencils, and tablet were tucked away inside
her desk; and she sat very still, her feet flat on the floor and her

hands folded on her desk, so the teacher would not scold, exactly as her sisters had told her she must do. At recess time she played "Jack-stones," "Wolf Over the Ridge," and "Crack the Whip." But she never tore her stockings or dress and she always kept her dress clean.

Although Papa had not sold the farm, he said the family would move anyway, before the school year was to begin in late September. He would stay on the farm until the crops were gathered and sold and the farm was sold. Mr. Calloway had told him that his daughter and her husband, one of the Lynch boys, wanted to buy the place if they could agree on trading terms.

In the dark, early morning of her birthday, she awakened, screaming—to escape from a funnel cloud of fire (with snakes and mad dogs swirling around her), sucking her down, down, down to bury her alive in quicksand in Shuffle Creek. Mama's hand on her forehead told her she was awake. Mama told her it was her birthday and brought the lamp from the kitchen so Dorothy could see to open her presents, wrapped in tissue paper, piled on a chair beside her bed: new clothes for all her dolls (from Grandma) made from the material of her own new school clothes with lace on the doll drawers and underskirts; a little gold flowerpin with a tiny ruby—her birth-stone—in the center (from Aunt Eddie); new shoes—button boots with a red tassel (from Mama); new black stockings (from Papa); a cane whistle (from Little Brother); a barrette (from Mary Lee); and a cigar box covered in tissue paper (from Eva Rita).

Mama sat on the edge of the bed helping her open her presents. Then she went to the kitchen to cook breakfast before Papa came from milking. Dorothy dressed in her clean birthday clothes hanging on the back of the chair before she brought her box of play pritties from under the bed. Again she sorted her old playthings, replaced them and added her new treasures, including the tissue wrapping paper carefully smoothed and folded.

She pushed the box back under the bed and stood up. Rising on tiptoe, she stretched her neck to be as tall as possible. Now she was, at last, eight years old. Motionless, she stood, waiting, for the morning light coming through the window to outshine the lamplight. At last, she turned the wick down, cupped her hand over the chimney, and blew. Through the kitchen and out the back door she ran as fast as she could to her Thinking Post to wait for the new day.

Catalogues

The Farm

Everybody in Sabine Bottom worked—except babies, who soon grew old enough to demand jobs to prove they were no longer babies: bringing in kindling, feeding chickens, gathering eggs or vegetables in the garden, and minding a new baby brother or sister. A boy's first initiation into manhood was being allowed to go with his father to slop pigs, milk cows, or open and shut gates when cows and horses were driven to stall and stable or let out to pasture again. There were no initiation rites for girls, who were born girls and stayed girls—with occasional exceptions. When the children in a family were all girls and a father despaired of ever having a son, he sometimes encouraged the youngest daughter to be a tomboy, taught her to do the jobs usually assigned to a boy, and boasted of her boylike accomplishments to neighbor men (who had sons).

The Mills farm and the farms surrounding held a community of families who, with preceding owners, were still clearing land of trees and guarding it against reversion to woods. The Mills farm consisted of one hundred acres of cleared and planted land in addition to woods, pastures, and new bottom ground where stumps were being burned and uprooted by teams of horses or mules harnessed to chains

wrapped around the resisting stumps, their roots grasping and clinging to rocks far underground.

Land clearing was a winter job that began after crops were
gathered (November) and lasted until spring plowing time (late
February). With a crosscut saw two men sawed and felled the post
oaks, pin oaks, and water oaks, trimmed off limbs, and hauled the
trunks to the sawmill beyond Shuffle Creek, where they were sawed
into lumber for buildings or into cross ties for railroads. The oak
limbs and the honey locust trees were good for fence posts. Other
trees — blackjack, hackberry, and elm — were cut into lumber or used
for log buildings: corncribs, pig sheds, log barns. Black walnut and
hickory nut trees were allowed to stand — often alone, silhouetted
against the sky in midfield — for their nut crops. Or, if they were cut,
they were sawed into boards, planed to glistening smoothness, stored
for curing, and saved to use for furniture or coffins. Elms, redbuds,
and seedling box elders were allowed to stand along fence rows for
shade, and often so were hackberries. Sumac bushes grew into hedges
along roadsides. And along creeks, branches, and pools, willow trees
drooped and leaned toward their drinking water.

When the men were clearing land on clear cold or damp cloudy
winter days, Dorothy had the job of carrying drinking water to the
working men unchallenged by her sisters (in school) and Little
Brother, too little for the job. With a gallon, tin syrup bucket two-
thirds full of fresh-drawn water she took off for the bottom, shod in
black high-laced shoes and black ribbed stockings bulged in lumps of
long underwear beneath; snug in a big sister's old, elbow-patched
jacket; toboggan cap pulled down to her eyes and wrapped around
her neck; stocking mitts on her hands made of old black stockings —
their feet beyond further darning — with the feet cut off and holes cut
for the thumbs.

Once the men had drunk the water, she was free to wander into
the cleared pastures hoping to find overlooked milkweed pods, skipping stones, jackstones, dead butterflies, old bobwhite nests, locust
shells, snakeskins, or small, sharp thorns (for needles) to drop into
her empty bucket and take home. Or she stayed in the bottom, playing in the creek sand, smelling the wood smoke rising from the
burning stumps, watching the horses strain, pulling the stump chains
taut until the taproots lost their hold on the earth, growled, and
broke into view spreading quivering tentacle roots like a giant spider
jumping into the sky; she waited until the dinner gong or supper

gong stopped the men at work and was allowed to ride a tired, hungry horse to the barn, holding the tin pail of play pritties carefully in front of her in one hand, holding the horse's mane in the other in case he decided to trot to his feed trough.

Carrying water to the working men extended from winter land-clearing through spring plowing into summer cultivation of planted crops, and on into the autumn crop gathering. In spring when the men plowed the cleared fields with a big turning plow, Dorothy followed the plowmen, stepping in their tracks, looking for nests of field mice turned up by the plow. She put the little pink, blind things in her empty bucket, took them home and hid them in a bureau drawer; tried to feed them grass; watched them die; buried them in match-box coffins in the peach orchard beside the graves of dead baby chickens.

In summer the men plowed the weeds from between the rows of growing crops, using a cultivator. And in autumn Dorothy was allowed to sit on the high spring seat of the wagon to guide the team down the rows of corn while two men, one on either side, gathered the ears and threw them into the wagon.

In winter, summer, spring, and fall—when work allowed—the children wandered the farm and adjacent roadsides.

In cleared pasture lands, thorn bushes sprang up among the grasses: crabgrass, Johnson grass, Bermuda grass. And between grass clumps the Jimsonweed, bull nettles, cockleburs, bitterweed, broom-weed, sassafras, mullein, and prickly pear grew. In cleared pastures, in spring and early summer, the children looked for sheep sorrel and sour dock to eat (and wild onions); and in the late summer and fall, pulled broom-weed for play brooms to sweep their outdoor playhouses marked off into rooms with sticks and tree limbs; and pulled sumac berries to suck the sour juice.

Along the roadsides and in the pastures they picked dried milk-weed pods, filling their apron pockets full; then sat in the shade patiently opening each pod, extracting tiny bits of gum from it, and—after an hour or so—collecting enough of the wax to make a substitute for a chew of store-bought chewing gum.

In the swampy land near Shuffle Creek they saw skunk cabbage and picked the tender leaves of poke salad, in early spring, to take home for cooking. In late summer they collected sweet-smelling water lilies and cape jasmine, hauling home loads of them in Little Brother's little red wagon.

In the heavy woods along the Creek, in late May or June, they hunted for hog plums for jelly making. In late July or August they looked for huckleberries to eat by the fistfuls. In September they knew the red haws and black haws were ripe for eating, and in late summer the wild grapes were right for jelly.

In early, early spring, when the winter turnip greens were almost gone, lambs'-quarters, growing in fence rows and corners, were gathered to be cooked with the turnip greens.

In field and pasture and by roadside they chased butterflies — yellow tinted and bold black-and-orange — blowing them with puffs of breath from flower to flower but never touching them (if a butterfly lost the powder on its wings, it could not fly and would die); caught snake doctors near branches, gullies, and pools; and in the waterholes of half-dry gullies and branches caught tadpoles, minnows, and wiggletails (when they were on their way home with an empty water bucket to put the catch in); searched for devil's knitting needles in the grass; hoped to scare up a nesting feelark (fieldlark) to watch it dart straight up, high into the sky, to hear its clear-noted whistling tune when it returned to sit on a nearby fence post waiting for the children's departure. Going toward the barn, they looked for doodlebug holes (where they sang to the doodlebugs to entice them out of their holes), and for tumblebugs rolling their little balls of animal manure along. When the children grew impatient with the tumblebug (because they wanted to find out where he took his tumble-ball), they played hide-and-seek with him by pushing — with sticks — his ball into the grass or behind clumps of dirt, sending the bug in frantic search for his manure-ball. When horses or cows were in the field (and when a child had an empty match box in her apron pocket — as she usually did, just in case), they caught horseflies by popping the box down over a fly while he was feeding on a horse's or cow's shoulder or flank, and shoving the box lid closed before he could escape. Inside, the horsefly buzzed frantically in low-pitched and high-shrill quivering tones. The children never turned a horsefly loose; they either let him die in the box or they later transferred him to a fruit jar (when they got home) so they could watch him beat his iridescent wings up and down. When summer-hot earth burned their bare feet, compelling them to rest in the shade of tree or bush, they listened to and answered the katydid: "Katy-did, Katy-didn't, Katy-did, Katy-didn't." Resting, they listened to locusts buzzing in the trees telling them summer was nearly over.

In the long twilight and growing dark of July and August evenings, the children, each equipped with a glass fruit jar, took to the yard, the road, and the orchards to catch lightning bugs to see who could catch the most. When they grew tired, they counted their fireflies. Then they turned them loose again or they put them all in one jar to make a big blue glow before they released them to blink into the night air filled with a chorus of tree frogs "peep-peeping" and distant bullfrogs "plump-plumping" in the pool beyond the barn.

At Christmas time the children gathered mistletoe from the oak trees, tied red yarn bows on bunches to hang about the house for Christmas decorations.

In the pastures and fields and woods, pain and danger lurked to strike suddenly anywhere, any time. Barefoot, the children stepped carefully to avoid sandburs that thrust hooked spines into the toughest foot sole and, if pulled out too hastily, left a crooked sticker to fester under the skin. They watched for stinging nettles that whipped bare legs and for cockleburs that clung and built clumps in the hair and clothes. They watched for the big red ant beds — little volcano cones spewing hundreds of fierce red ants that attacked legs and arms and ran under the clothes to sting, leaving throbbing red welts that sent the children running to the house to dab the stings with bluing. They watched for stinging scorpions living in decaying wood and ready to thrust hooked tails into a foot that stepped on them or a buttock that sat on them. They watched for wasps. They knew the harmless dirt dauber from a wasp, not only by its mud honeycomb nest but also by its size, color, and movement. The wasp was black, slender, with fast-flying wide wingspread; the dirt dauber, brown-gray, slower moving, heavier in body, lumbered harmlessly about its mud-house building, ignoring human observers.

They knew the sting of the bumblebee, the hornet, and the yellow jacket, and when they were too far away from the house to run for the bluing or baking soda, they made a mud pack for the sting by spitting on the soil. Sticktight fleas seldom bothered the children. They preferred cat flesh. But the hopping fleas that lived in the grass hopped, bit, and hopped away to leave a mild pinchy itch.

There were chiggers — always. From late spring to fall, there were chiggers. The children looked after themselves and each other for chigger bites because they were able to see a chigger and scratch it off either with a fingernail or a pinhead, after which they crushed the chigger between their thumbnails and watched its blood-full belly pop. The itch was relieved with a spit mudpack or a bit of butter. Grown-up people could not see chiggers and therefore had to remove them another way—usually by applying sulphur or coal oil repeatedly until the chiggers died. There were wood ticks, seed ticks, and dog ticks, which Papa or Mama removed. When the tick was embedded in the skin, Papa dug it out with the sharp tip of his pocketknife and the wound was soaked in turpentine or coal oil.

Always, the children were on the lookout for snakes and always carried a knotted stick as a ready weapon against all snakes except king snakes and garden and grass snakes. They knew to run from snakes but also to be prepared to kill the snake if they couldn't run. Ground rattlers, copperheads, diamondbacks, cotton-mouth moccasins, and spreading adders were the snakes most feared. The children knew those snakes when they saw them. And they also knew—though they saw them less frequently—western rattlers, water moccasins (which, it was said, would not strike under water), and the non-poisonous snakes: blue coach-whip, black racer, and chicken snakes (often found in the henhouse, swallowing little chickens and eggs—whole).

The king snake they knew from long acquaintance. Their pet king snake lived in the smokehouse for several years and kept the smokehouse clear of mice and rats. When Mama sent them to the smokehouse to bring her a slab of bacon or a jar of canned beans, they often saw him coiled on a shelf with a crack of sunshine glistening on his thick brown body. Once, in the hot summertime, he fell in the well and they discovered him lying on a brick ledge some twenty feet down, unable to scale the wall and get out. Papa let the well bucket down and guided it gently over to the snake. He coiled himself around the bucket and rope, was pulled to safety, and crawled off toward the smokehouse.

Another time when the children were in the hackberry patch gathering berries for a cobbler, they saw a pile of snakes and ran screaming to the house for Mama, who grabbed her hoe and came running. She discovered the pile of snakes consisted of a king snake wrapped and tied in a knot around a chicken snake. The king snake was in the process of swallowing the chicken snake. He had begun by swallowing the head; then he loosened the knot, let out a little more snake, and swallowed again. He continued until he swallowed the entire snake, stretched out, and crawled away while Mama and the children watched.

The black racers and blue coach-whips lived in the woods under piles of oak leaves and brush. Both were long, slender, fast slithering snakes. The blue coach-whip, an iridescent shimmering blue, was the most beautiful as well as the fastest of the two. Neither was poisonous but it was *said* that they could catch a child, wrap themselves around it, and whip it to death with their tails. One day when the children were playing in their stick-lined playhouses under the oaks beyond the barn, a black racer ran into Eva Rita's playhouse, chased her around from room to room as she tried to escape. Her screams brought the other three running with their clubs in hand but not before the black racer had raced away under the leaves.

One summer day Dorothy opened the closet door (privy or outdoor water closet) to see a chicken snake coiled on the seat between the two holes. She shut the door and ran for Mama, who got the hoe hanging on the garden fence before she ran down the path to the closet. When Mama opened the door, the snake uncoiled, crawled off the seat and onto the floor behind the half-open door. That made it necessary for Mama to go into the closet and close the door to be in a position to hit him with the hoe. When she did, the snake began to coil about her feet. Then she could not strike him with the cutting edge of the hoe because the hoe handle was too long to maneuver in the small space. Dorothy was on the outside listening to Mama stomping and screaming inside. She tried to open the door to get Mama out but Mama was against the door. She pushed and pushed with her whole body until finally, the door opened a few inches. She could see Mama jumping up and down and pounding with the hoe as the snake appeared then disappeared beneath Mama's skirt. The snake's head appeared in the door followed by his squirming body. Dorothy stumbled backward and fell as the snake crawled out and escaped into the grass and Mama came out, her hair flying, her red face dripping sweat, following the snake into the tall grass. She beat the grass with the hoe but the snake was gone.

The children were not afraid of lizards, toads, bullfrogs, or horned toads. Nor rabbits—jackrabbits or cottontails—nor squirrels, though they knew that a squirrel could bite and might be mad with hydrophobia. They knew how to make a possum play dead (though they knew that a possum had sharp teeth and could bite). They knew that many animals lived in the woods because occasionally they emerged into the fields: raccoons, bobcats, weasels, porcupines, armadillos, wolves, wild hogs (razorback hogs), panthers, and foxes.

There was nothing to fear from the birds in the sky except the chicken hawk and the hoot owl. They both stole chickens. The children knew a turkey buzzard from a chicken hawk by the color and markings as well as by the different ways of flying. Turkey buzzards soared in circles, circling above some dead animal discovered on the ground. They were black against the sky and heavy bodied. Chicken hawks had a wider wingspan and slenderer bodies, were lighter in color and streaked white on their breasts. They darted high in the sky and dived fiercely to the ground after their prey.

The harmless birds that filled the sky with color and song were: redbirds, blackbirds, red-winged blackbirds, feelarks (field larks or meadowlarks), English sparrows, bluebirds, scissortails, yellow-hammers, woodpeckers, thrashers, quail, crows, robins, and humming birds. Birds with whom the children could talk were: the mockingbird, the bobwhite, the hoot owl and the squeech (screech) owl, the mourning dove, the whippoorwill, the whippoorwill's widow, and the quarreling blue jay. In the spring wild geese flew silently north, high in the sky—hundred of them—following their leader in wedge formation; and in the fall, they came south, flying lower, cawing, cawing, silhouetted against the sky with a blue norther on their tail.

The children had learned that pokeberries, chinaberries, and toadstools were poisonous to eat; they knew poison oak when they saw it and knew by experience its dangers. But the wild flowers were theirs to pick in bouquets for their playhouse: buttercups, primroses, paintbrush, queen's lace, violets, Indian sage, red clover, and daisies.

The house faced a light, loose-clay yard, decorated with a chinaberry tree south of the front gate, one small rectangular flower bed on either side of the gate and a round one midway to the house and slightly to the north between the house and the stormhouse. The three flower beds held, from time to time, pinks and petunias, and always four-o-clocks, moss, sweet william, and forget-me-nots; and the beds were edged with bricks leaning on each other pointing a corner up to warm barefooted children. Along the edge of the front gallery on either side of the front steps, morning glories fought for life against daily trampling and climbed baling wire strung from ground to gallery eaves.

North of the stormhouse perennial hollyhocks came up every year, wandered each year farther into the old orchard north of the house; and in August, crazy-leaning, they fed bumblebees that the children could catch and hold in hollyhock cups and listen to as the bees buzzed angrily in their prisons. Honeysuckle grew on the road fence west of the old orchard; and a rose bush, gone wild, bloomed once each spring. For the rest of the summer it sprangled its thorny arms among fence row weeds to snag and hold children.

The house, yards, garden, orchards and berry patches constituted the women's province on the farm. With the exceptions of wood-chopping, garden plowing, shoe mending, and the heavy work of hog-butchering, women and children did all the work within that province, including scouring the closet and throwing lime down the two holes every Saturday. The closet was the eastern boundary of that province.

The men seldom used the closet. A woman or girl-child on her way to the closet always stopped at the woodpile to survey the landscape. If no man was in sight, she proceeded; but if a man was plowing nearby, she picked up a few sticks of wood, returned to the house, and waited for the plowman to disappear.

The rules circumscribing life and proper behavior for boys and girls were learned from precepts and example. The meanings of circumscriptions were often deep mysteries.

The Mills farmstead was bounded on the north by the road leading east then northeast across Shuffle Creek and on to Emory. The McKeithen farm lay north of that road with a lane joining house and road. The farm was bounded on the west by a road going south and north to join the Emory road (at the northwest corner of the farm) which ran west for half a mile before turning north to Woosley and to Point. Directly west of that north-south road lay Calloway land with Wes Driggers as renter. Running south, the road passed the Malloys', then the Harlans', Flats Schoolhouse, and Brother Dement's farm, then crossed the bridge over the Sabine and disappeared in the trees in Van Zandt County. The farm's south boundary was the Malloy fence. Shuffle Creek and the Malloy farm was the eastern boundary of the Mills farm.

Sitting high on a winter-bare limb of the hackberry tree in the back yard, a child could see through and beyond all the bare trees that, in summer leaf, enclosed the world of Sabine Bottom. They could see farther up the north road; the mail carrier in his buggy, a neighbor on horseback or walking, the Peddler who came in early spring and late autumn (as well as in midsummer) walking beside his wagon, or an occasional stranger.

A stranger approaching the Mills farm saw two dwellings, both facing west, both boxed and stripped houses under gabled roofs, each with a shed-room–kitchen and front and back galleries, alike except for size: the one to the south was the larger of the two. Looking east the stranger could see the roadside fields and pastures and the barns but not beyond into the depths of the farm extending east to Shuffle Creek. Nor would he know that the first house on the Mills land was called "The Miss Gussie House" because Miss Gussie and her husband and baby lived there for two seasons while the husband farmed on shares.

But the children, tree-sitting or walking along that road every day or playing in the fields and pastures, knew and in their minds could see, without looking, the depths of the farm. They could see inside and behind Miss Gussie's House. They saw, within her fenced yard, a smokehouse and henhouse; and northeast of the fenced yard, a log barn, once a dwelling. In the barn walls were loopholes through which early settlers had fired their muzzle-loading guns at attacking Indians. In the shed-room of the barn was a corn sheller. Papa let them turn the crank to shell the corn to take to mill and bring home ground into cornmeal for corn bread, hoecake, corn cakes and mush.

East, some fifty yards from the log barn, beyond a south-flowing branch, and in the middle of a field planted in corn, oats or kaffir corn, a crumbling stone-and-mud chimney rose tall against the sky, marking the spot where a house had burned to the ground. Each spring purple flags encircled a mound beside the chimney. And in the mound the children scratched and dug to find bits of colored dishes, a twisted piece of iron from an old stirrup or harness, and rusty tin from old milk buckets.

Some hundred yards east of the chimney was another mound where the children found arrowheads and pottery pieces. The unearthed treasures were wiped clean on underskirt ruffles and hidden in a hollow tree, a hole in a fence post, or any secret place, safe from prying sisters and brother, or they were dropped into an empty water bucket or stuffed into an apron pocket and carried home to be stored in the play-pritty box under the bed.

Beyond the barn, branch, chimney, Indian mound, and field around it, a row of shumeke (sumac) bushes marked the western border of new ground which increased in acreage each spring after

each winter's clearing diminished the woods along Shuffle Creek —
eastern boundary of the farm.

After Miss Gussie and her husband and baby moved away, her
house was never lived in again but was used to store hay, sacks of
stock feed, and fifty-pound sacks of flour (after the wheat had been
taken to mill and ground).

Beyond Miss Gussie's yard fence on the south, a pasture was
crossed by an east-flowing branch dammed to make a pool, and
beyond the pool, the branch ran into a plum thicket where it joined
the south-bound branch to meander southeastward to another pool,
after which it trickled to a dry ravine among the tall oak trees where
growing pigs rooted for acorns and slept on hot days under pig sheds.
The wooded hog pasture extended almost, but not quite, to the
Creek.

The Peddler, after leaving Miss Gussie's house, had to cross the
low plank bridge over the east-flowing branch — the bridge on which
the children often sat to fish for crawfish. And when his coming
coincided with their fishing day, the sight of his wagon up the road
made them drop their poles and race home to tell Mama the Peddler
was coming. Down the road they ran to the house, or under the
roadside fence they crawled to race across the pasture, crawl under
another fence, whip through the wheat field and stumble, out of
breath, through the peach orchards into the berry patches where
Mama was picking dewberries, blackberries, or strawberries.

East of the garden and potato patches lay more orchards, and
east of the orchards were watermelon and cantaloupe patches; then
pumpkins; then goobers, and east of the goober patch, sorghum
grew; and between the sorghum and ribbon cane along Shuffle
Creek, corn grew as tall as trees in the rich bottom land. North of
the goober patch and northeast of the house, smokehouse, and henhouse (about one hundred yards) were the barn and barn lots adjoining the wooded hog pasture on the east. The pasture extended almost
to the creek; a pool and pool pasture lay northeast to and adjoining
the barn lots.

The farm belonged to the children to roam at will in field and
pasture, but they were warned: not to wade in a pool without a
grown-up near; not to go into a boar's pen; to keep clear of mama
hens with chickens, mama hogs with suckling pigs, cows with sucking
calves; to keep away from horses' tails (because horses kick backward)
and away from cows' horns; to run from snakes but to carry a clubbed

stick to kill a snake if they were unable to run; to carry a pocketknife to pick out sandburs and splinters.

Most outdoor work and most tools for outdoor work were too heavy for children. But they were willing helpers, and when they were not needed specifically as helpers or errand runners, they were welcomed as companions by men working alone in fields or woods. Following a plowman, they pushed bare feet into the soft, damp, cool earth, leaving trails of tracks in carefully contrived patterns; they molded sand castles over bare feet in the sandy bottom, collected green foam from pool rims and branch water, made baskets of wild grape leaves fastened with twigs, and built miniature log pens, houses and barns from twigs searched for and carefully selected and collected in pocketfuls. Always they were within calling distance of a man working in a field.

Though the children could not plow a field or plant, cultivate or harvest a crop, they knew the names and uses of all the plows and cultivators: turning plow, middle buster, disc, harrow. They knew the broadcaster, corn planter, the drills, the hay loader, mower, reaper, binder, thrasher, scythe, and hay rake. They could not build a fence but they knew the auger, posthole-digger, wire-nippers, wire stretchers, mallet, and maul and how each was handled and used. They could not fell trees, pull stumps, or cut or chop wood but they knew axes (single-bit and double-bit), the bucksaw, bush hook, cross-cut saw (single and double), handsaw, ripsaw, and stump-puller.

They could not build a henhouse, pigpen, or sled (for hauling wooden water barrels) but they knew a chisel, file, hatchet, plane, pliers, monkey wrench, screwdriver, sledgehammer, brace and bit, and block and tackle. They watched the men use the road-scraper to scoop out the earth to form the pool; and again and again each spring when all the neighbor men scraped the winter-rutted road from Point to Sabine River, the children spent the day walking up and down the road as the turning plows ditched the road on either side; as the scrapers scraped the loosened earth and dumped it in the middle of the road; and as the men, driving two teams hitched by chains to heavy log-drags, stood on the logs and dragged and packed the earth to a rutless, smooth, slightly concave roadbed that would shed water into the plowed ditches.

They knew how and when corn was planted—and oats and wheat and sorghum and sugar cane and kaffir corn—how it was cultivated and how and when harvested. Wheat and oats were broadcast after the ground had been plowed, disced, and harrowed in early spring. Corn was planted later, in rows two feet apart so that a horse could pull a middle-buster plow between the rows to plow the weeds out. Corn, when knee-high, was thinned with a hoe to leave a space of fifteen to eighteen inches between stalks (that gave them room to grow). When the ears of field corn were half their matured size and still in green, damp shuck, they were pulled for roasting ears for family food. Most of the corn crop was left to ripen to be harvested in late summer or early autumn. Some was shelled (to be ground into cornmeal for family food). Some was fed to hogs (on the cob). Cobs were gathered for kindling and for use in the outdoor toilet. The cornstalks became winter fodder for horses and cattle.

The garden (after the initial spring plowing, harrowing, and turning into rows) was largely the province of the women and of the children learning to plant and hoe and harvest: lettuce, radishes, beets, shallots, Kentucky Wonder beans, butter beans, black-eyed peas, lady peas, whippoorwill peas, cucumbers, tomatoes, onions, red peppers, turnip greens, mustard greens, squash, cushaw, okra, sage, Irish potatoes, and sweet potatoes.

Irish potatoes were planted in rows of little hills (mounds of soil some fifteen to eighteen inches apart). Potatoes for seed were saved from the year before. At planting time Mama and the children sat on the back gallery with a dishpan full of potatoes on the floor and each with a syrup bucket in her lap. The potatoes were cut into pieces so that each piece contained an "eye." Then a child (with a bucket full of potato eyes) and Mama (with her hoe) went to the garden, where Mama hilled and scooped a hole in each hill for a potato eye which the child placed—eye up—in the hole. Mama raked the earth over the potato eye and tamped the soil down with the flat surface of the hoe.

Sweet potatoes were planted in beds instead of rows. They did not have distinct "eyes" as the Irish potatoes had. Sweet potatoes for seed were saved from the year before; they were planted in a shallow bed, kept watered, and allowed to sprout. Each potato put up many sprouts. The sprouting potatoes were unearthed and broken apart, each sprout becoming a "slip" to be planted in the sweet potato bed in the garden.

Kentucky Wonder beans were planted in hills and staked with bean poles five feet long crossed and tied together toward the top, wigwam fashion. Three or four beans were dropped in each hill. Other plants in hills were watermelons, cantaloupes, cucumbers, and squash.

Early black-eyed peas were planted in rows in the garden, harvested, and eaten as tender green plants. Later in the season black-eyed peas and whippoorwill peas (to be harvested dry for winter use) were planted between the corn rows after the corn had been plowed and hoed and needed no further cultivating.

Vine butter beans were planted by the garden fence and ran up and over the close-meshed chicken wire. Other vegetables were planted in rows, beginning with lettuce in early March (or even late February sometimes) and continuing on to the middle of May. In one corner of the garden a bed of sage was planted and a perennial mint bed sprouted each year in a flower bed in the front yard. Most of the garden vegetables were used for food during the growing season of the year. Additional crops of Irish potatoes, sweet potatoes, pumpkins, peas, popcorn, beans, and goobers harvested and stored for winter food were planted in the field south of the garden, in the orchards east of the garden, and in the field beyond (which included the watermelon, cantaloupe, and muskmelon patches). Papa planted and cultivated most of the vegetables outside the fenced garden.

During the growing season the daily routine for the children included going to the garden to gather a mess of greens, beans, beets, or squash; a few shallots, tomatoes, cucumbers, or radishes; or to dig up a mess of new potatoes. Whatever was gathered was brought to the house in the apron-front, caught up bunched and held in the hand to form a pouch or basket.

Those were morning chores. At other times they were sent to feed the chickens, to gather eggs, to bring stovewood from the woodpile or water from the cistern or rainbarrels at the corners of the house. Three times a day they washed and dried the dishes and set the table for the next meal.

Between chores in and around the house, the children lived outdoors—never far from where men were working. When the men built fences, they stood close by, handing tools to the men: wire-nippers, staples, or hammer; or they held wire upright while the men used the wire stretcher. They knew bobwire, chicken wire, hog wire; they knew a gap from a pole gate, wagon gate from a paling gate. When the men were ringing the pigs' noses to keep them from rooting under the fence, Dorothy stood by, her apron pockets full of rings, to hand a ring to a man holding a pig's slit nose in one hand while another man held the squealing pig immobile by his feet; then watched the pig (with the ring in his bleeding nose) released to run away grunting in anger.

The children watched the men use chloroform and creosote on pigs and hogs festering with screwworms. They watched a drenching administered to a sick horse; they knew that a foundered cow had to be punctured. They watched Grandma Gray grease baby chickens to kill chicken mites and put "copperas root" in the chicken water to kill maggots (in case the chickens ate maggots from decaying animals they found in tall grass). They helped Mama rake the henhouse earth floor clean of chicken doings and spread lime on the walls and floor to kill mites.

Though the children were never given the entire responsibility for feeding the stock, they knew what food to give each animal and how much. Chickens were fed food scraps, grain, and corn (shelled or on the cob). Horses were fed oats (unground, in husk), corn (unshelled), fodder, and hay (made of grass, pea vines, or goober vines). Cows were fed cottonseed meal (cottonseed, hulled and ground), bran (ground wheat without the chaff), and cottonseed hulls. Hogs were slopped with leftover table food in liquid; mash made of shorts (wheat with hulls, ground together) and liquid; and surplus milk.

Year-round all livestock foraged in fields and woods. Hogs rooted for acorns and roots. Horses were turned into stubble fields when pastures were grazed out in winter. Cows were pastured in empty grain fields in winter to eat caves into the strawstacks which the threshing machine the summer before had spouted into hemisphere piles.

The children could not milk a cow (though they were allowed to try), but they could bring the cows in from pasture for milking. And they stood by with a broomweed broom shooing the flies away and watched the milkers' fingers clamp a cow's teat high against the udder, then stroke the teat downward; and saw and heard the stream of milk hit the tin bucket on the ground. They watched until each teat was milked dry then each teat stripped. Then two children, one on either side, carried the full foaming bucket to the house for Mama to strain through a thin cloth stretched over a tin milk-strainer into a crock set on the back gallery shelf to cool.

They could not saddle or harness a horse but they could catch and halter one and bring him in from pasture. They could bridle one (by standing on a stall to reach his head) and assist at saddling or harnessing. And they could curry cockleburs out of a horse's mane (but *not* his tail). They knew a buggy shaft from a wagon tongue from the tongue of a plow; a single tree from a double tree. They knew names and uses for various parts of harness: bridle and bit (and, maybe, blinders), checkreins, hip strap, crupper, and lines; breast strap, hame and hamestrings, breeching, traces, spreading strap, and ring; saddle cinch, saddle strings, stirrups, spurs, rowels. They knew why the blanket went on before the saddle. They knew the way to hold the lines to guide a horse to a buggy or a team to a wagon. They knew how to guide a horse with a halter or a bridle when riding bareback or in a saddle (the lines, held in the right hand, pulled to the left, made the horse go to the left because the line touched his neck on the right side). In driving a team, the lines were held in the left hand and the right hand was used to pull the right line taut to turn the team to the right or the left line taut to pull the team to the left. In driving a buggy or wagon, they knew how to jerk and slap the lines on the horse's flank—signal to go. They knew how to flick a buggy whip on a horse's flank—and the ends of the two long wagon lines first to the right horse then to the left with a crack. Though they never drove oxen, they knew how it was done because they followed and sometimes rode the log wagons that rolled along their road hauling logs from Sabine woods to the sawmill beyond Shuffle Creek. And they watched every movement of the ox-driver as he curled, unwound and cracked the long blacksnake whip almost— but not quite—touching an oxen's ear. They watched so that they some day could do the same when they were old enough.

When the children followed the men about the barn, they learned the difference between a hayfork (long handle with three tines) and a spading fork (shorter handle with four tines used for gardening). They learned the difference between a spade and a scoop (a large, deep shovel for scooping food into troughs).

They learned to differentiate kinds and breeds of cattle: Jerseys, Holsteins, Longhorns, cows, muly cows (or polled cows), calves, heifers, yearlings, steers. Kinds and breeds of hogs: Poland China, Durock Jersey, and razorback; boars, sows, pigs, shoats. Kinds, breeds, and sizes of chickens: bantams, leghorns, Domineckers, Barred Rocks, Plymouth Rocks, Rhode Island Reds, Blue Hens, roosters, hens, broodie hens, layers, fryers. They knew horses, mules and donkeys: roans, piebalds, ponies, mares, colts, fillies, jacks, and jennies. They knew that a mule had a jenny mama and a horse papa but they didn't know how nor why and learned not to ask.

Some learning came by living day by day, watching and listening to what was said (and how) and to what was left unsaid (and how) as well as to what was done (and how). Day in, day out. Week in, week out. Month in, month out. Green spring, violent summer, smoke-hazed fall, and gray winter. Some learning came once a year by season: winter ground-clearing; spring road-grading; late-summer threshing under hot sun; and sorghum syrup making by October lantern light. When the bees swarmed, all work was dropped until Papa could settle and hive the bees. Time for robbing the beehives was also decided by the bees.

Threshing time came late June. Harvesting equipment (the reaper—which cut and bound the grain into bundles—and the thresher, powered by a steam engine) belonged to Mr. Williams (owner of the gin at Woosley), who went from farm to farm hiring his machinery and labor to a farmer and taking pay in a share of the grain harvested. The reaper was a cylinder of rotating blades (the blades were some six feet long, the diameter of the cylinder probably six feet, and the blades probably numbered a dozen). It was drawn by a team, and the operator rode, sitting high in a "cultivator" seat. Beneath the driver's seat was a box of gears that made the cylinder turn as the team moved forward. The grain stalks were cut off four to six inches above the ground by the rotating blades, which threw the stalks into a "binder," formed to receive, assemble, bind them into bundles, and drop the bundles to one side on the ground. Men walked behind the reaper, collected the bundles, and built them into shocks. A shock consisted of six to eight bundles, one bundle standing upright surrounded by five or six bundles leaning inward. One bundle was placed horizontally on top to cap the shock, which was built to shed rain, because the shocks were left in the field for two weeks or more before threshing. During reaping season the air was fragrant with new-cut grain from all the farms while the children impatiently awaited the day the thresher would arrive. Each morning they listened and looked up the north road. They looked for puffs of smoke and listened for the clack-whack-hissing noise of the magic monster—steam-powered—moving mysteriously without horses, its long neck ending in an open, round mouth, swaying dangerously as if looking for children to gobble up, chew, and spit out into the strawstack (where they would be buried forever in a strawstack grave).

At last the day arrived. At sunrise the thresher moved slowly down the road from the Calloways' or McKeithens', through the gate and to the middle of the field. Meanwhile the neighbor men were arriving in their flat-bedded wagons to help gather and haul the shocked grain to the thresher and take turns tending the machine. Soon after, the neighbor women and children arrived by families, the women and older children carrying baskets and bundles of food: frying chickens cut up and ready to fry; peas and beans shelled and snapped, ready for the pot already bubbling with a hambone in; new red potatoes washed and scraped with their eyes flicked out by knife point; coconut cakes; lemon meringue pies; jars of cucumber pickles and chow chow, sweet-pickled peaches and watermelon rind preserves.

With the women settled to talk and cook and sweat in the kitchen and on the back gallery (their nursing babies deposited on quilt pallets on the floor in the cool front room) and the men sweating in the hot sun of the grain fields, the children were sent to play, with the older ones assigned the responsibility of minding the younger. Minding little brothers and sisters limited big brothers and sisters to playing in the yard or the road in front of the house in order to keep the little ones there. The iron rule (punishment for violating it was a "blistering" for children—big and little) was: no child set foot inside the grain-field fence where the thresher stood, shook, snorted, and vomited out the strawstack.

From early to mid-morning the children stood spellbound in line along the wheat-field fence, each older child gripping the hand of a younger one, whimpering in fear and squirming for freedom. At last the rhythmic monotony of the retching creature broke the tension. With subsiding tension, hot sun, and burdensome little ones, the children all drifted back to the hackberry shade of the yard, the shady west side of the house and the front gallery to games of Mumble Peg; Club Fist; Hull Gull; Going to Mill; William, William, Tremble Toe (for the older boys and girls); and Ring Around the Rosie for little ones circling and singing under the thick shade of the chinaberry tree.

At noon the older boys and girls took turns hammering the broken plow sweep (hanging by a wire from a hackberry limb) to call the men to dinner. The younger children, escaping the tyranny of the older ones, were clinging to their mamas' skirts, weary and hungry. They were fed first and palleted on the front-room floor where they fell asleep, freeing the big brothers and sisters until late afternoon.

The sweat-wet men came from the fields, washed faces and hands at the wash shelf on the back gallery, let down their overall galluses off their shoulders, and filed into the shed-room-kitchen to the long table crowded with food. A table for the children, made of boards across sawhorses, was set up under the hackberry tree. The women waited on the tables while the men and children ate, bringing platters and bowls of hot food and plates of hot biscuit and corn bread to add to the light bread and all the bowls crowding the table. The children ate ravenously at first—and silently, as required. But when appetites waned to casual nibbles, then whispering, giggling, pinching, and winking brought scoldings from the mamas waiting table and banishment for the boldest bad boys.

Dinner over, the men returned to the fields. The women cleared the tables, sent the children to empty slop buckets into pigs' troughs and bring them back to be filled again. Then the women filled their own plates and ate. Some sat eating, nursing a baby first at one breast then the other. For a baby a year old, a mama chewed food and gave the baby the chewed food from her own mouth. Emptying the slop buckets was the last chore required of the children until evening, since the women washed and dried dishes on threshing day and carried drinking water to the threshers.

So it was to the barn, the pool, the woods, pastures, and the creek—far from adult sight and hearing—that the children raced, reckless in their freedom from parents and younger brothers and sisters—to double-dog-dare each other to swing a grapevine over the creek, climb the highest tree to a fragile, bending limb that sometimes cracked and broke and dropped a climber to a limb below, all in a moment of freezing terror that gripped the climber and his grounded darers. Within that same moment, fear changed to silent admiration and envy of the carefully descending hero. High-swinging, high-climbing, knee-deep wading in a pool or creek, snake-hunting with clubbed sticks—all the forbidden pleasures were dared and done before the children settled to safer games: "Hide and Seek" in the canebrakes or fishing for crawfish in pool or creek.

The sound of the thresher followed them wherever they went, all day, comforting assurance that the parents were all too busy to interfere with children's play. But as afternoon play-energy dwindled and afternoon shadows lengthened, the thresher reminded them that pants legs and dress bottoms, wet from wading, must be dry before the return to adult domination and late-afternoon lemonade awaiting them in the kitchen. Hence the last rite of the free afternoon was sitting in the edge of the barn shade with wet pants legs and skirt bottoms extended into sunshine to dry while all swore vows of secrecy about afternoon activities. The twelve-year-olds threatened the six and eight-year-olds with dire consequences to tattletale and the younger ones were required to swear with "Cross my heart and hope to die, I won't tell."

The sinking sun sent the children, dry and weary, straggling back to the house, past the emptied grain fields, past the dissonant thresher —no longer the fearful morning monster—back to lemonade and to minding the awakened, fretful baby brothers and sisters while the mamas got supper in the kitchen.

Finally, daylight gone, the men came to supper, silent, smelling of straw and sweat. Sat. Ate. The older children, holding babies, ate, again under the hackberry by light of a lantern hung on a lower limb. The thresher had belched its last sparks for the day into the evening sky and shuddered to silence.

Supper over, wagons, one by one, were brought up from the fields, loaded with women and children, and driven into the quiet night. The strange, exciting sounds of that special day were gone.

Tomorrow the thresher would go to the Malloys and Papa and his wagon with it. And later, Mama and the children, arms loaded with food, would trek down the road to join the other families again. From the Malloys the thresher would go to the Harlan farm. Then threshing time would be over in the Woosley-Flats community.

But before the thresher left the Harlans' to head north for Woosley again, other community gatherings had been planned for the rest of the summer: a fish-fry on Sabine; a Fourth of July picnic at Woosley; two protracted meetings, first at Woosley, then at Flats. The men who raised sorghum and ribbon cane made plans to bring their cane and sorghum to the Mills' sorghum mill to end the summer season.

The mill under the oak trees east of the barn was mounted on a platform three feet square, five feet off the ground, supported by four posts. The long pole sweep to which the horses were hitched was some ten feet long and bent to hitching level at the outer end. The cooking vat for the cane and sorghum juice was a little distance away —maybe forty feet—under another tree, a shallow galvanized pan perhaps five inches deep, four feet wide, and six feet long, mounted on bricks at the corners and middle. It sat some eighteen inches off the ground. Under the vat a fire was built and tended to keep a steady bed of hot coals while the juice bubbled for hours, it seemed, and was skimmed of foam with the long-handled skimmer, tested, and finally run through the small spout in one corner into bright-shining, gallon tin syrup buckets. The vat belonged to Mr. McKeithen.

Three or four families joined in making their ribbon cane syrup and sorghum molasses. The process started in the afternoon when the men arrived in their wagons loaded with cane or sorghum, to oil the mill, set up the vat, and start the fire; and lasted into the cool night lighted by lantern and pine torches. Men and older boys did all the work. The other children peeled joints of purple-striped ribbon cane, pretended it was candy, and sucked the sweet juice until hands, face, and clothes were sticky-stiff—and took turns, when permitted, riding the long sweep as the horses circled the mill. The women seldom appeared, but gathered at the house to nurse and pallet the babies and sit in undisturbed conversation around the lamp-lit kitchen table and send food and drink to the men and boys working. The fire had to be tended and the mill had to continue grinding buckets of juice to be ready for the next boiling-down. Gradually, as the night grew older and colder, the children hovered around the glowing vat, grew satiated with juice and uncomfortable in grimy dirt clinging to sticky bodies and clothing. And one by one and two by two, without being told, they drifted to the house to be washed off and palleted.

Early the next morning before breakfast, a child went to the smokehouse for the last slab of bacon hanging from a rafter, and saw, lined up on the shelves, the rows of shining tin buckets of syrup and molasses for winter use and extra to be used for trading.

The empty rafter hooks were ready to receive the coming year's supply of bacon, ham, and sacks of sausage. And the children could look forward to hog-butchering time.

As October turned into November, Papa talked about chances for an early winter. Neighbor men talked of the acorn crop—light or heavy. Daily the northern sky was scanned for sight of wild geese going south, flying high or flying low. And nightly all ears were alert for their faint, distant, high cries or low-flying cawing and whirring wings in a great rush as they cleared the treetops and the house, a leader's plaintive voice rising above the winged chorus. Thus men reckoned by the geese, for the geese knew how far behind the cold north wind trailed them.

Daily the men looked to the north for signs of blue-black clouds low on the horizon — clouds that would rise, a black monster, pounce on a summer-hot autumn afternoon and, overnight, freeze it into early morning skims of ice on water buckets and hog troughs. The geese and the clouds told Papa when to butcher hogs.

A month before butchering time, hogs to be butchered were penned and fattened. Sometimes they were turned into the goober patch to root. Always they were fed extra corn. And by the time they were butchered they weighed three hundred to four hundred pounds.

When the first cold spell came early, only one hog was killed and most or all of the meat was eaten fresh, immediately, by the family and neighbors. Little or none of it was cured. Neighbors took turns at butchering and sharing fresh meat, both pork and beef. Not until dependable winter weather came — usually not before Thanksgiving and some years as late as Christmas — did butchering and curing meat for future use take place.

Butchering always took place on an afternoon before a cold night was expected. Two or three men — neighbors or hired men — worked together. Fires were built under the washpot and under extra tubs of water so that the water would be boiling hot when the hogs were dead and bled. A work table made of planks across sawhorses was set up near the boiling pots in the back yard, and the children were sent to gather a supply of tow sacks and pile them by the work table.

Near the hogpen beside the barn a heavy crossbeam was nailed between two trees some seven or eight feet above ground. A sledge-hammer was used to knock the hog in the head to stun him (one blow in one special spot knocked the hog unconscious and immobile). Then his hind feet were clamped by tongs and a block and tackle hoisted him to the crossbeam, where he dangled, head down, to have his throat slashed with a butcher knife. He was left to bleed. Three or four hogs were butchered when a hard freeze was expected.

When the carcasses had dripped free of blood, they were dropped from the beam onto a sled and hauled by horse to the work table in the back yard. A hog was hoisted onto the table, covered with tow sacks, and a tub of boiling water was poured over him to loosen the hair for scraping. Scrapers made of old knife blades with a contrived handle at either end were used to scrape the hog's skin free of all hair. Sometimes it was necessary to leave the hot, wet sacks on for a while and replenish the scalding water before the hair came away clean. The clean-scraped hog, lying on his back with his four short clean feet sticking straight up, was slit from throat to tail, the head cut off, the feet and tail cut off, the body disemboweled and dis- membered: hams (hind legs and thighs), shoulders (front legs and thighs), backbone with ribs and some loin attached, and slabs of side meat for bacon. After cutting out and saving the bladder and liver, the men tossed the entrails into an empty tub nearby and buried them next day in the orchard—so deep the chickens could not scratch them up and eat maggots.

After the butchered hogs were cut up, a ladder was brought from the barn and the meat was carried to the back gallery roof and to the smokehouse roof; spread out and safe from wild animals, it was left to the freezing night. Meanwhile one of the men had washed and dried and blown up the hog bladders for the children. And the chil- dren went to bed contented with a new play pritty, resolving to play carefully next day with the bladder-balloon-balls (not to kick them too hard; not to let the wind carry them into the berry patch to be pricked and broken).

Next morning, after a breakfast of fresh hog brains, the men set to work salting down the hams and bacon or hanging them in the smokehouse for smoking. The women prepared to make sausage, souse and liver pudding, and to render lard. Days ahead of time, the sausage sacks made of lightweight, unbleached domestic, had been cut and sewn into long, pillowslip-like tubes some eighteen inches long and three inches across. The sausage grinder was clamped to the edge of the kitchen table. The women cut the lean hog shoulders and other lean meat into pieces small enough for the grinder, and the children took turns feeding and turning the grinder. They watched the cutters grab the meat chunks, chew and swallow them, and excrete them in a curling mass on the flat pie pan set beneath to catch them. When the pan was full, Mama removed it, placed an empty one in its place, and dumped the ground meat into a big crock to be seasoned with red pepper, salt, and sage and stuffed by hand into sausage sacks, later hung from the smokehouse rafters.

Meanwhile the souse and liver pudding were simmering in their separate pots on the stove. In the souse pot the hog heads (minus brains and eyes) and feet were boiled in water seasoned with vinegar and salt until the broth would jell; then the souse was poured into tin bread pans which molded gelatin loaves as the broth cooled. Souse was sliced and served cold for supper. In the liver pudding pot the ground up hog livers simmered in water seasoned with salt and red pepper. When the meat was done, cornmeal was stirred into the pot with the liver to make a cornmeal mush. And the mush, when done, was poured into bread pans to cool and set in loaves, which were sliced and eaten cold or fried in bacon fat and served hot for supper.

Two or three days after hog-killing, lard was rendered in the big black washpot in the back yard. First, the leaf lard was made—the purest and best—of fat pulled in sheets from the inside of the hog's abdomen. The fat was cooked on a slow fire until the grease separated from the meat fiber and became liquid, which was poured through a cloth strainer into gallon tin buckets (syrup buckets), where it solidified into lard as it cooled, to be marked and stored on the smokehouse shelves. Cracklings, the crisp meat fiber left after lard-rendering, were drained dry, stored in crocks, and used to season corn bread (crackling bread). After leaf lard, odds and ends of fat from all parts of the hog were thrown into the lard pot and rendered into ordinary lard used for everyday cooking but not for the best cakes and pie crust and biscuits.

While women worked in the kitchen on sausage, souse, and liver pudding, the men worked in the back yard and smokehouse. Bacon slabs and hams were hung from the smokehouse rafters; a smoke fire of hickory, built in the middle of the earth floor, produced a heavy smoke all day and all night and sometimes was continued for two or three days. Thin ribbons of blue smoke curled through the smokehouse cracks to cover the whole farm with blue, fragrant cold air.

The children, bundled into winter clothes, ran with their hogbladder balls up the north road to the corner, turned the bladders loose to be carried south by the wind, followed, protected the bladders from gusts that would carry them into or over the barbed-wire fence and against thorn bushes, guided them south as the wind willed.

Their hands grew stiff with cold though mittened in mittens knit by Grandma Gray or in mitts contrived by her from worn-out stockings. For a while they could shelter their noses by wrapping the tobaggan-cap tail around the throat and face up to the eyes. But eventually the tail grew frozen stiff from their breath. Legs were snugly warm under long underwear wrinkling under long black stockings that were almost, but not quite, held up by elastic garters above the knee and always lapping over the tops of high-laced shoes with shoelaces that forever came untied and dangled. And bodies were warm under the ribbed, long-sleeved union suit that was under the drawers and gray flannel underskirts that were under the cotton check apron that was under the hand-me-down coat with elbows patched and sleeves too short.

One by one, as the days went by, the bladder balls burst or were carried up over the treetops and lost to the wind, or gradually shriveled to hard knots of viscera lying on the floor behind the kitchen stove. But the loss of the transient play pritty dwindled in importance as anticipation of Christmas grew and as looking at the Sears and Roebuck catalogue consumed more and more time and controlled their daydreams of Santa Claus and Aladdin.

Bladder balls were not forgotten. Next year would bring hog-butchering again. Bladder balls were stored at the bottom of their memory beneath Christmas, Easter (with Easter egg hunts), birthdays, summer picnics, fish-fries, protracted meetings, threshing time, and syrup making. The year would make another circle.

Sunday Clothes and Everyday Clothes

Sunday clothes eventually became Everyday clothes after being handed down and darned and patched beyond respectability for Sunday school and church. Clothing made for everyday use was seldom handed down because six and one-half days a week of wear on everyday clothes with all the tears, darning, patching, and repeated washing and scrubbing with lye soap and ironing sent most garments to the ragbag before they could be passed along to a younger sister. All clothes were worn until they were past further darning and patching; and the rags were used until they were worn to shreds. Woolen rags from old coats were saved for Sally Anne rags (for chest colds); yarn from worn-out socks and mittens was raveled and saved for reknitting (if usable) or to make string-balls for the children.

Sunday clothes were worn to Sunday school and church services, to Fourth of July picnics, to singing school, and for any dress-up occasions, but were changed to everyday clothes on the return home before the children were allowed to go out to play. That was the rule. When paying visits to neighbors either on Sunday or weekdays the children and Mama and Grandma put on clean everyday dresses (or rompers). The men in their neighborly visits during the week

123

never changed from dirty working clothes. On Sunday afternoon visits, however, they wore clean overalls.

Everyday dresses were the same the year round. Underlayers were added as the weather grew colder. The girls wore "aprons" made of "cotton-checks," a sturdy checked or plaid cotton material. These were dresses which hung from the shoulders in a one-piece front and buttoned all the way down the back. They had two big patch pockets below waist level in front, long sleeves, a round Buster Brown collar, and a sash (called apron strings) about three inches wide sewed into the side seams on either side at the waist and tied into a bow at the center back.

In summer they were worn over the straight-legged drawers made of unbleached domestic, without ruffles or lace, buttoned on to homemade suspenders of unbleached domestic in doubled strips. Two strips — one over each shoulder from waist front to waist back — were held in place by a cross strip across the chest and another across the shoulders. A third strip was a waistband that anchored the suspenders and held the buttons to which the drawers were buttoned. The drawers and apron came to below the knees. The children went barefooted and bareheaded except when the midday sun sent them to the house for bonnets.

In winter the cotton-check apron covered a gray cotton outing underskirt over the drawers attached to an outing bodice instead of the summer suspenders. Underneath, next to the skin was the long-legged, long-sleeved union suit with drop seat. Over the long legs of the underwear, black-ribbed cotton stockings were pulled to above the knees and held by round garters made of black elastic webbing about one inch wide. High-laced black shoes (shoestrings dangling, usually) were worn from the first cold snap through the Easter cold spell (Grandma said Easter always brought the last sharp norther). Once donned in the fall, the shoes were worn every day until spring. Going barefoot in early spring was a gradual process. First the child was allowed to play in the house in stocking feet on a warm day. Then the child was allowed to play outdoors in stocking feet in old, worn-out stockings. Finally, when the spring sun and weather signs indicated no more brisk northers, the stockings were discarded. The child was free at last for the summer: free of the bulky union suit; free of the outing underskirts; free to feel cool, spring earth under tender foot-soles; free to turn apron strings loose and let the breeze billow the apron into a balloon child with the real child tingling inside; free of the dark house. Free and wild with escape, to run and run and run until exhausted; then to lie down and roll over and over down the grassy knoll near Miss Gussie's house, grasping at grass clumps to hold on to and stop just in time before rolling into the branch running full with spring rain.

Free except on Sunday. On summer Sunday mornings the children put on their shoes and white stockings and their Sunday underwear when they got up in the morning (while their feet were still clean from the Saturday night bath). A clean everyday dress was worn until — breakfast over — dressing for church began.

First, the patent leather, one-strapped slippers were shined by rubbing them with half a biscuit (the soft part) left over from breakfast. Next came hair combing. Mama or Grandma sat in a kitchen chair beside the kitchen stove with the child to be combed standing before her. The hair was brushed vigorously all around and hung down over the child's eyes in front. Each tangle brought an ouch; if the ouches were convincing, eventually Mama or Grandma held the strand of tangled hair above the tangle while brushing it out. The comb was dipped into a pan of warm water to dampen the hair and ease out the last little tangles before the hair was parted and plaited or curled. The two older girls wore their dark brown hair parted in the middle from forehead to the nape of the neck and plaited into two plaits doubled back and tied with blue or pink satin ribbon bows, one behind each ear. Dorothy's blond hair, parted in the middle from forehead to crown, was divided into strands and curled into a dozen curls that hung around her shoulders. The front curl on either side was fastened back with a bow of ribbon to match the dress she wore. Her summer Sunday dress of light blue or pink corded dimity was cut with a yoke and full gathered skirt hanging below the knees. The short, puffed sleeves ended above the elbows in a band of lace and the same lace edged the low-cut, square neck. The Sunday underskirts and drawers were bleached domestic or cambric banded in rows of tucks, insertion, and embroidered ruffles or ruffles edged in lace.

Dorothy's Sunday summer hat, which had belonged to the oldest sister and to the next sister before it was hers, was a leghorn sailor. The large brim was topped by a shallow crown circled in blue and pink forget-me-nots sewed to a blue velvet ribbon band (the blue matching her eyes, so Dorothy was told) that extended into two hanging streamers in the center back. An elastic cord under her chin held the hat on as it sat on top of her curls, streamers flying in the wind as the buggy raced along to Woosley and Sunday school.

Winter Sunday dresses were made of dark plaid and checked gingham or suiting, cut long-waisted, with a full skirt gathered to a waistband, long sleeves and a high neck and rounded bertha collar. Winter-time underwear was the same for Sunday and every day; changed every Sunday morning after the weekly bath the night before. Sunday shoes were the everyday shoes shined with shoe blacking or Shinola on Saturday night before the baths. On their heads the children wore velvet or knitted tam-o-shanters—except in extremely cold weather, when they wore their toboggan caps with the long tails wound round their necks. There were Sunday cloaks and everyday cloaks. Everyday cloaks were old Sunday cloaks, outgrown, torn but patched, and handed down from one child to a younger one and remodeled to achieve the best fit possible. Made of dark green, brown, red, or blue wool broadcloth, herringbone tweed or storm serge, they were cut double breasted and trimmed in a row of brass buttons down each side of the double breast. A shoulder-cape collar, trimmed with a row of sutache braid around the edge, buttoned close around the neck and gave added warmth. The cloaks were store-bought—either in Point or ordered from Sears and Roebuck. But by the time they had been handed down, patched and discarded, they were more homemade than store-bought.

Little Brother's Sunday suit was white, tan, or brown linen crash made with straight-legged pants extending below the knees, buttoned onto homemade suspenders of unbleached domestic worn under a sailor blouse, long-sleeved in winter, short-sleeved in summer. The blouse had a drawstring (running through the hem below the waist-line) which was pulled and tied to make the blouse blouse. The blouse with its square-shawl sailor collar, trimmed in navy blue soutache braid, came to a low-neck V in front and the shield inserted in the V was embroidered with an anchor or ship's wheel in navy blue. For Sunday, both winter and summer, Little Brother wore long black stockings fastened under his pants legs to the suspenders, and high black shoes either laced or buttoned. In summer shoes and stockings were put on him amid stormy protests and always came off on the way home.

In winter time knit union suits with long sleeves and long legs were worn every day (under his rompers) as well as on Sunday under the sailor suit, and were changed to clean ones every Sunday morning after the Saturday night bath (and during the week when he "had an accident"). Over the union suit and sailor suit, Little Brother wore a double-breasted wool jacket made of gray imitation chinchilla and a gray wool cap with bill and bloused crown or his gray toboggan cap in the coldest weather.

Every day except Sunday, from May (or earlier) through October (or later), Little Brother went barefooted. His only garment in summer was a pair of rompers made of sturdy dark solid colored chambray. The short-sleeved waist and pants (all in one) had a drop seat worn, most of the time, half buttoned or misbuttoned, for he resisted his sisters' efforts to keep him buttoned up. Summer nights he slept in a short nightshirt made of unbleached muslin, with short sleeves. In winter he slept in an outing nightgown long enough to be tucked over and around his feet.

Mama, dressed up, was elegant winter or summer. She sat up straight, her corset strings laced tight at the waist. Her face was rice powdered, solemn and dignified under the gold-brown pompadoured hair under the winter hat of dark green satin built on a wire brim, tilted up on the left. Two brown ostrich plumes blew in the wind, fastened by a jet buckle, center front, in the middle of a green satin rosette. The hat was pinned to the pompadour with two long gold-headed hat pins—one in back and one in front. The plumes swept up and back to the left, drooping over the brim behind Mama's ear, the tip of which showed above the turned-up round collar of a brown broadcloth cape embroidered with curlecued black soutache braid. Under the cape was a suit of iridescent green silk (Mama's wedding suit). The skirt billowed out on the right (when the plume billowed out on the left in the wind), showing the gores and the bell-shaped flounce at the bottom.

In summer Mama's Sunday dress was white lawn. Its full gathered skirt with rows and rows of tiny tucks running horizontally around its bottom, billowed out by two stiff-starched flounced underskirts. Rows of insertion ran between groups of rows of tucks. The waist had a yoke with perpendicular tucks and lace insertion and a large bertha collar or flounce falling over the shoulders. Whether bertha or flounce, it was tucked and edged in lace. Mama's summer leghorn hat rode high on her pompadour, tilting high to the left. The mushroom crown of maize-colored chiffon lay coiled in folds atop the brim; and brim and crown were topped by a bed of pink rosebuds sprouting wiry green leaves. Mama, in summer dress, always held in her outstretched hand her blue ruffled parasol, her handkerchief, or her china-silk fan, unfurled.

Underneath Mama's Sunday finery were layers of underwear (topped by her small duchess bustle riding her hips and rump) differing with weather and season. In winter the layer next to her skin was a fleece-lined cotton knit union suit (open seat). Next came cambric drawers (open seat) with embroidered ruffles reaching below the knees. Over the drawers a boned waist corset was worn, laced in the back to pinch the waist in. The corset extended to the hips, dipping in front to press the stomach flat and rising above the waist to the breasts. The low-necked corset cover worn over the corset was a mass of tucked horizontal ruffles trimmed with lace edging and insertion. Two waist underskirts, gored and flounced, were always worn, winter or summer. In winter the one on the bottom was white cambric and the other black taffeta or sateen. In summer both underskirts were white, trimmed with tucks, lace or insertion or with embroidery, and a lightweight cotton knit vest was substituted for the union suit.

In summer or winter Mama's stockings and shoes were black. Her summer stockings were lightweight lisle and in winter, heavy mercerized cotton. Her Sunday stockings—winter and summer—were fastened to supporters hanging down from her corset, front, side, and back. In summer she wore black, high-heeled slippers with one strap. In winter she wore high-buttoned shoes with medium heels.

On Sunday morning Mama dressed the children first, then set each one on a chair and warned each one separately to sit quietly and stay clean while she dressed. Thus imprisoned, watching Mama comb her hair offered the only diversion from the tedium of sitting still. Her waist-length hair (dampened and rolled up on rags on Saturday night) was unrolled to hang in long corkscrews about her head until she brushed it and brushed it into a feathery brown mountain. Then, brushing her hair forward over her eyes, she placed the pompadour rat across the top of her head and pinned it in place with big black hairpins before she brushed the front hair up and over the rat, pulled it together, twisted it, and pinned it into a round, coiling knot at the crown. Next she combed the back hair up, twisted it, pinned it, coiled it to make the flat crown-knot larger, and stuck hairpins in the coils around and around and around. Last, the two tortoiseshell back combs, two side combs, and neck comb were anchored in place, their amber brilliants glittering in gilt settings.

Relieved, the children knew that Mama soon would be ready to go for they knew that under her dressing wrapper she already wore her clean Sunday underwear. They watched her wiggle her bustle into place and could see her polished Sunday shoes peeping from under ruffled Sunday underskirts. The dress or suit went on over the head, carefully. Then everything was buttoned and her gold brooch was fastened at her throat beneath her chin. As Mama put on her hat (and cape or cloak in winter time) the children slid off their chairs and ran for the front door to be first to the buggy hitched at the front gate.

Returning home after church — after sitting still between Mama and Papa without a whisper or a fidget during Brother Dement's long sermon and longer (it seemed) final prayer — they were first out of the buggy at the front gate and into the house to change to every-day clothes (underwear and top clothes) and freedom. Mama followed, removed her Sunday dress but not her Sunday underwear, and put on an everyday blue-printed, red-printed, or green-printed calico dress with instep-length skirt gathered at the waistband and attached to a waist with plain, unpuffed sleeves and a small, round collar. The front buttoned opening and placket extended from the collar to about eight inches below the waistband. Over her dress she tied an everyday cook apron made of checked gingham or calico, gathered to a waistband that extended into a long sash tied in a bow at the back. The apron covered the entire front of her skirt. When there were Sunday dinner guests — the preacher, neighbors, relatives — Mama put on a Sunday apron made of white muslin or lawn with hem-stitched hem or insertion and tucks and lace edging across the bot-tom.

Monday morning Mama put on her clean everyday underwear for the week: plain muslin drawers — no ruffles and no lace; plain under-skirts of unbleached muslin in summer and gray outing in winter. Mama wore her corset only on Sunday so on weekdays she wore no corset cover but, instead, a sleeveless cotton knitted vest in summer and a muslin or white outing chemise in winter. The vest was hip length. The sleeveless chemise hung loosely from the shoulders to below the knees. Mama's everyday shoes were old Sunday shoes. In cool or cold weather she wore a shawl or fascinator over her shoulders indoors and over her head and shoulders outdoors. In extreme out-door cold she wore an old black beaded cape (losing its beads). In summer weather she wore one underskirt, and in extreme heat, left off that one, as well as her summer vest, and dressed in nothing but a muslin chemise and an old Mother Hubbard (a yoked dress with full-gathered skirt hanging loose from the yoke) made of calico.

Outdoors in summer women and girls wore sunbonnets to shade their faces from sun and thus prevent freckles and suntan (a milk white or "peach" complexion was the criterion of beauty). For the same reason they wore, over their hands and wrists and arms, fingerless mitts made of legs of old stockings. The simplest everyday sun bonnet was a slat bonnet of calico or gingham — simplest to make and simplest to launder. Without lace, ruffles, or bloused crown, it was cut in one big piece that opened flat for ironing. The slat bonnet was worn for work in the garden and yard. Fancier bonnets were made for afternoon visits to neighbors, for picnics, and for semi-dress-up occasions. Fancy bonnets were cut in two pieces of dimity, lawn, or muslin, white, pink, light blue, or flowered, with embroidered ruffles or ruffles edged in lace. The stiff brim was quilted in close rows of machine stitching, the crown gathered to make a semicircular blouse framing the brim. All bonnets from the simplest to the fanciest were gathered at the back with a drawstring loosened for laundering. And all bonnets had cape tails to protect the neck and shoulders.

The children never saw Grandma Gray in Sunday clothes except when she went away to visit relatives in Emory, Sulphur Springs, or Campbell. She did not go to church and Sunday school because she was a Seceder Presbyterian and no Presbyterian preachers ever came to preach at Woosley or Flats. When she went visiting, Papa put her little black alligator satchel or her larger black valise (depending on the length of her visit) in the back of the buggy and drove Grandma to Point, where she took the train.

Grandma was a tiny woman, not much taller than her oldest granddaughter (at age twelve). And since she was a widow, her best clothes were all black and her everyday dresses were gray printed calico. Her coal-black hair was always parted in the middle. When she dressed up to go away, she wore it in a knot on top of her head between two puffs made by ratting (teasing) the hair on either side of the center part. Every day, her hair was combed straight back to a low knot above her neck, center back.

Her Sunday hats (of black horsehair lace in summer and black felt in winter) were brimless mushroom crowns extending forward to make a semicircular frame around her solemn white face and black hair. A black velvet bandeau, loosely attached, was fastened in the center back with a velvet bow. Her dress, always black taffeta over a black taffeta underskirt, swished and whispered as she walked (the children following) from the house to the gate to get into the buggy. Over the black taffeta dress she wore (in winter) a long black broadcloth cape embroidered with black soutache braid and she carried her unfurled black parasol by its crooked handle as if it were a walking cane. Her right hand hidden in its black kid glove walked the parosol-cane before her while her left hand held the strings of her black satin reticule close to her waist — a white point of linen handkerchief peeping from its drawn top.

Thus dressed she rode away and, dressed in the same clothes, she returned weeks later or months later if she had stayed away to nurse a sick relative through a long illness. The day of her return was as important as any birthday. And after the children had helped Papa hitch Old Red to the buggy to go to Point to meet her, they kept watch swinging back and forth on the front gate until scolded twice and then ran up the north road searching the roadline for the dust cloud, heralding her approach. Any dust rising had to be watched and analyzed to decide whether it was the dust of a single horseman or of a horse followed by four wheels, each wheel boiling its own swirl of dust in the patterned cloud. Once the buggy was in sight they ran ahead to meet it. Papa stopped so that they could climb the spokes of the back wheels into the box behind the seat to ride home standing, holding on to Grandma and Papa with arms around their necks. When Grandma and her satchel and valise were all in the house and the hugs and kisses were over, the children waited impatiently for Grandma to change into everyday clothes, knowing that in her satchel, under the clothes, would be presents.

Out came the unbleached domestic nightcap and nightgown to be hung on a nail behind the cretonne curtain in the corner but only *after* Grandma had finished changing clothes. Next came the ankle-length drawers, chemise, and plain undershirts, all of unbleached domestic. Then the gray calico dress with a round white cambric collar with crocheted or knitted lace edging. Finally out came the big gray cook apron.

Undressing and dressing followed a set procedure. Grandma taught that procedure to her three granddaughters, a technique for undressing and dressing without exposing to view any part of the body from the neck to the ankles. In undressing, the nightgown — a long, full skirt gathered to a yoke — was pulled over the head of the fully clothed girl-child or woman. The arms were not inserted into the sleeves. The gown was buttoned down the front. In this manner a tent was formed under which the child or woman removed her garments one at a time and brought them from under her tent or stepped out of them, leaving a pile on the floor to be picked up and folded on a chair or hung up. She then slipped her arms, one at a time, into the sleeves and was dressed for bed.

In dressing, the procedure was reversed. The child or woman in her nightgown simply slipped her arms out of the sleeves and created the tent under which to dress: union suits, drawers, underskirts, dresses. The gown was then unbuttoned. It dropped to the floor and out of it stepped the fully clad (though unbuttoned and barefoot) girl-child.

When Grandma dressed and undressed, she sent the children from the room. She nevertheless followed her safe-dressing procedure, as the children made occasions to observe when doors were left open a crack. After she had returned from a trip, they were the most watchful of spies, waiting for the moment the presents would appear: a new rag doll or a new set of clothes for an old doll (drawers, underskirts, dresses with buttons and buttonholes), a bean bag for Little Brother. Rarely but sometimes a bought toy: a painted tin tea set with teapot and cups and saucers and a jumping jack for Little Brother.

Grandma, having distributed the presents, tied her big cook apron over her long, full-gathered skirt and went to the kitchen to help Mama. The world seemed more serene and safer with Grandma home again. Papa never yelled at Grandma and Grandma never yelled at anybody and nobody yelled much or very loudly when Grandma was present. Her quietness soothed and dominated the assembly so that nobody wanted to shout.

The presents from Grandma's satchel did not end the pleasant surprises she brought back with her. When the season arrived for sewing clothes for winter or clothes for summer, she opened her valise and brought out piece goods — gingham, handsome plaids in reds, greens, blues, pinks, and yellows — a piece for each of the girls and ofttimes grown-up clothes from Aunt Bertha, Aunt Eddie, Aunt Lou, or Cousin Lutie — capes, cloaks, dresses — to be made over into

Sunday clothes for the girls.

Grandma's satchel, valise, and trunk were treasure chests to feed the children's imaginations. Nobody opened them — ever — nobody but Grandma. She had no rule about it. Nobody ever thought of going into them on the sly. Somehow the game of wondering and waiting for Grandma to snap the catch, open the lid, and bring out the surprise gave as much pleasure as the treasures themselves. There was no agony in the waiting, no fear that the surprise might be bad, but serene confidence that — whether a big surprise or a little one for "Shut your eyes and hold out your hands" and receiving a cigar box (from Uncle Robert's cigars) or a broken amber comb (from Aunt Bertha) — the surprise would be a happy one. Hence the object became a souvenir of the happy anticipation, a keepsake or memento of experience, a token of Grandma's comforting devotion, and — keeping it as a treasure — an act of contract in a relationship with Grandma. Whatever Grandma gave became a treasure *because* Grandma gave it: a piece of string produced at the moment a child desperately needed a piece of string; spools to make wagon wheels for a match-box wagon; a man's old handkerchief or a rag to stretch over willow fronds to make a covered wagon; a nail to drive through a spool to make a top.

Grandma never said, "No! Can't you see I'm busy?" (She *was* busy, always.) Instead, she said, "Let me finish darning this sock," or "When I finish this row of knitting, I will mend your ball," or "I will make flour-paste for your kite." But when a child appeared with a bleeding, stumped toe or crying from a red ant sting, knitting or darning was put away at once. No hurt or sick child waited for Grandma's attention.

So when Grandma brought out a piece of gingham for a girl-child's dress or an old garment to be made over for a child, her magic was sewed into the resulting garment to make it a favorite. Then, too, there were the scraps left over from each girl's dresses (kept in scrap bags, one for each girl, holding only scraps from her own dresses) pieced into quilts later. Each granddaughter helped Grandma piece and quilt her own quilt and was allowed to choose the pattern, but was advised to choose among the simpler patterns with the promise of making more complicated patterns later.

Papa's everyday clothes consisted of indigo blue denim bib over-alls and blue chambray shirts over ribbed cotton knit union suits or ribbed cotton knit undershirts and drawers (long-sleeved, long-legged, summer weight, or winter weight). In winter an extra undershirt was worn and also an extra outer garment—a jumper—a blue denim jacket (with two big patch pockets) reaching to the hips. Heavy gray socks were worn in winter under high-cut black or brown shoes of tough leather laced with rawhide laces through five or six pairs of brass-rimmed eyelets, then hooked over three pairs of brass hooks, drawn tight, and tied in a bow knot over a soft leather tongue. The big overalls had five pockets; one on the left-hand side of the bib, two large, deep ones high on either side of the pants front for holding pocket knives, nails and small tools, and two large hip pockets, one of which always held a turkey-red or indigo blue printed pocket handkerchief some twenty inches square and the other which sometimes held a pipe and leather tobacco pouch or a plug of chewing tobacco.

In heavy rain men wore brown or black slickers, sometimes called "oil slickers" (long coats to the ankles, fastened with hinged metal buckles that clamped through large, brass-rimmed eyelets). Sometimes men wore caps of the same material, with bills over the forehead and attached capes over the neck and shoulders. But usually an old felt hat served as a rain hat. In winter rain men wore rubber-soled arctics over their shoes (high, water-proofed black cloth overshoes that fastened with hinged buckles), and in summer rain, storm rubbers cut low at the instep but cut in a high, rounded tongue to protect the foot and ankle.

Men's Sunday suits, winter and summer, were made of gray, blue or brown worsted (sometimes in herringbone weave), blue serge, or cheviot. The suit had a coat, vest, and pants—and sometimes two pairs of pants. An extra pair could always be bought, and was, if necessary. The six-buttoned, collarless vest, single breasted, came to two V points at the waist. On each side of the buttoned front were two lip pockets, one above the other. From the lower left of the four pockets—the watch pocket—the gold watch chain dangled, in a loop, attached to the watch in the pocket and fastened at its other end in the pocket buttonhole.

Telling the time of day involved a ritual: the coat was unbuttoned; the watch was extracted with thumb, forefinger, and middle finger of the right hand; it was pulled straight forward until the watch chain was taut. The ornamental lid was snapped open with the thumb nail of the right hand, and there the watch remained, held stationary while the owner appeared to forget it momentarily; then suddenly remembering, he lowered his eyelids, paused, pronounced the hour, snapped the lid closed, and returned the watch to the pocket.

The round cutaway sack coat with a small lapel collar was single breasted, usually had four or five buttons and one flap pocket waist-high on either side. The pants were held up by elastic web suspenders trimmed with ornamental sliding buckles to shorten or lengthen the suspenders to fit the wearer. They were worn under the vest. The pants had a fly front opening, a deep, inverted pocket in either side, two inverted hip pockets and a small watch pocket on the left front side an inch below the waist. The uncuffed, skimpy pants legs ended below the shoe tops at the ankles.

Getting into and out of a man's pants became a ritual fascinating to spying children. First, the collarless white muslin shirt, with its two collar buttons inserted front and back, was put on and buttoned down the front while the wearer stood in clean, long cream underwear in his sock feet. Next, holding his open pants before him about knee-high — suspenders dangling — he leaned forward, balanced on his right foot, lifted his left foot high, inserted it into the left pants leg (meanwhile hopping a little hop or two to regain balance). Third, changing weight to the clothed leg, he inserted the right leg into the right pants leg and stood upright, again pulling his suspendered pants up with him. At that stage his white shirttail billowed out around his middle. His first step in controlling the shirt was to hold his pants with his left hand, reach behind with his right, and push the shirttail down as far as possible into the seat of his pants. That done, he pushed his left front shirttail into the pants and, changing hands, made a victorious swipe with his left hand pushing the right tail into place.

Finally, a thumb caught under each front suspender, he hoisted them over his shoulders, snapped them a time or two into place, buttoned up his fly, and stood fully clothed except for shoes — already shined — soon put on, laced up, and tied in a bow knot. The stiff, white linen collar was buttoned on and the four-in-hand tie was pushed under the collar. Holding the left end of the tie in place, Papa threw the right end under, then over and under again, bringing it up behind the knot-to-be, slipping it under the fold, drawing both ends down tight, and fastening the tie down with a gold stickpin.

His sack coat went on last. Then the black felt hat with a six-inch crown above a brim with a fourteen-inch diameter. He placed his folded handkerchief in his hip pocket, his leather money purse in his left side pocket, watch in his watch pocket, and he was ready for church.

That was in winter. When winter changed to spring and late spring, the cutaway sack coat was left at home and Papa went to church in vest and shirt sleeves, with rubber band sleeve holders worn above the elbows to pull up his sleeve cuffs to keep them clean. When summer came, the coat and vest were left at home. Then the gold watch was transferred to the pants watch pocket and the fob was fastened to the suspenders loop.

But the time-telling watch ritual was the same, winter or summer. And the big black hat was the same—perched high on Papa's black curly hair or pushed back so he could mop a hot forehead with his white handkerchief, or in winter pulled low over piercing blue eyes in clean-shaven face as he sat beside Mama in the buggy and drove toward Woosley into a stiff north wind.

Mama and Grandma made all children's clothes, women's clothes, and shirts for the men, but not men's white linen collars, coats, capes, and jackets, which were bought in Point or ordered from Sears, Roebuck. They made all sheets, pillowcases, dresser scarves, table runners, and tablecloths. Grandma knitted lace and insertion from fine sewing thread to trim Sunday underskirts and drawers but lace was bought to trim yokes of Sunday dresses. Most stockings and socks were bought, though Grandma, when she had time, knitted stockings and socks from black yarn as well as colored mittens for the children.

Sewing seasons were early spring and early fall. Before the treadle sewing machine was opened and the bobbins threaded, an inventory was made of clothing needs of each family member: who had grown out of what that could be shortened, lengthened, patched, remodeled, and made to fit a child for another season; who needed what new garments made of what material; how much of what material was on hand and how much must be ordered from Sears, Roebuck: domestic—bleached and unbleached—for clothing as well as for sheets and pillowcases, batiste, broadcloth, calico (oil-boiled), cambric, challis (wool), chambray, cotton-checks, dimity (cross bar and plain), dotted swiss, foulard, gingham, huck toweling, eiderdown (wool), lawn, linen crash, linen, longcloth, nainsook, outing (cotton flannel), percale (printed), poplin, taffeta, sateen, shepherd checks, storm serge, and voile. Few patterns were bought. Patterns were borrowed from neighbors and duplicated, cut out of newspapers. Basic patterns were altered and changed to fit for size and style. Grandma, who could cut by chart, made most of the patterns by measuring a child and placing the measurements on her chart. After patterns for garments were decided upon, estimates were made of thread, buttons, and trimmings to be ordered: cambric embroidery edging, Nottingham lace and beading, ruching, soutache braid, Swiss embroidered edging and insertion, and torchon lace and insertion.

Garments made were: aprons (everyday dresses for the three girls), cook aprons (for Mama and Grandma), bodices, bonnets, chemises, corset covers, drawers, dresses, nightcaps (for Grandma) nightgowns, rompers, saques, shirts (for Papa, blue chambray for every day and bleached domestic for Sunday), suspenders, underskirts, and wrappers (dressing gowns).

Grandma made patterns for doll clothes by drawing small squares on a piece of brown wrapping paper or old newspaper and then cutting the pattern by the "chart" method. She taught the children how to cut their own doll clothes, how to sew with very fine stitches a flat-fell or French-fell seam and why. Grandma made the buttonholes on the doll clothes, because they were very, very small. But she taught the girls how to make buttonholes by allowing them to make them for the large buttons on their everyday aprons. First, Grandma made the top buttonhole as an example, explaining how and why at each step. She chose the top buttonhole to make sure the apron would stay buttoned. Thereafter, with Grandma's supervision and help, a child made the remaining lower buttonholes (which Papa sometimes teasingly called "pig eyes").

Winter time was quilting time, when quilt tops pieced in spare minutes throughout the year were brought forth from Grandma's trunk along with quilt bats carded by Grandma with the help of the children and stored in layers between newspapers in the rafters. Papa brought the quilting frames from the smokehouse (four boards about nine feet long, two inches thick, and three inches wide with holes bored at three-inch intervals the entire length of each board). He clamped the boards together with carpenter's clamps to form a frame to hold a quilt six and a half by eight feet. Into the frame the quilt lining of unbleached domestic was sewed with strong cord; a darning needle laced the cord through the holes. Stretched taut, the lining was covered with the carded cotton bats. The pieced quilt top was stretched on top of the layer of bats and laced to the frame. Then Papa contrived a pulley contraption to raise the framed quilt to the ceiling and out of the way when quilters were not at work: four strong hooks in the ceiling (one at each corner of the frame) held small ropes (attached to the four corners of the frame) in such a way that they could be pulled or released to raise or lower the quilt to about thirty inches from the floor, a comfortable height for quilters.

The stitching or quilting patterns were usually diamonds or shells, drawn on the surface with white chalk. For drawing diamonds a piece of string pulled taut, guided the hand. For drawing shells, a compass was made with a piece of string tied to a piece of chalk. The left hand held the string to a specified point on the quilt's edge while the right hand moved the chalk to describe and draw an arc—say, a third of a circle with a diameter of twelve or fifteen inches. That done, the string was shortened one inch to draw a second arc inside the first, shortened another inch to draw a third arc inside the second, and the process continued until the string made a radius of one inch. Thus a shell was formed.

A second shell was drawn to dovetail with the first, and a third and on until a row of shells extended the length of the quilt. When an entire row of shells had been quilted, the cords fastening the quilt to the frame were loosened and the frame was rolled under, rolling the row of quilted shells with it. Then a second row of shells was drawn, quilted, and rolled under, and a third until the middle of the quilt was reached. Quilters usually quilted a row on one side, then a row on the opposite side, thus rolling under alternately until the middle of the quilt was reached and the quilting finished.

When the quilt was quilted and taken out of the frame, it then was bound by hand. The domestic lining (about two inches larger than the quilt top) was brought over the quilt edge, turned under, and whipped down with coarse cotton thread (O.N.T. number thirty or forty). The finished quilt was folded and put away in the big wooden box chest to be a company quilt until it was needed every day. When quilts grew old and faded from washing with lye soap, they were used as quilt pallets for children and babies and for camping when Papa and neighbor men went on week-long fishing and hunting trips to Caddo Lake.

Piecing quilts was a spare-time activity the year round and so was knitting and darning. Grandma's big, round, sweet grass sewing basket, on the shelf in the kitchen, on the center table in the front room, or on the floor by her rocker, usually held a few quilt squares and quilt scraps along with two or three socks or stockings for darning and her knitting needles (side by side, thread or yarn wrapped around them) attached to mittens, tobaggans, socks, stockings, or lace, cast on; the finished portion was neatly rolled.

Grandma pieced each quilt square on a paper foundation — a square cut from old newspaper — that kept the cloth pieces from puckering or stretching. When the squares were put together into the quilt top, the paper backing was torn off.

Grandma taught the girls how to piece and quilt the simpler patterns. The star patterns were among the most difficult: Lone Star, Morning Star, Star of Bethlehem, and Star of the East. Other difficult patterns were Sunburst, Cherokee Rose, and Irish Chain. Simpler patterns were Log Cabin, Golden Stairs, and String Quilt. The girls learned how to briar-stitch and featherstitch on patchwork pillow-covers, covers for doorstops (brickbats), and patchwork pincushions made of velvet, satin, or woolen scraps.

Making quilts was all done by hand, both piecing and quilting. Clothing, except for baby clothes, was made on a Singer treadle sewing machine, except for basting, buttonholes, and hems-on-the-bias. The machine was moved from one front room to another and placed near a window for light (when it was in use). Closed and not in use it sat before the front window in the north front room with an embroidered round doily on top.

Dorothy longed to use the sewing machine but was forbidden to do so for fear she might hurt herself. One day when she was almost six she could no longer resist the temptation (with Mama and Grandma both in the kitchen). She placed her doll dress under the needle, lowered the needle and the needle foot. Then she found she had to stand to treadle the machine with one foot while balancing on the other and holding the cloth in place with both hands. Ready to start sewing, she heard the kitchen door hinges squeak. In fright and haste, she raised the needle foot and needle to remove the doll dress. But her foot went down on the treadle at the same time, bringing the needle down and through her finger. Pinioned to the machine, she screamed and jerked her finger away, breaking the needle. When Grandma appeared in the doorway, Dorothy stood before her weeping and holding up the bleeding finger with the needle protruding on each side. Grandma used Papa's pliers to pull the needle out. Dorothy sat holding her finger in a tin cup of turpentine for a long while, worrying about the coming punishment for disobedience. But when Grandma finally bandaged the finger, Mama scolded her and said she hoped Dorothy had learned her lesson. Dorothy knew, without a doubt, that she had.

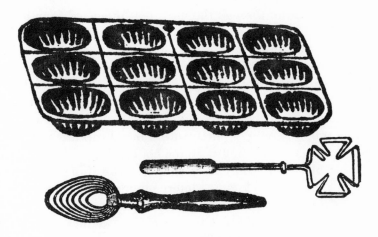

The Home

Year in, year out, the kitchen was haven: the safest room in the house and the source of food and companionship. In winter it was haven from outside north wind that chafed hands and lips till they bled; and inside a haven from cold bedrooms. By daylight or lamplight the kitchen was always warm on cold days. And on summer days the hot stove could be endured in anticipation of its rewards.

Year round, it was a haven from darkness. Before daylight, Papa lighted the coal oil lamp sitting high on the kitchen shelf before he built the fire in the stove. When the kitchen was warm, he called to Mama before he took down the lantern hanging on a nail by the door, lit it, and went to the barn to milk.

The stove ruled the kitchen. From its skillets (sizzling) and pots (boiling) on top, and from its oven underneath, promises floated out to fill the kitchen and the house, and whisked on hot air through the kitchen door across the yard to children playing. Interest in play dissolved in the smell of yeast bread to be spread with butter fresh from the churn and eaten, still oven-warm. Or turnovers or sweet potato pie — maybe cinnamon-spiced — or angel food cake, vanilla flavored, or sausage (sage-seasoned), ham, or chicken, frying. Or Kentucky

Wonder beans with new potatoes boiling in hambone broth in the two-gallon black iron pot crowning the stove.

The stove stood in the center of the north wall, to the left of the door to the staircase leading to the loft room above. The tin stove-pipe went straight up through the shed roof, protected from catching fire by a surrounding tin sheet. Standing on cast-iron splay feet on a decorated tin pad (four feet square) to protect the floor from stray coals, the stove opened its small firebox door (on the left) and its clanging oven door (on the right). The iron hearth extending the length of the firebox held pots and pans of cooling food. The entire top of the stove could be removed in sections: six round caps, set in removable frames, could be lifted with a metal cap-lifter. A padded potholder protected the hand from the hot cap-lifter.

The big black stove wore its black-pot crown (full — or clean and empty) on the right back cap, winter, summer, day, and night like Old King Coal with his merry old soul. Beside the pot, the iron tea-kettle (full of water) crowned his queen. On a rack above, three flatirons resting on their handles, turned points upward to top the throne, and above the throne three black skillets hung on the wall. Sooner or later a child learned, painfully or by observation and admonition, that the merry old soul could — without warning — lick out a fiery tongue to singe hair and clothes, and could blister a finger (which had not been spit on first).

Next in importance was the kitchen cabinet (sent as a surprise for Mama, after Papa wrote a letter to Mr. Searsanroebuck). Standing against the east wall, with shelves above for spices and small utensils, the cabinet asserted its importance with its protruding flour-bin belly.

To the right of the cabinet, high sliding windows gave a view of the well pulley and the smokehouse roof. And to the right of the window the kitchen safe stood, its tin door panels punctured in star designs and its doors hiding loaves of bread, pies, cakes, syrup pitcher, and bowls of leftover food. The long dinner table stood parallel to the west wall, surrounded by a long bench on either side, a split bottom chair at either end, and Little Brother's high chair at the corner next to Mama's chair. A fourth of the kitchen space was free for churn and churners and for sitting pea-shellers, bean-snappers and potato-peelers. Grandma's low armless rocker stayed in the southeast corner in front of the safe except when she moved it to the back gallery to escape stove heat in summer or into a front room for quilting in winter.

A door in the center of the south wall led to the back gallery; and the door in the center of the west wall led into the north front room. Dorothy's favorite door, however, was the staircase door leading to the loft room.

The loft, extending the length of the house, received daylight from low windows in each gabled end. On either side of a center path of light, beds and cots were pushed into the shadows under the rafters. There the hired men slept. Sometimes in winter, however, the hired men were away: they had been paid off, fired, or had gone to Arkansas to visit homefolks. Then Dorothy was allowed to play upstairs alone, free from Little Brother, who was not allowed upstairs for fear he might fall out of a window or punch his eye out with Dorothy's paper-doll scissors. On a winter afternoon the sun on the roof warmed the cold loft, and on a dark, wet day Dorothy could snuggle down on a cot by the chimney—at the north end—and undisturbed, read, "The Wide, Wide World." Playing paper dolls, however, was her favorite pastime upstairs. For there, in the entire length of that center pathway of light, she could set up a whole community of paper-doll families, with an unlimited supply of fathers, mothers, children, uncles, aunts, cousins, grandparents, cut from old *Ladies' Home Journal*s and Sears and Roebuck catalogues and augmented by the store-bought paper dolls sent by Aunt Eddie from Dallas.

Seldom in summer did Dorothy play upstairs. The sun on the roof made the loft an oven, even with a breeze blowing down the path of light between the open windows. When a sudden summer shower brought an order from Mama to "Run upstairs! Quick! And close the windows!" the hot air sent her scampering down again. But a slow summer rain on the roof all night and all day made the loft a welcome hideout in a house-prison full of quarrelsome sisters and brother. When she tired of dolls and reading, she could stand on a cot and touch the roof, keeping time with the rain put-putting on the shingles.

However, when night fell, summer or winter, the staircase was no longer an escape. The coal oil lamp hanging on the wall at the top of the stairs, shining against its tin reflector, was no friendly beacon but a dangerous lure to a black den of silent mad dogs, snakes, wildcats, panthers, and wild boars, ready to snarl, hiss, and scream when they pounced on her.

The door to the stairway was kept closed (because of Little Brother's unpermitted wandering) except on the hottest summer days, when it was opened to allow hot kitchen air to escape, and on the coldest winter nights to allow kitchen stove heat to warm the loft.

The kitchen lamp, first to be lit in the morning, was last to be put out at night. At bedtime, after the children had been put to bed, Mama turned down the wick, cupped her right hand at the top of the chimney, and thus directed a big puff of breath down the chimney. The flame disappeared, leaving the wick a faint glow in utter blackness. A nightgowned child, still awake (for a drink of water), clung to Mama's hand and was led through the door to the north front room to be tucked into bed.

This was called "*the* front room." In the southeast corner (south of the door to the kitchen) a wooden bedstead stood, its carved headboard standing high against the south wall. The north wall had two windows (one on either side of the old fireplace chimney) giving a view of the peach orchard and the road north to the McKeithens. In the north half of the room three rocking chairs were grouped to face the stove (in winter), attached by elbowed pipe to the old fireplace chimney. The shoat-nosed wood-burning stove had a firebox about two feet long, sixteen inches wide, and eighteen inches deep. The top was completely removable in five sections including two round caps. An iron hearth about six inches deep extended across the front end underneath the firebox door. Bas-relief lions' heads decorated each rounded side of the shoat-nosed firebox. The stove rested on lion-clawed feet on a padded tin square. On warm spring days when the stove was cold (before it was taken down to be stored in the smokehouse for the summer), the children traced the lions' heads through tissue paper to make masks to scare each other.

North of the door to the kitchen, in the northeast corner of the room, a low door led to a closet under the kitchen stairway to the loft. There, the featherbeds were stored for the summer.

In summertime, the three rocking chairs faced the center table in the middle of the room. The undershelf of the table held the Bible on top of folded copies of *The Christian Observer* and the *Rains County Leader*.

Strips of grass matting, tacked down, covered the floor. The walls were papered with a heavy building paper, rose-pink, held to the wall by tin brads (one inch in diameter) spaced one foot apart. A child sick in bed could trace imaginary lines making diamonds climbing to the grooved wooden ceiling.

The west wall held one window looking up the road west to the Driggers' place and, south of the window, a door leading to the front gallery. Between the door and windows stood a large dresser with a high-standing mirror resting on two long drawers and guarded on either side by three small drawers that rose halfway up the mirror's height.

Against the south wall, west of the door leading to the south-front room, a bookcase with glass doors held *Pilgrim's Progress,* a set of Dickens' novels, a set of Thackeray's novels, the complete works of William Shakespeare, Longfellow's *Poems*, and a novel—*St. Elmo*.

The south front room had two doors and two windows. One door on the west led to the front gallery, and the one on the east to the back gallery. The windows were centered in the west and south walls.

White iron bedsteads stood on either side of the south window and parallel to the east and west walls, and sometimes a cot was placed under the window against the south wall, between the two beds. Winter and summer, when the beds were made each morning, they were covered with white counterpanes. Pillows, their wrinkles smoothed out, stood upright against the headboards. In winter time, featherbeds (beaten, fluffed, and smoothed) under the white counterpanes made white mountains on top of which children were not allowed to play. Nevertheless, dark caves underneath invited games of Chicken Little, Aladdin, and made-up stories that could happen only once. In summertime featherbeds were stored and children went outside to play other games until geese flew south again trailed by a blue norther. Featherbeds were brought out again and children remembered again their land of the white mountains.

Other furniture in the south-room included a large hump-back trunk at the foot of each bed, a dresser against the north wall (west of the door from the north room), and a washstand holding a pitcher and washbowl against the east wall by the door leading to the back gallery. The chamber pot, kept behind the washstand doors in daytime, was placed under a bed at night. Flowered cretonne curtains stretched catty-corner across the northeast and northwest corners of the room, hiding coats and hats hanging on nails in the wall. The wall telephone was by the north-wall door, about five feet from the floor, and underneath it was a split-bottom chair for children to stand on. The floor, like the floor of the kitchen and back and front galleries, was wide pine boards scrubbed white with lye soap.

The front gallery on the west (cool in summer-morning shade) extended the length of the house. The back gallery on the southeast (cool in evening shade) extended one-third the length of the house.

Between two gallery posts (next to the kitchen door), a shelf rested on cleats about thirty inches above the floor. And the shelf held an enamel washpan, a tin water bucket, and tin dipper. A hucktowel hung on a nail on the wall above.

On rainy days children could chase each other in a circle from the back gallery into the kitchen, into the north front room, onto the front gallery, into the south front room and onto the back gallery again—faster and faster—until Mama said, "Slow down before you get hurt," or bathed a child's bumped head and suggested a game of "Hull Gull" or "Going to Mill," before she went back to her work in the kitchen.

Mama ruled the kitchen. Under her full-skirted calico dress covered by a big gathered apron, she was tall and slender. Her crown of dark hair combed over a rat above her forehead and coiled in convolutions on top of her head added grace and authority to everything she said and did. Dorothy, sitting quietly with clean-washed face and hands, waiting for the goodies Mama would soon bring from the fragrant pot or oven, pretended to be a princess—happy ending to a morning of being Cinderella, required to run one errand after another with no time for play in between. When her sisters were at home, they shared the chores, but when they were in school all the errands, including minding Little Brother, fell to Dorothy's lot. From her sisters she had learned a grumbling verse to comfort herself in the Cinderella role:

> *It's Dorothy this and Dorothy that*
> *And Dorothy skin the old gray cat.*
> *The same old thing every day.*
> *I never, never can go play.*

But she never recited the verse within Mama's hearing.

When Dorothy was told to "go get a cake pan, colander, slaw-cutter, shoe last, jar of preserves, or bucket of molasses," she needed no instructions on where to find anything. She knew.

High on the east wall, north of the kitchen cabinet, the round wooden dough tray (twenty inches across) hung by a leather thong. Flanking it were the wooden dough board (a rectangle some eighteen by thirty inches) and the wooden rolling pin, both hung by leather thongs. Nearer the cabinet and lower on the wall hung the blue graniteware colander and the ten-quart, tin dishpan. A ten-quart galvanized iron slop bucket sat on the floor beneath the dishpan.

The top shelf of the shelves above the kitchen cabinet held two glass coal oil lamps (in the daytime). At night when they were lit, one was placed in the center of the dinner table and the other on the center table in the front room. The lamp in the front room had a decorated pressed glass bowl above a slender glass stem resting on a round, glass foot. The plain glass bowl of the kitchen lamp rested on the table. The blue graniteware coffee pot was kept on a lower shelf (along with the gallon milk pitcher), except when the pot was on the stove and the pitcher on the dinner table. And the coffee grinder was kept on the bottom shelf.

Inside the cabinet, the tin flour-sifter was kept in the flour bin. Behind the cabinet doors (next to the bin) blackened tin roasting pans, cake pans, and pie pans were stacked, large ones on the bottom. The sausage grinder with its three cutting attachments was kept in a cabinet drawer with the wooden potato masher. Another drawer held the butcher's knives, butcher's cleaver, kitchen knives, graniteware cooking spoons, steel-tined kitchen forks, steel cake turner, egg beaters, grater, and tea strainer. The bottom drawer held the fluted silver spoons (Mama's wedding present) and the extra case knives and forks used on the dinner table.

Milk vessels were stored on the back gallery — for fresh air and sunshine. All milk vessels were washed and scalded after each use. The five-gallon crockery churn sat on the floor. Above it, on the wall, hung the butter molds (round, one-pound size), butter paddle, and churn dasher along with the tin milk strainer, milk pans, milk buckets, and milk coolers.

A galvanized, five-gallon coal oil can sat in the corner of the back gallery, just outside the kitchen door, with a tin funnel — bottom side up — over its spout.

In the smokehouse, the east and west walls had shelves below and on either side of centered windows. Shining tin buckets of syrup were lined up on the top shelf. On lower shelves were rows of glass jars of fruits, vegetables, pickles, preserves, jellies, and crocks of sauerkraut. On bottom shelves Mama kept empty crocks, and the kraut and the sausage stuffer; and Papa kept his equipment for mending shoes: the iron lasts (three sizes), iron stand, sheets of thick sole leather (which he cut into shoe soles, using the worn-out sole as pattern), tack hammer and puller, an awl, heel nails (longer), and clinch nails (shorter). Cured hams, bacon slabs, and long sacks of sausage hung from the rafters. An old bottomless kitchen chair (with boards nailed on for a seat) was used by the children to stand on to reach upper shelves.

Another storage place for canned food was the old stormhouse, northwest of the house — until its roof caved in during a heavy rain. Then Papa removed the rotten roof timbers with a crowbar, dug out the wet dirt from the sunken earth roof, and the children rescued the muddy jars of food from the shelves lining the stormhouse walls, washed them clean in a tub of water by the well, and stored them in the smokehouse.

The dinner table was the family meeting place three times a day: for breakfast (before dawn), dinner (at noon by the sun), and supper (after dark). The children were allowed a midmorning and midafternoon snack. The basic snack menu was bread and butter (corn bread or light bread). To that was added, in spring and summer, fresh garden radishes, shallots, lettuce, and turnips. The children liked to fill their pockets with buttered bread, then go to the garden to pull radishes or shallots out of the ground, wipe off the dirt on the under side of an apron hem, and eat them — a bite of vegetable and a bite of bread, alternating. Sometimes in winter Grandma sprinkled the buttered bread with a little sugar and a smidgeon of cinnamon. The snack ended with a glass of milk — either sweet milk from the morning milking or buttermilk from the morning churning.

When the meal was cooked (and keeping warm in oven or pot) one of the children was sent to beat the broken plow sweep hanging by a wire from a limb on the hackberry tree, to signal the men in the fields. They came to the house one by one, washed face, hands and arms (with rolled-up shirt sleeves) on the back gallery. Papa led the way into the kitchen, where the children waited — not allowed to sit down until Papa sat down at the south end of the table. Mama and Grandma sat at the north end (near the stove) and the three girls and hired men sat on benches along each side. Little Brother sat in a high chair beside Mama until he was three: then he sat beside Dorothy on the bench next to the wall. As soon as Papa sat down, the children scrambled over the benches and sat, heads bowed, ready for Papa's mumbled blessing and "amen." Plates were turned up to wait for food to be passed along. Children were required to eat a little of every dish — especially vegetables — and *all* of the food on the plate. Hence, experience soon taught them to take small helpings of dishes they did not like. They could always ask for seconds. They were not

allowed syrup, molasses, honey, pie, tea cakes, cake, jam, jelly, preserves, or any sweet food until vegetables were eaten. They were
admonished to alternate a bite of bread with a bite of vegetables or
meat, to chew each bite thoroughly, and to swallow each bite of food
before taking a drink of milk. They were not allowed to whistle or
sing or scuffle or play at the table. Though they were allowed to talk
quietly — with permission — they were not allowed to linger over food.
At the end of the meal they were not allowed (except with special
permission on special occasions) to leave the table until Papa got up.
So the children sat imprisoned on the bench, waiting for Papa to
take his last bite, cross his fork and knife on his empty plate, push his
chair back, and stand up.

After each meal, dishes were removed, the flowered oilcloth
tablecloth wiped clean, the dishes washed, and the table reset for the
next meal. Plates were turned face down to protect them from dust.
The knife and fork, side by side, were placed to the right of the
plate. Tablespoons. and teaspoons stood upright in the spoon holder
in the center of the table — handles down, spoons up, spreading into
a bouquet. To keep the table and dishes free of dust and flies, a
porous cloth tent was spread over the table with the spoon holder
serving as a center tentpole.

Breakfast consisted of ham, bacon, sausage, or calf brains or hog
brains (at hog-killing time), eggs, scrambled or fried, and biscuit —
always biscuit, coffee (for adults) with cream and sugar, sweet milk
(for the children), and ribbon cane syrup or sorghum molasses in the
syrup pitcher sitting in the middle of the table in the cluster with the
pepper sauce bottle and the spoon holder. The biscuits were made
with buttermilk, soda, salt, lard, and flour by a recipe in Mama's
memory and never written down. Breakfast ended with biscuit and
molasses or syrup. The molasses was poured over the open biscuit,
and the biscuit cut into bite-size pieces.

Dinner at noon, suntime, consisted of vegetables cooked with
meat (a piece of salt pork on the rind — or skin) about six inches long,
two inches wide, and two inches thick. The meat was sliced to the
rind (but not severed) in slices a quarter of an inch thick. The meat
boiled in a pot of water for an hour before the vegetables were
added: greens (turnip greens, mustard, lambs'-quarters, or poke
salad); beans (Kentucky Wonder, wax beans, green or dried butter
beans, dried navy beans); green or dried black-eyed peas and green
or dried lady peas. Sometimes a piece of ham or hambone with meat

on it was substituted for the salt pork. Fresh leaf greens were available almost the year round, with a winter turnip greens patch supplemented by wild lambs'-quarters and poke salad in early spring before the spring turnip greens were ready to eat. Lambs'-quarters grew along the garden and field fences and was sometimes mixed with other greens. Poke salad greens were the young, tender shoots of the poke berry bushes growing in the creek bottom. They were never cooked with other greens. To make them edible, they were cooked in several changes of clear water to remove the strong taste before they were added to boiling meat.

Irish potatoes, another standby on the dinner table, were usually mashed. Peeled and cut into chunks, they were cooked in clear water, drained, and mashed with a wooden potato masher. Then thick cream and butter, salt and black pepper were whipped into them with a fork before they were piled into a bowl and brought to the table. In early spring, small new potatoes were scraped instead of peeled, and their eyes cut out with the point of a knife; they were then dropped into the pot of Kentucky Wonder beans boiling with the hambone or salt pork.

Dinnertime vegetables eaten raw were lettuce (washed clean and piled in a bowl), green onions, shallots, radishes, and tomatoes (peeled and sliced).

Corn bread was always served with vegetables at dinner and supper, along with a few slices of light bread on Monday, Tuesday, and Wednesday (until all the bread from Saturday's baking was gone). The yellow cornmeal was made from corn raised on the farm and ground into meal at a mill on the Emory road. To make corn bread, Mama added salt and soda to buttermilk in a crock and then stirred in the cornmeal to make a thin batter (the amount of soda was reckoned by the sourness of the buttermilk). Shortening (lard) was melted in a skillet and added to the batter. Then the skillet with a small amount of fat still in it was heated until the fat began to smoke. The batter was poured in and the skillet placed in a moderately hot oven to cook (twenty to thirty minutes, depending on the oven). At hog-killing time and thereafter for a while as long as cracklings were available, a handful of cracklings, crumbled, were added to the corn bread batter to make crackling bread. When the skillet was brought from the oven, the corn bread was cut into wedges (like pie wedges). A plate was placed over the skillet and the skillet turned upside down to transfer the crisp, brown-crusted circle of wedges onto the plate; it was carried immediately to the table so that each diner could slit his wedge and slide in a sliver of butter to melt and seep into the warm porous bread beneath the scrunchy crust.

Dinner ended with a slice of light bread (or a wedge of corn bread) covered with honey, pear or peach preserves, plum or grape jelly.

Added to that basic menu of bread and vegetables were, at different times of the year, chicken, ham, beef, squirrel, rabbit, and catfish. During the winter the chickens to be eaten (full-grown roosters or hens) were stewed until tender, and dumplings, made similar to biscuit dough, rolled thin and cut in strips, were dropped a few at a time into the simmering broth. The pot was uncovered for a few minutes until the dumplings were set, then covered and allowed to cook slowly for fifteen or twenty minutes. When it was done, butter and black pepper were added.

In the spring, chicken was fried. The young, tender chicken was gutted and cut into pieces (legs, thighs, back, pulley bone, breast, neck), washed, salted, and allowed to stand several hours (preferably overnight). The pieces were rolled in flour and fried slowly in a heavy iron skillet in melted fat about one-half inch deep. The pieces were turned with a fork constantly so that they would brown evenly. When all pieces were brown encrusted, a few drops of water were added and the skillet was covered for about five minutes to make the chicken tender before it was removed from the skillet. Gravy was made by adding more flour to the fat residue in the skillet and stirring and mixing it with the browned flour left from the chicken. Then milk and black pepper were added and the mixture brought to a boil, stirred, and quickly removed from the stove.

In the fall, when spring chickens had grown too large and tough to fry, they were baked with dressing. The dressing was cooked separately from the chicken in a pan or skillet. The chicken was gutted, and the heart, gizzard, liver, and leafs of fat were stewed to make a broth with which to mix the dressing, made of stale corn bread (one-third) and stale light bread (two-thirds) crumbled. To the crumbled bread, salt, black pepper and sage were added—to taste. Onion chopped fine was added and then the chicken broth, to make a soft but firm mixture. Last, lumps of butter were stirred into the dressing before it was put into the skillet or pan and a few pats of butter were dabbed on top before the pan went into the oven with the chicken to bake.

The dinner drink for all the family was buttermilk—fresh and cool. At midmorning when churning was done, the fresh-churned milk with sweet butter flecks floating, was poured into tin coolers (buckets) and the coolers were lowered into the cistern by small ropes to hang three-fourths submerged, with the ropes anchored, each to a strong spike in the well frame. At noontime one cooler at a time was drawn up as needed and the rest left to keep cool for supper. Buttermilk left over from supper (saving enough to make biscuit and corn bread for the next day) was poured into the slop bucket and fed to the hogs. Beside the coolers of buttermilk hanging in the cistern, a two-gallon cooler of sweet milk from the morning milking hung, along with syrup buckets holding butter molded into rounded mesas with a pine cone design on top. For seven months of the year or more, the cistern was ringed with milk coolers and butter buckets. Mama took care that no cooler leaked. Such an accident would have ruined the drinking water for a long time.

Supper was always eaten by lamplight, summer and winter. Through the hottest summer months, the meal was cold food left over from dinner. (The fire in the kitchen stove was allowed to go out after dinner.) A favorite ending for summertime supper was corn bread crumbled into a glass of sweet milk, stirred into a mush and eaten with a spoon.

Winter-time supper consisted of warmed-over food from dinner with freshly cooked hot foods added. The favorite was *cornmeal mush* served in a bowl, sprinkled with sugar, covered with cream, and eaten with a spoon. To make cornmeal mush, a pot of salted water was brought to a hard boil and the cornmeal added slowly and stirred constantly to prevent lumps. The pot was moved to a cooler stove lid to cook slowly, being stirred constantly until it began to thicken. Then it was done.

Variation in daily fare for dinner and supper was determined by the season (of necessity) and by choice according to the day of the week or special occasion like birthdays, visitors, or picnics. On Monday (wash day), on hog-killing day, lard-rendering day, or soap-making day—when Mama worked in the back yard or smokehouse—the food chosen was sauerkraut or turnips and greens or some other food that could be boiled in the big iron pot and required little time and attention.

Bread made from wheat flour, cornmeal, or a combination of the two accompanied all three meals every day of the year. Breads were leavened with soda (when buttermilk was used), baking powder (when sweet milk was used), and yeast. Grandma made the yeast cakes from light-bread dough rolled very thin, cut in strips about two inches wide and four inches long, dipped in cornmeal, dried in the sun, and stored in a glass jar in a cool, dry place.

Wheat and corn grown on the farm were taken to the mill on the Emory road and ground into flour and cornmeal. The mill owner kept a share as pay. Flour brought home in fifty-pound bags was stored in the barn loft (enough to last the year).

When the supply of cornmeal ran low, corn was taken to the mill (cornmeal could not be stored safely — from weevils — for long periods of time). The farm produced most of the family food, even the seed for the next year's planting.

The few store-bought foods came from the Peddler, the Raleigh man, or from Point when Papa made his monthly trip to town. The bought food included coffee (Arbuckle's), tea, sugar, salt, soda (Arm and Hammer), baking powder, pepper (black), ginger, nutmeg, cinnamon, and allspice, vanilla, lemon and almond flavoring, and sage. Papa always brought back a five-cent sack of peppermint striped candy for each child. Occasionally he came home with a package of dried navy beans, of dried apples (for turnovers), or of Baker's shredded coconut. Sometimes — but seldom — he bought Packers Tar Soap or Fairy Soap, cheese, canned salmon, a box of apples, a whole coconut, a stalk of bananas (shared with neighbors), and — near Christmas time — a box of apples. Oranges, in Christmas stockings, were brought by Santa Claus.

Saturday was baking day. The baking process began Friday night before supper when a yeast cake was dropped in a small bowl of warm water and placed on a warm back shelf of the stove to dissolve while supper was cooked and eaten. With dishes done, the big dough tray was placed on the kitchen cabinet and a mountain of flour was sifted into it. With her fist, Mama punched a crater in the flour mountain and poured the yeast water in. Then she added melted lard, salt, and sugar. With the fingers (of her right hand) she stirred and mixed the pool of stiffening liquid, stroking in flour from the surrounding crater's edges. When the mixture was too stiff to stir with one hand, Mama used both hands to knead the dough, fold the outer edges in, and turn it over into a hard white featherbed which she punched hard with both hands until she flattened it. Then she began folding in the edges again. The longer the bread was kneaded, the finer the grain of the bread, Mama said. Finally, the dough was placed in a greased crock, covered lightly with a clean dishcloth, and set in a warm place to rise overnight.

The next morning the kitchen was full of fragrant yeast smell and the dough mushroomed over the crock top, bursting in waxy yeast bubbles. After breakfast Mama put more flour into the dough tray, poured in the mushroomed dough, kneaded in more flour, covered and set it back in a warm place to rise again—this time in the dough tray. When twice its original size (two hours, maybe), it was punched down with the fists, pinched off, and shaped into loaves, which were placed in tin bread-loaf pans and allowed to rise again before baking in a hot oven for a half-hour to three-quarters. When the loaves were brought from the oven, their brown crusts were coated with melted butter.

Sometimes before Mama shaped the dough into bread loaves, she pinched off small pinches and shaped them into rolls, dipped each roll into melted fat, and shoved the rolls against each other in a large flat pan to bake for Saturday dinner.

Other breads of cornmeal—beside corn bread—were *hoecakes*, *hotcakes*, and *cornmeal pancakes*. To make *hoecakes*, cornmeal and salt were sifted together in a bowl. Boiling water was added and stirred in to dampen the meal into a stiff batter. When the batter had cooled enough to handle, pieces were pinched off and shaped by hand into hoecakes one-half inch thick the size of the palm of Mama's hand. Hoecakes were cooked on a greased griddle or skillet until brown on one side, then turned and browned on the other. Papa could make *hotcakes*—the only food he knew how to cook. So whenever Mama and Grandma were both away or when Mama was sick, Papa made hotcakes of cornmeal, buttermilk, soda, salt, and eggs. The batter was very thin and the hotcakes cooked to crisp, brown lacy edges. *Cornmeal pancakes* were made with equal amounts of flour and cornmeal, sweet milk, baking soda, sugar, salt, two eggs, and shortening. First, the flour and meal, sugar, salt, and baking powder were sifted together into a bowl. Then the eggs, milk, and melted shortening were added to make a thin dough, spooned onto a hot, greased skillet to brown and turn and then to eat with honey or molasses.

Whole corn was made into *hominy* to substitute for potatoes when the potato supply was exhausted before the new crop came in. To make hominy, lye had to be leached from wood ashes. Then shelled dry corn was boiled in water (to which lye had been added) until the corn was tender and the husks came loose. The husked grains were rinsed in cold water several times, to remove the husks and lye, and brought to a boil again in salted water. The boiling hot grain was poured into glass jars, sealed, and stored on a smokehouse shelf. The big iron washpot in the back yard was used for making the hominy.

Any day of the week except Sunday (when no cooking was done) and Monday (wash day) unexpected changes happened in the daily fare to bring children within smelling distance of the kitchen. They were always ready to lick the cake pan, or to be given a syrup bucket lid for a cooking utensil and granted scraps of bread dough to form tiny loaves, or leftover piecrust to be flattened out with the palms of the hand and sprinkled with sugar, or slivers of tea cake dough left from the tea cake cutter to be patted into miniature tea cakes to be baked in the oven with Mama's or Grandma's baking. The miniatures were carried outdoors to the playhouse table and placed on "play party" dishes of broken china or the tiny tin plates of a toy tea set, and eaten.

Wheat flour was used for cakes, tea cakes, pie crust (for pies and cobblers), and thickening for puddings, sauces, and gravy. Pies with bottom and top crusts (fluted with a fork around the edges and slit with a knife on top to make a flower pattern and to allow steam to escape) and with a filling of blackberries or dewberries in between were made for Sunday or company meals. But *cobblers* were made for everyday eating—with fresh or canned blackberries or dewberries; fresh, canned, or dried peaches; or fresh hog plums. For cobblers, a pie crust made of flour, milk or water, salt (and maybe baking powder) was rolled thick, cut into long strips about two inches wide, and baked until done but not brown. For cobblers made of dried peaches or fresh plums, the fruit was cooked with sugar (and plum seed removed). Fresh fruits and berries were precooked with sugar before putting the cobbler together. Cobblers were baked in a shallow rectangular tin pan some eight inches wide by twelve to fifteen inches long and three inches deep. Strips of precooked pie crust were laid the length and width of the pan's bottom in a latticed pattern. A layer of fruit or berries was poured over the bottom crust. Another latticed crust layer went on top of the filling and another layer of filling on the second layer of crust. The cobbler was completed with a top lattice liberally dotted with pats of butter to melt and run over the crust and into the filling while the cobbler baked and browned twenty or thirty minutes on the top shelf of a warm oven.

Turnovers were everyday fare too, sometimes made fresh for supper in winter and for school lunch buckets the next day. They were individual-sized pies made of dried peaches (home dried) or apples (store-bought) stewed and sweetened and seasoned with cinnamon and butter. Circles of pie crust the size of a saucer (in fact, a saucer was used as a pattern) were cut. A large tablespoonful of cooked fruit was placed on one half of the pie crust circle; the other half was folded over the fruit to form a closed half-circle pie. The edges were pinched to seal the filling in and also to make a fluted edging. The turnovers were fried slowly and turned to brown evenly on both sides.

Butter rolls were an everyday supper delicacy made when pie crust or biscuit dough in some quantity was left over — say from cobblers at dinnertime or biscuit from breakfast. Or when no crust or dough was left over, Mama or Grandma might — when the children begged — make fresh crust or dough for butter rolls. Pie crust was rolled thin, dotted with butter, and sprinkled with brown sugar. From that stage there were three different ways to complete the process before baking: the thin pie crust was folded over to enclose the sugar and butter and the edges pinched together; it was rolled into a roll with ends pinched together; or it was rolled into a roll and sliced into pieces. The folded or rolled dough was placed in a pan and sprinkled with a mixture of flour and sugar. A smidgen of hot water was added to the pan before the butter rolls were placed in the oven.

Gingerbread and molasses tea cakes were two of Grandma's winter-time, suppertime, midweek specialties and *molasses candy* an after-supper treat on a bitter cold night when the children could dash outdoors to cool the candy for pulling — on rare occasions, by setting the pan in the snow — and dash back in again shivering. For molasses candy, molasses, vinegar, and butter were boiled together until it reached the stage to harden into clear, teardrop globules when dropped into cold water. Then a pinch of soda was added and the mixture poured into a large platter to cool enough to handle. Thereupon each child greased her hands with butter and was given a handful of candy to be pulled, twisted, doubled and redoubled, and pulled again and again until it grew lighter and lighter in color and stiffer and stiffer. At last, when a child's tired hands could pull it no more and the candy was a silken coffee-cream-golden strand, Grandma laid the strand on the oilcloth-covered kitchen table and whacked it into small pieces with the back edge of the butcher knife. Both sorghum molasses and ribbon cane syrup were used, though the cane syrup was preferred. It made better candy.

Molasses tea cakes and *gingerbread* both called for molasses. The tea cakes required buttermilk, soda, eggs, flour, shortening, and molasses (sorghum). The thick rolled-out dough was cut with a biscuit cutter into round cakes which spread and rose and browned in the oven and came out lopsided circles about four inches in diameter, sorghum-fragrant, scrunchy, and chewy.

Gingerbread required shortening (usually butter) and sugar creamed together with a beaten egg and molasses added. The dry ingredients—flour, soda, cinnamon and ginger, ground cloves and salt—were mixed together, stirred into the first mixture, and a little hot water added to make a semi-stiff batter soft enough to pour or rake into a greased, rectangular tin pan some eight by fifteen inches. Gingerbread was baked in a hot oven for three-quarters of an hour, more or less, depending on the oven. To test gingerbread to see if it was done, Grandma pulled the pan from the oven and struck a broom straw down in the center of the cake. If the straw came up bringing dough or crumbs clinging to it, the gingerbread was placed in the oven again for a few more minutes. But when the straw was clean, the watching children knew the waiting was over, and as quick as a cat could wink his eye, Grandma had that gingerbread cut into squares, a square on each of four saucers, and a child sitting before each saucer at the table with a glass of sweet milk to wash the gingerbread down.

Mama's special weekday treats were *sweet potato pie, sweet potato pudding*, and *pumpkin pie* (because Papa liked punkin pie). *Sweet potato pie* was made with cooked, mashed sweet potatoes, sugar, butter, sweet milk, eggs, and cinnamon and allspice to taste, mixed together and baked in an under pie crust which Mama fluted around the edges by pressing down with fork tines. *Sweet potato pudding* consisted of ground or grated raw sweet potatoes, sweet milk, eggs, butter, sugar (according to the sweetness of the potatoes), salt, cinnamon, and flour, mixed and baked in a round blue and white mottled graniteware pan.

Pumpkin pie followed the directions for the sweet potato pie. The raw pumpkin was first peeled, cut into small chunks, stewed, and mashed. Sometimes, when the pumpkin was large and fibrous, Mama put the mashed pumpkin through a sieve before mixing it with the sugar, butter, eggs, sweet milk, cinnamon, and allspice.

Cakes were baked only on Saturday for Sunday dinner when the preacher and other visitors were expected, when Aunt Eddie or Aunt Della and the Dallas cousins were coming to pay the family a visit of a week or more, and for special community or neighbor gatherings like threshing time, picnics, and fish-fries. Mama was the cake maker. When she made an *angel cake* she also made a yellow cake, using the egg whites for the angel cake and the yellows for a layer cake to be filled with *caramel* or *coconut-cream filling*. The angel cake, baked in a round cake pan with a funnel in the center, was cooled and covered with icing made of egg whites and sugar beaten together with a fork to a stiff froth and spread and smoothed over the cake with a case knife.

Caramel filling was made with sugar, milk, and butter. About two cups of sugar, one cup of sweet milk, and butter the size of a small egg were placed in a graniteware saucepan to boil. Another cup of sugar was browned in a skillet by constant stirring and then poured into the boiling mixture. The mixture was stirred and cooked until it was as thick as honey, then removed from the stove and beaten with a fork until cool enough to spread on the cake—usually three layers cooked in three tin cake pans about nine inches square.

Coconut-cream filling, used for either a yellow or white layer cake, was made of sugar, a little flour, an egg, and butter, mixed and stirred into a cup of sweet milk cooking in a graniteware saucepan sitting in a pan of boiling water on the stove. The mixture was stirred and cooked until thick, then removed, and with flavoring and coconut added, was allowed to cool before being spread between the cake layers and over and around the entire cake. The coconut was store-bought in Point or from the Peddler (shredded or whole). The shredded kind, which came in cardboard boxes, was emptied into a glass fruit jar immediately to keep it from becoming stale and dry. When Papa brought home a whole coconut, the children were allowed to play with it, rolling it about and pushing it with their bare feet until Mama was ready to use it—whereupon Papa took it to the back gallery, punched a hole in the coconut's eye with a tenpenny nail, and drained the milk into the children's waiting cups in equal portions. Then he took his hammer and broke the coconut open and into jagged segments of shell lined with moist white meat. These pieces, put in a waiting pan, were sent (by one of the children) to Mama in the kitchen.

Drawn by the smell of cream filling being cooked and of vanilla flavoring, the other children followed to watch and wait for the bowl-licking when the cake was filled and done. Mama peeled off the coconut's shaggy shell and cut off the thin, brown inner lining before she got out her grater and grated the chunks of white coconut meat into squirming white slivers that grew into a mound. The mound was dumped into the saucepan of filling, stirred, and set aside to cool. By that time, the arguing about whose turn it was to lick the bowl was over, the two losers had left the house, and the two winners waited, spoons in hand, in whispered argument about whose turn it was for the first lick.

Ice cream was the greatest treat of all in summer, and make-believe *snow ice cream* in winter. Each winter whenever snowflakes began to fall, the children watched with faces flattened against windowpanes, waited and hoped for snow deep enough for snow ice cream. Most winters brought hopes betrayed. Hence, the rare rewards were all the more exciting. At the first snowflake, somebody shouted, "It's snowing! It's snowing!" After that, all morning and all evening, over and over, the children ran to Mama or Grandma: "Is the snow deep enough?" And each time Mama or Grandma said, "Ask your Papa." But Papa was not there and so they had to wait and listen for Papa's stomping feet on the back gallery and race to the door to meet him with their question. That always happened at suppertime, so that on the rare occasions when his answer was yes, the yes was qualified with, "After supper, we'll make snow ice cream." Supper-time thus became an endless agony of waiting for Papa to take his last bite, cross his fork and knife on his plate, push his plate forward and his chair back and say to the children, "Get your cups ready and I'll light my lantern." By the time the lantern was lit, each child stood at the kitchen door in toboggan and cloak, each holding a spoon in one hand and in the other a tin cup in which Mama had put sugar and vanilla flavoring. Mama handed her flour scoop to Papa, and together Papa and the children went to the back yard to make snow ice cream. Papa brought a ladder from the smokehouse to climb to the smokehouse roof or to the back gallery roof from which to scoop up clean snow for the waiting cups below, in which the vanilla and sugar had been stirred and stirred and would be stirred some more when the clean snow was dumped in. Snow ice cream had to be mixed and eaten in a hurry outside. That the chil-dren learned by experience. A shivering child who ran into the house hoping to finish her snow ice cream by the kitchen stove found nothing but sweetened vanilla water in her cup.

Real ice cream in summertime was another story, with no betrayed hopes. When Papa left for Point in the wagon with an empty washtub and an old duck cotton sack behind the spring seat, the children knew that he would bring home a hundred pounds of ice wrapped in newspapers inside the old cotton sack inside the tub, and that Mama would have the ice cream custard cooked and ready to go into the freezer.

Ice cream custard of milk, cream, sugar, eggs, and vanilla was cooked slowly and stirred until the mixture coated the spoon. After it cooled, it was poured into the freezing can of the ice cream freezer. Crushed fresh peaches or berries (when in season) were added and stirred in. The paddle (dasher) was lowered into the can and anchored. The tight lid was fastened on the can and the can locked into place under the gear that made the crank turn. Meanwhile Papa, on the back gallery, had crushed the ice in a tow sack, smashing it with the side of a hammer. He brought the freezer to the back gallery and packed layers of crushed ice and layers of salt around the freezer can while one of the children began turning the crank. When crushed ice had settled down to a compact mass, the tow sack was folded and laid on top of the freezer for the child to sit on while she turned the crank—a job the children gladly took turns at. During the process, Papa from time to time added ice and drained off water through a stoppered hole near the bottom of the wooden freezer bucket. As the ice cream thickened and the freezer crank grew harder and harder to turn, the youngest crankers gave up, then the next and next until Papa had to take over. At last, when the custard was frozen stiff and Papa could not turn the crank one more turn—even with two children sitting on the freezer—the ice cream was done. The children whose turn it was to lick the paddle ran to the kitchen for a big bowl and spoons. Papa unfastened the crank latches, opened the freezer can, pulled out the paddle dripping with blobs of ice cream, and put it in the big bowl on the floor for the lucky lickers. The lid went back on the freezer can, the freezer was drained of water for the last time, extra ice was packed around and over the freezer top, more salt was added, and old newspapers and a tow sack were tied over the top. Then the freezer was set in cool shade for an hour or so to allow the ice cream to ripen.

After Dorothy was five, she helped more and more (along with her older sisters) in planting, harvesting, gathering, and preserving food for the family.

Preserving food for winter began as soon as crops produced a surplus not needed for the dinner table. Preserving methods included canning, drying, salting down, and smoking. Fruits, berries, and vegetables were canned in Ball glass jars in gallon, half-gallon, and, rarely, quart sizes, covered with glass-lined metal lids screwed on over rubber bands to seal them. Jellies were put up in half-pint jelly glasses and sealed with melted beeswax. Peaches and young field corn (still in tassel) cut from the cob were sun-dried. Clear-seed peaches—for drying—were washed free of fuzz, cut in halves, and spread in the sun on an old sheet on the flat roof of the henhouse. During the day they were turned over. At sundown they were gathered into the folded sheet and brought in for the night and put out again day after day until they were completely dehydrated and ready to be stored in a flour sack in the smokehouse.

Black-eyed peas, whippoorwill peas, and butter beans were left on the vine until the shells were dry and brittle, then shelled, aired to remove any residue of moisture, and stored in flour sacks after having "highlife" (carbon disulfide) poured over them (and dried afterward) to keep the weevils out. Later, before they were cooked, they were washed thoroughly to remove all traces of "highlife."

Pork was smoked or salted down in barrels, and Irish and sweet potatoes and pumpkins were stored in cool places. Sometimes Papa dug a trench, bedded it in straw, put in sweet potatoes and turnips, and covered them with more straw, then with earth. They were dug up as needed.

Canning came first in the season and continued throughout the summer as food became available. On canning days Mama started early in the morning as soon as breakfast was over. She cleaned the empty jars by washing them thoroughly with lye soapsuds and rinsing and scalding them. Then she put a three-gallon graniteware kettle half full of water on the stove and poured in cups and cups of sugar to boil into a syrup in which to cook the peaches.

Meanwhile Grandma and the older girls sat in chairs in a circle on the back gallery, each with a pan in lap and a washtub full of peaches (gathered the day before) and the crock churn on the floor in the center. Each peeled peaches: a small, sharp-pointed kitchen knife was held just so, to ream the stem, then continue peeling in one long curl circling the peach until the peel dropped off into the pan.

The peeled peach was quartered, deseeded (seeds were cut from clings; broken out of clear-seeds), and dropped into the churn. The peelings went into the slop bucket and the slop was fed to the hogs.

When the churn was three-quarters full and the syrup had boiled to the right consistency, the peaches were dumped into the boiling mixture and cooked slowly until tender but still firm. At that point Mama took a clean jar from the row on the kitchen cabinet, put a rubber ring around the top, set it in a pie pan on the stove beside the boiling peaches, swathed it in an old wet dishcloth to keep the glass from breaking, placed a graniteware funnel in the jar, and poured in cup after cup of cooked peaches until the jar was full and the syrup running over the rim. She wiped off the surplus syrup from around the top of the jar before screwing on the lid, lifting the swathed jar to the kitchen table and removing the swathing. That done, she was ready for the second and third and on and on until the bushel or two of peaches were peeled and canned in rows of glass jars, cooling before they were to be stored on smokehouse or stormhouse shelves.

Canned peaches were used for cobblers. Mama also made *peach preserves, peach butter,* and *pickled peaches.* For *peach preserves,* firm, ripe peaches were peeled and cut into small pieces and placed in a crock with an equal amount of sugar to stand a few hours so that juice would accumulate. Then they were cooked slowly until tender and the juice was as thick as honey before they were canned and sealed. For *peach butter,* very ripe peaches were peeled, removed from seeds, mashed or cut into very small pieces, and cooked with an equal amount of sugar to a mush before canning and sealing. Small, firm cling peaches were used for *pickled peaches.* Each peeled peach (left whole) had several whole cloves stuck into it. A syrup was made of water, sugar, and vinegar, and a stick of cinnamon was added for each jar. The whole cloved peaches were dropped into the syrup and cooked until tender but still firm, then canned and sealed.

Blackberries and dewberries were canned for cobblers and pies and made into jams; wild grapes and wild plums were made into *jellies,* and hog plums were made into *plum butter.* Hog plums were cooked in a small amount of water until tender. Then the seeds were removed, sugar added to the pulp and skins, and the mixture cooked slowly until very thick (constantly stirred) and canned. Wild grapes and wild plums were good for jellies because they were sour. The whole grapes and plums were each cooked in a mild sugar water until cooked to a mush, then mashed through a strainer. The strained juice, with equal amounts of sugar added, was cooked slowly to a thick syrup. It was tested by dropping drops into cold water. If the drops coagulated, the jelly was done and ready to be poured into jelly jars and sealed.

For canning berries, a thick sugar syrup was made and the clean-washed berries dumped into it to be cooked a very, very short time. For jams, the berries were cooked longer — until they were the consistency of mush. That meant constant stirring so that the jam would not stick to the bottom of the kettle.

Pear preserves were made by the peach preserve method. A firm, hard pear was best for preserving.

Vegetables canned were Kentucky Wonder beans, green black-eyed peas, green butter beans, tomatoes, sauerkraut, and beets. Beets were also pickled, as were cucumbers. And chow chow was made just before frost to make use of the green tomatoes before frost got them. Kentucky Wonder beans were snapped and shelled, washed, parboiled for a few minutes, then cooked until tender in water to which salt, vinegar, and a pinch of soda had been added. They were usually put up in gallon jars. Before they were used, they were washed to remove the vinegar flavor. Green black-eyed peas and green butter beans were simply cooked until tender in salted water and canned. Tomatoes were cooked in a very small amount of salted water.

Making sauerkraut was a long, smelly process. The cabbage was shredded and put to soak for about a week in crocks of brine in the smokehouse. As the days passed, and when the wind was in the east, the odor permeated the whole house day and night. In spite of the smell, the children sneaked into the smokehouse for fistfuls of briny, crisp kraut to eat raw. Finally the kraut was removed from the brine, washed several times to remove most of the salt, and cooked in clear water until tender, then canned in gallon jars to be brought forth on Monday wash days.

When *beets* were canned, they were cooked in their skins in salted water, until tender. After the skins were peeled off, the beets were dropped into jars, covered with boiling beet water, and sealed. When they were to be pickled, the boiled and skinned beets were dropped into a boiling mixture of half vinegar and half water, to which sugar and spices had been added, and cooked for a minute or two before canning in half-gallon or quart jars.

For *cucumber pickles*, the cucumbers were peeled and sliced across and soaked in brine for a day and night, then rinsed and cooked until tender in water seasoned with vinegar, salt, and sugar.

Chow chow consisted of cabbage, green tomatoes, onions, and small green peppers, all ground in the sausage grinder (using the coarse blade). The ground vegetables were sprinkled with salt, put in a crock, and allowed to stand overnight. Then the salt water was drained off and vinegar, sugar, and spices were added. The mixture was cooked until tender and canned in quart jars.

In spring and fall weather when days were warm, nights cool, and milk plentiful (no cows dry), Grandma occasionally made *curd cheese* from clabber. She bagged the clabber in a cloth bag made from an old sheet and hung the bag on a high-reached limb of the hackberry tree in the back yard for several days. The whey dripped from it less and less each day until the children could report to Grandma that the cheese was done — that it dripped no more and the cloth bag was dry. Then the bag was taken to the kitchen and opened up. Salt and pepper were added to the curd lumps and the cheese was stored in glass jars. It was a favorite supper dish.

After canning season ended (with the first heavy frost) and after the first hog-killing (with sausage, souse, and liver pudding to keep the women busy), the time came for making *lye soap*. For weeks Grandma had been leaching ashes for lye, storing it in a sealed syrup bucket on a smokehouse shelf too high for children to reach.

Lye soap was made of hog fat — residue left after the best lard had been rendered for cooking. The fat was cooked until the oil separated from the meat fibers; then the oil was strained through a porous cloth and poured into the pot. Lye and some water were added and the mixture was stirred constantly for hours over a slow fire until it thickened to mush. The fire was raked from under the pot, and the mixture was allowed to cool and solidify overnight. The next day Mama or Grandma turned the pot upside down, dumping the solid lye soap hemisphere on an old clean sheet spread over boards laid on the ground beside the pot. With the largest butcher knife she sliced the hemisphere into four-inch slices, next cut the four-inch slices into four-inch strips, and last, cut the four-inch strips into four-inch lengths, thus creating three or four dozen four-inch cubes of soap with half that many curved odd pieces formed by the pot shape. The cut soap was left in the sunshine and fresh air for a day or two, then spread on a smokehouse shelf to cure for a month or two before it was ready for use. Lye soap was used for washing clothes and dishes. Sometimes a mild lye soap was made and used for the children's required nightly foot washing at bedtime. But, usually, Packers Tar Soap and Fairy Soap were used for bathing.

Lye soap, nevertheless, was the foundation of family cleanliness. Clothes, dishes, and cooking utensils were washed in lye soapsuds. In the kitchen, boiling water from the black iron teakettle was poured over a cake of soap in the big, round graniteware dishpan on the kitchen cabinet. Dippers of cool water from the water bucket on a nearby shelf were poured into the hot water. Then the dishrag was rubbed on the soft lye soap and swished about to form a foaming suds. After the cake of soap was removed and placed in the ironstone soapdish always sitting at the back of the kitchen cabinet, the washing began. Dishes were washed and set to drain in a second pan beside the dishpan. The two older sisters took turns washing dishes. Dorothy wiped the dishes and reset the table for the next meal: turning plates face down, placing a knife and fork side by side to the right of each plate, and dropping the spoons (handles down) in the spoon holder in the center of the table. Extra dishes and bowls and platters were stored in the safe.

The dishrag was just that—a rag square torn from an old sheet, pillowcase, or underwear, unhemmed and fraying. For drying dishes, a hemmed flour sack about three feet square was folded once.

Twice a day, morning and night, milk vessels (including strainer cloths) were washed in clean dishwater, then placed in the drainer pan and scalded by pouring boiling water over them. Undried, the milk vessels were taken to the shelf on the back gallery to dry in clean sunshine and the strainer cloths were hung on the wire above the shelf.

After the milk vessels and dishes were washed, the pot vessels were scrubbed. When pots would not come clean with soap and water they were taken to the back yard and scrubbed with sand or brickbat dust (as were rusty knives and forks). Occasionally a pot was put to soak on the back of the stove and washed clean after the next meal.

Three times a day, without delay, when the meal was over, dishes were scraped clean (all food scraps going into the slop bucket), stacked, washed, and wiped. The table was reset and the kitchen floor swept onto the back gallery, the back gallery swept onto the back steps, the back steps swept onto the ground, and the little pile of debris swept under the steps to stay until Saturday. The wet dishrag was hung on a nail behind the stove and the wet dishcloth spread to dry on a galvanized wire stretched between two gallery posts above the wash shelf on the back gallery.

On Saturday, sometimes, the kitchen floor was scrubbed. But usually that was done on Monday—wash day. After Monday dinner dishes were done, hot suds—in which white clothes had been boiled in the iron pot in the back yard—were brought to the kitchen in galvanized buckets, poured on the floor, and the wet floor scrubbed with a broom. In dry, warm weather all floors in the house were scrubbed, then rinsed with clear water. Excess water that did not seep through cracks and knotholes was swept back onto the back gallery (also scoured) and onto the ground where it splattered into dust-covered drops. Floors scrubbed regularly with lye soapsuds turned lighter and lighter in color until they were almost white.

On Monday morning before breakfast Papa propped up the iron wash pot (by placing two or three brickbats under each of its three legs), filled the pot full of water, and built a fire under it. He then took down three galvanized tubs hanging on the outside smokehouse wall, placed them on a bench against the wall, filled two tubs, and poured two buckets of water into the third. After breakfast Mama took the full, dirty-clothes bag from its nail behind the kitchen door, put a small kitchen knife in her apron pocket, sent a child to the smokehouse for a cake of lye soap and the washboard, and headed for the washpot and tubs behind the smokehouse.

By that time the water was boiling. She dipped out two or three buckets full and poured them into the half-empty tub, leaving the pot half full of water with room for the clothes to be put in later. Then with her kitchen knife, she shaved slivers of lye soap into the boiling pot, stirring it occasionally with a broom handle. A child was sent to bring more stovewood and the fire was built up before Mama put the washboard into the tub of warm water and began to scrub the white sheets, pillowcases, Papa's white Sunday shirt, white dresses, chemises, corset covers, underskirts, and drawers before dropping them into the boiling pot and stirring them with the broom handle. The children hung around hoping and waiting for the day when Mama would say they were old enough to stir and punch the boiling clothes down.

After all white clothes were scrubbed, boiled, lifted from the pot on the broom handle, and dropped into the first rinse water, the colored clothes (all but black stockings, which were washed last) were put to soak in the suds tub while white clothes were being rinsed. (Colored clothes were not boiled.) Clothes were rinsed through one tub of water to remove soap and through a second to which bluing was added to whiten clothes. Lump bluing (bought from the Peddler) tied into a white cloth pouch was swished through the water until the water was sky-blue. When the children, allowed to put the bluing in the water, became fascinated with trailing swirls of blue, the family slept on blue sheets for a week.

Beside the tub of bluing water, two dishpans sat on the bench: one dishpan with cooked starch in it, and the second dishpan to receive the rinsed, starched clothes ready to go on the wire clothes-lines stretched from the smokehouse to the henhouse to the hackberry tree and back again to the smokehouse. Dishcloths and towels were spread on berry bushes and broom-weeds and left overnight to be bleached by dew. But clothing, bedclothes, and tablecloths were brought in off the line before sundown.

After supper on Monday the kitchen table was not reset for breakfast as usual, but was left clear and the oilcloth washed and wiped clean in preparation for sprinkling clothes down for Tuesday's ironing. The starched clothes had been piled on a bed in the front room. And after Mama had placed a washpan full of water on the corner of the kitchen table, she brought the garments in, one by one, spread out each garment on the table, dipped her hand into the water, and slung her wet hand about above the garment, flinging off drops from her fingertips until the cloth was thoroughly sprinkled and the garment ready to be rolled into a tight ball and deposited on a folded white sheet on a kitchen chair. When all garments were sprinkled, rolled, and piled on the folded sheet, the sheet was folded over and wrapped about the lot, and the sprinkled garments were left to dampen overnight to be ready for ironing early Tuesday.

While breakfast was cooking Tuesday, the three flatirons were heating on the back of the stove. And as soon as breakfast was on the table, two or three sticks of stovewood were added to the fire and the irons were moved to the hottest stove caps to be sizzling hot and ready for ironing as soon as breakfast was over and the kitchen table cleared of food, dishes, spoon holder, and pepper sauce bottle, and wiped clean.

Mama brought out the ironing board from behind the kitchen door (beside the dirty-clothes bag), placed one end on the table and the other on the back of the chair holding the sprinkled clothes.

Then she made cold starch in the washpan to starch Papa's white Sunday collars, after which she tested the irons to see if they were hot enough to begin ironing: with a potholder she grasped the iron handle, turned the flat side up, spit on her left forefinger, and touched it quickly to the iron; if it sizzled, the iron was just right; if it made no sound, it was not hot enough; and if it made a frying sound and burned her finger a little, it was too hot and was set on the back of the stove, leaning on its handle to cool.

From time to time the iron had to be cleaned of starch accumulation, especially cold starch. For that purpose a lump of beeswax the size of a goose egg was tied into a pouch made of white rag. The beeswax was applied to the hot iron's surface; as the wax melted on the iron, the iron was moved back and forth several times on several layers of brown wrapping paper which absorbed the wax, taking with it the starch and leaving the iron clean.

Ironing occupied Mama, Grandma, and the older sisters most of the day. An iron was used until it began to cool; then it was exchanged for a hot iron on the stove. Starched clothes, tablecloths, napkins, and dresser scarves were ironed first and spread over beds, table, and chairs (to dry out completely) until the ironing was done. Unsprinkled everyday dresses, underskirts, drawers, and pillowslips were pressed. Seldom were sheets ironed completely; they were folded when taken from the clothesline, and the folds and hems were pressed. Ironed, folded linens were stacked in neat stacks on the tables and the children were allowed to put them away, carefully, in dresser drawers. Towels were seldom ironed; dishclothes, never.

At the end of the ironing day, Sunday dresses (to be worn next Sunday) were pinned to an old sheet stretched behind the cretonne curtain in the south-room corner. Other garments were folded carefully and placed carefully on top of folded linens in dresser drawers.

Saturday night baths took place in the kitchen. (In summer weather, the men bathed in the creek, the pool, or the smokehouse.) With supper dishes done, a tub was brought from the smokehouse and placed close to the stove, on which a full kettle and extra pots of water were steaming. A washpan with warm water and washrag sat on the stove hearth and beside it the soapdish. Water—cold, then hot—was poured into the tub until it was half full, and its temperature was tested with Mama's elbow. The children were bathed first, beginning with the youngest.

Everybody but Mama and the child being bathed left the kitchen to sit in the front room by the stove (in winter) and on the front gallery (in summer). In winter the kitchen doors were closed for privacy, but in summer the doors were open for ventilation and a privacy screen was made by throwing a sheet over two chairs standing three feet apart. With the washrag and soap and water (in the washpan), Mama scrubbed Little Brother down from head to foot. Then he sat in the tub while Mama (with a soap-free rag) squeezed water over his head and shoulders, rinsing his whole body. Clean, he stepped from the tub and stood on an old towel on the floor to be rubbed dry before Mama put his clean nightgown on him and carried him to bed.

Dorothy's turn was next. Undressed to her drawers, she stood before Mama with her eyes squeezed shut to keep out the soap while Mama washed her face, neck, body, legs, and feet and then handed her the washrag and said, "Now wash your down-be-low." Mama turned her back while Dorothy took off her drawers, scrubbed, got in the tub, swished around the rag — imitating Mama — and climbed out, dried herself, and put on her clean nightgown hanging on the back of a chair.

After the children's baths, the women bathed; and last, the men.

Babies, small children, and people sick in bed were given sponge baths every day; but the word "bath" was used for both soaped-sponging and tub-bathing. When Little Brother was a baby, Mama bathed him in the morning after breakfast dishes were done, soap-sponging him, then dipping him in the dishpan of warm water sitting on the kitchen cabinet. When Mama had dried Little Brother and dusted him with rose talcum, Dorothy handed her a bird's-eye didy folded — a square folded into a triangle, then folded into a smaller triangle — which Mama pinned on him with three safety pins: one below the navel and one on each leg. His other garments — all hand-sewn in fine stitching — were a flannel shirt of soft wool, brier-stitched in blue; a nainsook undershirt that hung loose from his shoulders; a nainsook dress long enough to tuck over his feet shod in socks (store-bought), and hand-knitted bootees; last — and last put on — a soft cream flannel sacque, cut with butterfly sleeves, embroidered in blue. Bathed and dressed, he was bundled into a soft wool blanket. Mama placed the blanket on the bed, placed Little Brother on the blanket (catty-cornered), folded the bottom corner over his feet, the side corners over the folded bottom corner, and the top corner over his head. Then she rocked him to sleep in the rocking chair while he nursed at her breast. If, while she bathed him, he cried from hunger, she gave him a sugar tit to suck until nursing time and sang to him, "Two Babes in the Woods."

That was winter-time bath ritual for babies. In summertime, the baby four months old or older wore only didy and dress.

Bathing a sick patient required special precautions against drafts and cold. A small area of the body was uncovered, sponged, and re-covered; then another small area, until the entire body had been bathed. Before a doctor's expected visit, the patient was bathed and clean sheets and pillowcases put on the patient's bed.

People who did not bathe every Saturday and change to clean underwear and outer clothes, who did not require children to wash their bare feet before going to bed, and all people who did not wash face and hands before each meal and comb the hair once a day or more, were classified as "trashy." Respectable shaven men shaved once a week or more. Respectable mustached men trimmed and pointed the mustache and shaved once a week or more. Bearded men who lived in the woods along the river were looked down upon as trash.

Soap-and-water was the basis of the prevention and cure of sickness and injury as well as of cleanliness (and therefore decency). Clean washed rags were stuffed in the ragbag hanging behind the kitchen door. Ragged pillowcases and sheets were saved for bandages for cuts and bruises. Grandma tore old sheets into strips one inch wide and rolled the strips into rolls of bandages ready to bandage cut fingers and stumped toes. She also cut strips two inches wide and four inches wide for skinned shins and knees. The bandage rolls were wrapped in tissue paper (to keep them clean) and kept in the bottom of the ragbag.

Grandma knew the art of tying on a bandage so that it would stay, whatever or wherever the part of the body involved. For a bruised or cut fingertip (or toe tip), for instance, after the finger had been washed clean and soaked in turpentine or coal oil, the bandage was wrapped tightly around it with enough left over to anchor the finger to the wrist. Grandma's bandages stayed on all day, and at night—before bedtime—she cut off the dirty cloth to put on a clean bandage for the night and next day.

Most injuries happened to fingers, toes, arms, and legs. Bandages for body injuries were made of old knit underwear. They were wrapped around the body or head and pinned with safety pins.

Many injuries called for doctoring but no bandages: wasp stings, red ant stings, scorpion stings, chigger bites, sandbur pricks and prickly pear spines, poison oak. First aid to the injured began with washing the injury thoroughly with soap and water.

A doctor was not sent for unless the patient was seriously ill — running a high fever for several days or delirious or unconscious. People with broken bones went to the doctor's office in Point, carried there lying on the bed of a wagon or sitting in a buggy (for broken arms or collarbones). Little Brother broke his collarbone when he was four. He fell out of the wagon while he and Dorothy were playing "Doctor," using the wagon bed as the playhouse. Little Brother was the patient lying ill; Dorothy, the doctor, had departed after taking the patient's temperature with a stick thermometer when Little Brother stood up in the wagon and called, "Doctor! Doctor! You forgot your temperature." He leaned over the wagon wheel to hand Dorothy the stick and tumbled to the ground, breaking his collarbone on the wagon step. Mama, standing in the kitchen doorway, saw him, heard him scream, came running, sent Dorothy running to the field for Papa, who came running, felt Little Brother all over, pronounced the break a "green break," put Little Brother in the buggy with him (after Mama had bathed and dressed him in his Sunday sailor suit), and they drove off to Point to the doctor's office. Dorothy sat on the back steps all afternoon, full of dread that Little Brother might die. And Mama and Papa might blame her because she had forgotten the stick thermometer.

Before suppertime they returned, Little Brother's shoulder bandaged in splints, his arm in a sling, and his face and sailor suit pink-stained and sticky from the striped peppermint candy he had been eating all the way home.

At the supper table, while Mama fed Little Brother (because his arm was in a sling), she told Papa and Grandma exactly how the accident happened. When she repeated Little Brother's "Doctor! Doctor! You forgot your temperature," everybody laughed including Little Brother, who then began to shout, as he laughed, "Doctor! Doctor! Doctor! Doctor!" until Mama had to say, "Hush! That's enough of that! Don't be silly!"

When everybody laughed, the dreadful woe Dorothy had felt all afternoon disappeared. She knew then that Mama and Papa did not blame her for Little Brother's broken collarbone. And she knew he would get well.

In late winter and early spring of 1907, when the whole family —

one by one, and finally, three at a time — had smallpox, the doctor came to the house day after day during the three months the yellow quarantine flag fluttered on the front gatepost. The oldest sister came down first in early February; then the second; next Mama; and last Papa and the two youngest (neither of whom was sick enough to be put to bed).

Mary Lee caught smallpox at school from a schoolmate whose big brother had come back from Indian Territory with a mild case, undiagnosed. The doctor, on his first visit, diagnosed the disease as typhoid fever and prescribed calomel, leaving powdered calomel folded in little tissue paper doses for Mama to funnel into capsules later. Not until Mary Lee broke out in pus-filled sores circled in red and her fever rose again, did the doctor know his mistake. Then he brought the county health officer from Emory. The diagnosis was smallpox and the health officer nailed the yellow flag on the front gate. Eva Rita was put to bed with fever before Mary Lee was up and soon became so sick that the doctor stayed one whole day and night and Mama stayed up night after night, all night, bathing Eva Rita's feet with sweet oil and keeping wet bandages on her entire body.

The county health officer brought the state health officer to the house to see her. He pronounced the case the worst he had ever seen and took a picture of her to print in the state medical journal.

Neighbors could not come in to help as was the custom when a patient was sick enough to require attention around the clock. They brought food and other necessities, leaving them on the front gallery or at the front gate. And they wrote letters to the family's relatives to let them know the situation: mail could come in but no mail could go out of the quarantined house. Neighbor men took care of the livestock (milking and feeding) and of the farm work during the six weeks Papa was sick. And the county health officer found a man who had had smallpox who agreed to nurse Papa while Mama took care of the two oldest children recovering and the two youngest contracting the disease.

Grandma was away visiting and could not return because of the quarantine. Mama could not write to her, but Grandma wrote letters telling about Uncle Robert (her son) who had gone to Indian Territory to sell lumber, had caught smallpox from the Indians, had been put to bed in a pest house. She had heard no further word. She did not know whether he was alive or dead.

All night long Little Brother cried in his sleep and all day long he stumbled round and round dragging the sodden toothless eyeless sleepy doll (gift from a girlhood friend of Mama's) whose eye sockets were eyeless when she arrived and whose teeth had been punched out when Little Brother and Dorothy fed her crackers and water to keep her from getting smallpox.

It was on a morning in late April, near Easter, that the county health officer came to take the yellow flag down. Neighbors had already bought and brought a big bag of powdered sulphur in preparation for fumigating; and new mattresses for all the beds had been bought and piled on the front gallery. A late spring norther had blown in the night before and the children gathered on the leeward side of the henhouse to watch the old mattresses brought from the house, piled in a heap (with the eyeless doll thrown on top), splashed with coal oil, and set on fire to burn slowly all day, warming the cold back yard. The washpot was boiling and Mama was busy all day washing bed linen and clothes. Papa sealed door and window cracks with folded newspapers and set sulphur afire in a pan in a tub of water in the middle of each room. All day, the children playing in the yard smelled sulphur fumes escaping. At noon and evening they ate a picnic dinner and supper of the food brought in by neighbors. And before bedtime Papa had opened and aired the house and Mama had washed each child down with carbolic acid water and dressed each child in a clean-washed, sun-dried nightgown ready to go to bed on a new mattress, to sleep between sheets clean and fragrant from lye soap, wind, and sun, under new quilts aired in the sun all day.

When the children had chicken pox, measles, and whooping cough, the doctor was not called. Mama and Grandma knew what to do. When a child was fretful and its forehead warm or hot to touch, the child was put to bed and kept there until free of fever for one whole day. Whatever the disease or ailment, the bowels must be kept open. That was the basic premise underlying all medication. To diagnose a child's illness, Mama or Grandma placed the palm of her hand on the child's forehead and judged the temperature as "none," "light fever," "fever," or "hot fever"; looked at the child's tongue (a coated tongue meant biliousness); and inquired if the child had had a bowel movement that day. Constipation or biliousness called for a cathartic or purgative.

In the corner of the highest kitchen wall-shelf over the kitchen cabinet, all medicines and remedies for people, animals, and plants were kept—all except butter, cream of tarter, honey, lard, soda, tallow, and vinegar (kept with foods): bluing, coal oil, copperas root, and Paris green (kept on a high shelf in the smokehouse); axle grease, highlife, chloroform, and creosote (kept on a ledge in the barn); Papa's whiskey bottle (hidden in different places in the barn); Grandma's blackberry wine (kept in a jug in the stormhouse); mud (made by spitting on dirt wherever the patient—stung by red ant, bee, or wasp—happened to be); and the madstone (somewhere in Texas where a patient bitten by a mad dog was taken in a hurry).

On the kitchen shelf were calomel (powder wrapped in papers in doses) in a small cardboard box, a cathartic; chill tonic (bitter, clear green liquid in a bottle); camphor (clear liquid in a small bottle); capsules (two bottles; one for 5 grains of calomel or quinine; one for 10 grains); carbolic acid (clear liquid in a tall bottle with skull and crossbones on the label); castor oil (thick clear liquid in a big bottle); Eagle eye salve (in a metal tube); flax seed (in a little glass jar); laudanum (yellow-clear liquid in a very small bottle); liniment (yellow clear liquid in a huge bottle); mullein leaves (dried and crumbled, in a glass jar); oil of cloves (thick yellow liquid in a small bottle); paregoric (brown liquid in a small bottle); pine tar (dark brown liquid in a bottle); quinine (powders in paper doses, in a small cardboard box); salts (Epsom: crystals, in a glass jar); sassafras (dried roots, kept in a glass jar); sulphur (powder, in a crock); sweet oil (thin oily liquid in a small bottle); syrup of figs (brown, sweet thick liquid in a brown bottle); and turpentine (clear liquid in a large bottle).

Minor injuries, ailments, symptoms, cures, and, sometimes, preventatives were:

ant stings (from big red ants) Bluing was dabbed on the sting with a clean rag. When stung far afield, the child made a mud patch and held it on the spot until the sting subsided.

bee sting First the stinger was removed with the fingernails of thumb and forefinger or tweezers formed by the blade of a pocketknife and thumbnail of the left hand. Then bluing or mud was applied.

biliousness Symptoms were: (1) a dizzy headache, (2) nausea, and sometimes (3) vomiting. The standard cure was salts dissolved in a glass of water, syrup of figs, several doses of calomel or two tablespoons of castor oil.

chigger bite Powdered sulphur rubbed on arms and legs prevented chigger bites. The cure involved: (1) removing the chigger and (2) soothing the itch. Children with good eyesight could see the chigger, scratch it off with a fingernail, and mash it between the two thumbnails to watch the spurt of blood. Grown-ups who could not see a chigger covered it with butter, lard, or axle grease so the chigger could not breathe and would therefore die. A dab of turpentine or coal oil disinfected and soothed the itch. When a child scratched the skin off along with the chigger, Mama washed the place before dabbing it with turpentine.

chills and fever (malaria) First the body was seized by cold chills that made the victim shiver and shake. Fever followed. The chills and fever attacks usually came on in the afternoon and evening. By morning the fever was low or gone and the patient weak. The attacks were repeated every day or every other day, gradually weakening the victims more and more. The cure was quinine or chill tonic (Grove's Chill Tonic was one brand used).

cold (chest) A Sally Anne rag was the standard cure, made of a double-ply wool flannel piece some eight by twelve inches dipped in a pan of a heated solution of turpentine and tallow or lard, applied to the chest (as hot as the child could stand) at night, pinned with safety pins to the child's nightgown. The Sally Anne rag was pinned high around the child's throat. If the cold was not much better in the morning, the rag was reheated and reapplied. Sometimes a child wore a Sally Anne rag for several days and nights.

cold (head cold) Mullein leaves, dried and crushed, were smoked in a corncob pipe to relieve a stuffed-up nose and watery eyes. Quinine in 5-grain doses was given.

cough Honey and vinegar was Mama's standard cough remedy. Papa's (Mama disapproved) was honey, pine tar, and whiskey.

crick in the neck The cure was rubbing with liniment or hot compresses.

croup The Sally Anne rag was standard remedy for croup, in addition to breathing steam from camphor water. Boiling water was poured over camphor in the washpan. The child— head covered with a towel—breathed the fumes until the water cooled. Mama or Grandma held the child to prevent it from turning the washpan over.

cut, scratch, or *abrasion (from splinters, thorns, stickers, prickly pear spines, bobwire, nails, knives)* The injury was first washed clean with soap, then soaked in turpentine and bandaged if necessary. When the skin had been broken by a nail, wire, or other metal, the soaking was lengthy. Splinters, thorns, and stickers were removed by picking them out with a needle (*never* a pin), sterilized by holding it over a flame. When the splinter or thorn had penetrated too deep to be removed with a needle, Papa cut it out with the sterilized point of a pocketknife blade.

earache Sweet oil was warmed, dropped into the ear, and the ear filled with cotton. Or cotton was saturated with warm sweet oil and stuffed in the ear.

fever blister (on the lip) Camphor was applied again and again throughout the day.

head lice The child's hair was washed (daily for a week) first in hot coal oil water to kill the live lice. After each washing, Mama combed the child's hair with a fine-tooth comb, combing out the nits and dropping them into a cup of coal oil. Each day she parted the hair into small strands and examined every hair. The daily process continued until the head was clear of nits for two or three days. Dorothy was the only Mills child so infested.

hiccough The victim was given a cup of water to drink ten big swallows without taking a breath between swallows. Before drinking the water, the hiccougher said:

Right up, straight up Jacob
Nine sips of water in a teacup
Will cure the heecup.

loose bowels Bowel movements were described as: constipation; "running off at the bowels" or "Flux" (diarrhea); or "loose bowels" (somewhere between the two extremes). For loose bowels, Grandma's blackberry wine—three or four tablespoonfuls—was the happy remedy. When bowels were "running off," paregoric in water was the distasteful remedy. Children hoped for the blackberry wine prescription. The cure for constipation was a cathartic or purgative; children described their symptoms to avoid that diagnosis as long as possible.

lumbago Papa had lumbago. It struck him suddenly, doubling him in pain so that he could not straighten his back. Mama rubbed his back with liniment and he stayed in bed until the pain left as suddenly as it came.

poison oak The poison oak splotches were bathed with strong lye soap and greased with axle grease.

scorpion sting The stinger had a hooked barb on the penetrating end; it could not be pulled out and therefore had to be cut out with a pocketknife blade. The wound was then soaked in turpentine and bandaged if necessary.

sore eyes If the eyelids became inflamed, Eagle eye salve was applied. To remove a cinder or speck of dust, a flaxseed was placed under the eyelid. The flaxseed made the eye water, and the tears brought both flaxseed and foreign object to the corner of the eye to be removed with the corner of a clean handkerchief.

sore throat (or hoarseness) Sugar moistened with turpentine was held in the mouth and allowed to trickle down the throat.

stomachache Baking soda in water was the cure for a mild case. Paregoric was given to babies and small children for bad cases of colic.

toothache Oil of cloves (warmed) or laudanum dropped in the tooth cavity killed the pain. Cotton was pushed into the cavity to hold the medicine in place.

tooth pulling A string was tied securely around a child's loose baby tooth; the other end was tied to a doorknob or an open door. Then the child slammed the door, jerking the tooth out.

warts Castor oil was rubbed on a wart twice a day or more often until the wart disappeared. Neighbors advised rubbing a wart with a very dirty dishrag, then burying the dishrag in a secret place. As the dishrag rotted in the ground (so they said) the wart would gradually disappear. Mama and Grandma preferred the castor oil cure.

wasp sting (black wasp) The stinger was removed and bluing or mud was applied to the spot.

yellow jacket sting The stinger was removed. A wet compress was applied and renewed to keep swelling down.

When spring rolled around and it was time to shed winter underwear, it was also time for a spring tonic for all members of the family.

If there had been little sickness during the winter, sassafras tea sufficed to "thin the blood." If not, sulphur was mixed with cream of tarter and sorghum molasses, and two tablespoonfuls dosed out to each member of the family each morning for three or four mornings.

Though the "seven-year-itch" (scabies), considered a serious malady, was epidemic among Woosley schoolchildren from time to time, no Mills child ever caught the disease. Some neighbor children wore bags of asafetida on strings around their necks in the belief that the foul smell prevented the disease.

The most dreaded of all accidental ailments probably were snake bite and mad-dog bite. Fortunately no member of the Mills family was ever victim of either. Papa recounted times when fellow fishermen had been bitten by moccasins, copperheads, cottonmouths, or rattlers. The victim was stretched out on the ground and the wound was slashed across several times with a pocketknife to make it bleed profusely. The escaping blood carried with it some of the poison. The wound was sucked by mouth to further "draw out the poison." Whiskey was administered generously (internally) while the patient was being carried to a doctor — unless the distance to a doctor was too great, in which case the victim survived or died without further medication.

Every spring when weather began to turn warm, mad-dog scares occurred. Neighbor men loaded their rifles and shotguns, took to their saddles, and rode in posses looking for dogs on the loose. The phone carried the general signal to all parties on the party line and the ringer would say, maybe, that one of the Harlan boys had seen a mad dog, foaming green saliva, loping through their pasture. Mama rounded up the children, sent them into the house, beat the dinner sweep long and loud to bring the men from the field, and shouted to them when they reached the barn, "Mad dog! Mad dog!" In minutes the men were off.For days they watched the cattle, horses, and pigs for signs that they might have been bitten by the mad dog. Usually the dog was sighted and killed. Sometimes it disappeared into the wooded creek and river bottom to die (so the men said). No person in the Woosley or Flats communities was ever bitten. A story was often told of a child in Van Zandt County who was bitten and taken by train to some far place in Texas to be treated by the madstone treatment. That was the only known cure.

Colds in winter and chills and fever in summer were the principal recurrent complaints. Papa poured a coal oil skim on rain barrels and pool to kill the wiggletails so they could not hatch into mosquitos. But in a wet spring or summer, standing water in ditches and branches produced too many breeding places to control. Hence the whole community suffered "poor health" which extended into the winter months.

Play Life

This catalogue of games and play activities (arranged alphabetically for easy reference) begins with "Anty Over" and ends with "Wring the Dishrag." "Wring the Dishrag" required two players (no more, no less) and no equipment except the acrobatic bodies of the two players. "Anty Over" required (for equipment) a ball and a building to throw it over; it also required two teams of players (though sometimes only two children played — just for practice). From "A" to "W," the games and activities listed and described include the outwardly simple play of children alone, and of children together in pairs or groups, with and without external play equipment. They are listed as the children knew and named them.

Manufactured (store-bought) toys were rare among the children in Sabine Bottom except in the fairy-tale pages of the Sears, Roebuck catalogue. Play tools included sticks, stones, dirt, water, wind, sky and clouds, leaves, flowers, vines, tree limbs, rope, string, spools from sewing thread, corncobs, cane joints, broken dishes, discarded coffee grounds, burnt matches, match boxes, shoe boxes, cigar boxes, scraps of cloth leftovers from dressmaking, rags from the ragbag and any needed thing or object borrowed or appropriated from farm and household equipment.

The word "toy" was not in the vocabulary of the Mills children. They had "playthings" and "play pritties." A "plaything"—a stick, for example—was not a stick but (metaphorically) a horse to ride, a thermometer for playing doctor, a writing or drawing tool for marking on the ground, a log for building log cabins, a boat to float down a rivulet from a spring shower, play candy, a shotgun for hunting, or another person. A "plaything" could be and was anything the mind willed—for a moment, an hour, for months or years. The definition, unarticulated, was communicated by action in a context common to and understood by all the players. Play was metaphoric action.

"Let's play like..." Dorothy would say. "Let's play like I am Mama." From that sentence the drama proceeded. Characters assigned themselves parts. Together the family constructed the setting according to circumstances: (1) a rainy day in the house; (2) play behind the smokehouse; or (3) play in the woods beyond the barn. The plot was determined by the setting: (1) in a play indoors, the children received spankings for being "bad" in whatever way a character chose to be "bad"; (2) in a play behind the smokehouse, the children were sent to feed the chickens, collect eggs, bring bacon from the smokehouse; (3) and in a play in the woods, the children were sent for walks or in errands through the woods, each carrying a club (a long tree limb with a heavy knot at the end) to kill snakes. On occasions, a real blue coach-whip snake or a black racer became the most important character in the play. And an irate hen, protecting her chickens, sometimes brought a play to an abrupt tragic end. Indoors, a play ended with a real spanking from a real Mama if the "bad" child became too inventive. Whatever the setting and plot, each character adapted his and her lines and actions without stage direction or prompting. Children of Sabine Bottom made little distinction between work and play. And, whenever possible, children and adults alike made play of work.

Children were aware of no distinction between traditional formula play learned from other children and from their parents and grandparents, and the play springing from their own individual and group imaginations. The most tradition-bound games (like "Mumblepeg," "Jackstones," and "William Tremble Toe") required adaptation to function in the lives of children in Sabine Bottom. A ball-and-bat game became "One-Eyed Cat," "Two-Eyed Cat," or "Three-Eyed Cat," depending on the number of players (the minimum was two). Children playing alone with no play tools but their own bodies available, selected what they needed from transmitted lore and devised and established for themselves patterns of play by hopping, skipping, jumping, turning somersaults, running in the wind, playing with shadows, or playing "Hide and Seek" with field larks and bobwhites.

Children in Sabine Bottom were not isolated from the adult world of work and play, nor isolated in age groups. Younger children learned from older ones and older children learned from their parents and grandparents. Grandma Gray taught the children to manipulate their hands and fingers in sunlight, moonlight, and lamplight to create wall-shadow plays; a donkey braying; a fox eating a goose; and a goose eating grains of corn and then sipping and swallowing water. With what Grandma taught them about the control of shadows, they experimented to teach themselves and each other. It was Grandma Gray to whom the children went for help in kite making. She gave them flour in a tin cup for flour paste; brought out the ragbag to let them choose the brightest colored rags for the kite-tail; lent them a ball of twine—which they promised to return; and helped them fasten the cross together, tie the harness, and fasten the tail securely. They then taught themselves and each other how to choose the best breeze for kite flying; how and where to launch the kite, maneuver it, and reel it in safely so that it would not get caught in trees.

Papa helped the children select the best board for a seesaw; but they learned together the secret of the fulcrum. He helped them choose the poles and stirrups for their stilts and helped to make them; but they taught each other how to mount and balance, how to do tricks and play games on stilts. He allowed them to ride the sorghum mill as a merry-go-round before he and a hired man built a "flying jenny" for them. He showed them how to hold a pocketknife for whittling; and how to hammer, holding and tapping the nail in place, yet removing the fingers from danger before driving the nail down.

After testing a hemp rope and selecting the best tree limb for a swing, Papa installed the swing and inspected it periodically for safety. The children taught themselves and each other all the ways to swing: how to "pump," sitting or standing; how to swing, two players together, either sitting or standing; how to "kill the cat" or "let the cat die"; the right moment to jump and sail through the air (and, most important, how to land).

Mama allowed the children to bake miniature pies, cakes, biscuits, and light bread on tin bucket lids, showing them how to insert the pans into a hot oven and how to remove them safely. In play, they made mudpies, using red brick dust to turn the mud to chocolate and foam from the pool's edge for icing. Mama gave them scraps of cloth for doll clothes; Grandma cut out the clothes for them; and they finished the garments (including buttonholes, which Grandma taught them to make). Mama allowed them to use old quilts for tents and covered wagons (props for "Going Out West" and "Going to Dallas").

Orphus Trailer, the hired hand, taught them to make a balloon of a man's handkerchief and to launch it high into the air.

Dorothy learned from her sisters the games and play customs they had learned at Woosley School—the playways of all the children of Sabine Bottom when the families gathered for picnics, fish-fries, and at threshing time.

In the process of learning to control their own bodies and to control their environment (animate and inanimate), those children learned the finite limitations of their bodies, the limitations of their power over the physical environment, and best of all, the infinite power of their minds.

ANTY OVER

The usual setting for "Anty Over" was the back yard; the players, Little Brother and Dorothy; the ball was thrown over the smokehouse or the henhouse and caught in the air or on one bounce. But this was an adaptation of the game they learned from their sisters and their sisters' playmates who occasionally came to play.

The game required two or more players divided into teams, a ball, and a building to throw the ball over. One team stood on one side of the building with one team member holding the ball ready to throw; the other team stood arranged on the other side of the building ready to catch the ball when it came over. The thrower called "Anty," waited for the opposing team to answer "Over," then threw the ball over the building. If a member of the receiving team caught the ball (the throwing team could not know whether or not that was so), he ran around the building and tried to hit a member of the opposing team with the ball. The throwing team fled to safety around the building and thus the teams changed places. A player hit by the ball became a member of the opposing team. And the game continued.

The game played with a large group of players of varying

sizes and skills was played on a larger scale. The ball was thrown over the house, the barn, or the schoolhouse. The older, skilled players threw the ball and pursued the opponents; the little ones merely ran, following the leader in pursuit or in escape.

Rules required that when a fair ball, thrown, was not caught, the receiving team was honor-bound to admit it by immediately calling "Anty" and waiting for the answering "Over." The honor of opponents was sometimes the subject of heated debate which ended in a draw and the end of a game.

Rules required that the ball must pass over the comb of the roof, either rolling over or flying over in the air above the roof within an area defined by the roof comb. The thrower aimed to throw the ball to clear the roof and reach its summit as far as possible beyond the roof comb so that its decline would send the catchers as far afield as possible. The catching team stationed themselves at staggered intervals across the length of the building and some twenty to forty feet away from the building, prepared to run forward for the catch or backward if necessary.

Rules also required that when the ball was thrown outside the defined area (above the roof comb), the throwing team relinquished one member to the opposing team (usually the smallest child). For the next play (after a "no fair" ball) the ball changed teams but the teams did not change from one side of the building to the other.

The ball used for "Anty Over," as well as for all ball games, was homemade of string, twine, or yarn raveled from an old sock or stocking. Grandma first searched for a small, round rock about one inch in diameter (used as the center of the ball). She then wound the string or yarn around the rock in a pattern, carefully darning it into place as the winding proceeded. The finished ball was about two and one half inches in diameter and had a limited bounce.

BEANSHOOTER

Beanshooters were hollow pieces of cane cut from the canebrakes in the bottom land along Shuffle Creek. A pocketful of dried beans or peas—black-eyed peas, lady peas, or navy beans—or tiny pebbles was ammunition blown through the cane, directed at chickens, pigs, cats (shooting at each other was forbidden for fear of a shot in the eye). An old hen or rooster intent on scratching and picking worms, breadcrumbs, or oats, suddenly hit in the tail with a bean, spluttered, flopped, or spread wings into the air, careened across the yard and raced into the berry patch or orchard squawking. A pig hit made one tiny squeak, then peddled away; and a cat made no sound as it scampered up a tree or under the house. Saturdays, after the front yard and back yard were raked clear for Sunday, the beanshooter war on the chickens began and was carried on intermittently all day, Little Brother in charge of the front yard and Dorothy of the back yard. When war-weariness did not overtake them before it was time for the chickens to go to roost, the Sunday sun arose on a back yard and a front yard that were, if not immaculate, then almost free of chicken manure (called "chicken doings").

BELIEFS

1. First speaker   *Bread and butter*
   Second speaker   *Come to supper.*
   Two children, finding that they had allowed a post, a tree, or any upright object to come between them as they walked, recited this formula as a charm to counteract divisive evil spirits. They believed that they would quarrel and their friendship would be broken if they failed to recite the charm.
2. "Cross my heart and hope to die."
   This was a pledge or oath of allegiance, constancy, secrecy.
3. Dress or garment put on inside out (accidentally), if worn so the rest of the day, brought good luck.
4. Dress hem accidentally turned up.
   Spit on the hem before turning it down to get a new dress.
5. Gap between teeth meant a generous disposition.
6. A mole was called a beauty spot.
7. First speaker   *Needles*
   Second speaker   *Pins*
   First speaker   *When a man marries*
   Second speaker   *His trouble begins*
   First speaker   *What goes up the chimney?*
   Second speaker   *Smoke*
   First speaker   *Hope this wish*
   Second speaker   *Will never be broke*

When two children accidentally said a word or words in unison, each crooked the little finger of his right hand; they hooked the crooked fingers, made a secret wish and recited the formula, believing the secret wish would come true.

BLACK MAN

There were two bases, which were circles four or five feet across scratched on the ground, with thirty or forty feet between bases. A player was safe inside a base or if he had one foot inside the base.

The players—all but the Black Man—stood inside one base while the Black Man stood somewhere between the bases to catch and hold any player daring to run between bases. Every player was required, sooner or later, to run across to the second base. Once a player left base he could not turn back: he had to run for the other base; and since no geographic limitations on the chase were set, the Black Man could pursue him far afield, in which case he tried to tire the Black Man and thus reach safety by default. Otherwise he tried trickery. Meanwhile, his playmates would have crossed between bases. Seldom did a Black Man accept the challenge of a wild chase but chose, instead, to let the first man pass and wait for later players.

Timid players, reluctant to leave the safety of home base, were goaded by the Black Man who called them "Fraidy Cat" and "Cry Baby."

A player, once caught, remained idle on the sideline until all players were caught or safely through the Black Man's territory. The first player caught was Black Man in the next game.

To catch a player, the Black Man was required to catch and hold him in a full stop. If the player could wrestle free from the Black Man's grasp, he was free to run on. The Black Man often found himself holding a buttonless shirt, half a shirt, torn jacket, or half of a girl's skirt or a sleeve of her blouse instead of the player who owned the garment.

When neighbor families visited, the boys and girls from five to fourteen years old played Black Man together in the pastures and along the road. The big boys and girls did most of the chasing and catching and allowed the small children safe passage made exciting by pretended attempts to overtake them.

BLADDER BALLOONS

At hog-killing time, the hog bladders were washed, blown up by mouth, and given to the children for a play pritty. The children punched the bladder balloon with their fists to see how high they could make the bladder go. If caught by an up-wind, it could rise and soar off into the fields, with the children racing wildly after it. It could be lost to a blue norther blowing strong. The children were not defeated easily, however, for a bladder made a good toy for many weeks before the membrane dried up, cracked, and disintegrated. Often, they tied a string to the balloon so that they could reel it out (or in when the wind fell).

BLINDFOLD

There were three or more players, indoors or outdoors, but usually indoors. One player volunteered or was chosen to be "It." A man's handkerchief or a square piece of cloth (perhaps torn from an old sheet) was folded into a blindfold: first folded into a triangle; second, the right angle folded over to the center edge of the hypotenuse; then folded once more. "It," with eyes covered by the blindfold tied around his head, cautiously stepped about, listening for noises made by moving players avoiding his grasp. When "It" succeeded in touching a player, the player stood still while "It" tried to identify him. "It" was allowed to feel the player with his hands, to measure his height and examine his clothes. When accurately identified, the player then changed places with "It" and the game continued. Before the game began, a limitation of the area of play was agreed upon: if outdoors, the game was limited to either the front yard or the back yard; and when "It" wandered outside the game space, all the players shouted to warn him, then scampered to change positions. The game continued until the players' interest was exhausted or until parents called players to work or to supper.

BOBWHITE

This was a hide-and-seek game played by one child and one bobwhite in a field of wheat or oats. A child, hearing a bobwhite call, started the game by crawling through the grain toward the bird—but not too near. Hidden, he answered:

Bobwhite
Is your wheat ripe?
No, not quite.

Then, as the bird answered and flew toward the mimic, the child crawled away at a right angle to the line of call, sat still a few moments, answered again, and crawled away again.

The game sometimes became an endurance test between a persistent bird and a persistent, tired child who did not want to admit defeat.

BUBBLE BLOWING

A pan of water and a cake of soap were all that were needed for bubble blowing. Sitting on the back gallery steps with the soap and water, a bubble blower lathered his hands until the palms were slick with lather; then, with wrists touching and fingertips touching, he cautiously opened his palms. If he found a film of lather closing the opening between his little fingers, he blew gently on it puffing it out into an iridescent bubble, which broke or disengaged itself to float with the breeze, followed by baby bubbles made by quick little puffs of breath. Sometimes a spool was used for a bubble blower. Then a good suds was necessary. The soap was swished back and forth in the pan until the surface was a mass of frothing bubbles. The spool dipped into the suds picked up a soap film to close the opening, against which the blower blew to force the bubble out and into the air.

BUTTON, BUTTON

Players sat in a circle. "It" (favored position) held the button between his hands, palms flat together, and anchored the button by pressing it between two fingers so that he could release it at will. He went in turn to each player, who cupped his hands (to make one cup) and held them out to "It." "It" placed his hands inside the cup, slightly opening his palms and either dropping or pretending to drop the button into the player's cupped hands, saying: "Hold all I give you." The receiving player, whether or not he received the button, closed his palms together as if he held the button.

When "It" had completed the ritual with all players in the circle, he stood in the center and said: "Button, Button, who's got the button?" He then called the name of an empty-handed child, who was required to open his empty hands before calling the name of another player. Regardless of the number of false calls, the button-holder always became "It" for the next game.

CATCHES

1. *Adam and Eve and Pinch me tight*
   Went over the river to see a cat fight
   Adam and Eve got back all right.
   Who didn't?
   Answer   *Pinch me tight.*
   The uninitiated child received a tight pinch and either returned it in anger or accepted it with tears. The initiated (1) refused to answer; (2) answered "Pinch me tight" and ran, challenging the trickster; or (3) answered "Pinch you tight" and ran.
2. *Crow's nest:* The older or knowing child extended two forefingers of the left hand, spread, and placed two spread forefingers of the right hand at right angles over the left hand spread fingers, making a hold or "crow's nest." He then said to the uninitiated: "That's a crow's nest. Put your finger in to see if there are any eggs in the nest." The greenhorn found his finger caught in a vice as the nest-owner closed his fingers.
3. First child   *I saw a dead chicken down by the henhouse.*
                   I one it.
   Second child   *I two it.*
   First child   *I three it.*
   Second child   *I four it.*
   First child   *I five it.*
   Second child   *I six it.*
   First child   *I seven it.*
   Second child   *I ate it.*
   The first child, usually older than the second, instructed the second child to say the formula and afterward laughed at his expense, raising his nose as if smelling a bad odor and shouting, "You ate it! You ate it!"
4. *Shut your eyes and hold your hands:* A child or adult with a small gift for another would say, "Shut your eyes and hold your

hands." The complier receiving the gift could then open his eyes to a surprise. This was usually a kind trick. When an unkind gift bearer placed a rock in the receiver's hands or slapped them, a chase and fight or pinching match ensued.

5. *Blindfold with hands over eyes:* A player crept up on another from the rear, placed his hands over the eyes of the unsuspecting player, remained silent until the blinded player could guess his identity. The blinded player was allowed to reach with his hands to feel the clothing of his unknown playmate but could not turn around.

CHICKAMY CHICKAMY CRANY CROW

Characters: Old Witch, Mother Hen (Chickamy Crany Crow), and her brood of chickens.

Places marked by a stone, tree, or tree limb were specified as "the well," "the witch's house," and "the chicken coop," the three usually located to form a triangle. The favorite place to play was under the hackberry trees across the road from the farm in late spring, summer, or early autumn days.

The game began when the Old Witch left her house and busied herself picking up sticks (or pretending to). At the same time the Mother Hen left her coop (to go to the well) and her chickens trailed along behind or beside her.

Chickamy, chickamy, crany crow
Went to the well to wash her toe
When she got back her blue-eyed
(or brown or black) chicken was gone.

Then the **Mother Hen** called   What time is it, Old Witch?
Old Witch   One o'clock.
Mother Hen   What are you doing, Old Witch?
Old Witch ⋅ Picking up sticks.
Mother Hen   What time is it, Old Witch?
Old Witch   Three o'clock.
The question–answer formula about time went on until the **Old Witch** shouted   Time to build a fire and cook me a chicken.
Mother Hen   Where will you get yourself a chicken, Old Witch?
Old Witch   I'll steal myself one out of your chicken coop.
The chickens, meanwhile, had formed themselves into a row behind their Mother, the first one locking her arms around the

Mother Hen's waist, the next one locking her arms around the first, and so on.

The Old Witch darted for the chicken at the end of the line while the Mother Hen spread her arms (wings) to protect her brood and moved herself, and her line of chickens with her, back and forth countering the Old Witch's movements. The Mother Hen's success depended on her brood's cooperative movements and usually the younger players were placed in the middle of the line and an older, more able maneuverer at the end.

When the Old Witch succeeded in touching a chicken, she took it to her house and shoved it in her pot. The game continued until all the chickens were caught and stewed, after which the Old Witch went through motions of eating each chicken, beginning with the ribs to tickle it and make it squirm — and flop like a recently beheaded chicken.

Players volunteered for the positions of Old Witch and Mother Hen to test their prowess. The chickens became chickens by default. When the Old Witch and the Mother Hen were too evenly matched, the game wore on too long for fun and disintegrated as the chickens tired and wandered away.

CLUB FIST

From three to seven players (or as many as could squeeze into the circle) played. The starter placed his left fist on the ground, floor, table, or knee, with his thumb sticking upright. A second player grasped that thumb with his left hand and stuck his own thumb up for a third player to grasp. When each player had his left hand in, then each player entered his right hand.

When all hands were stacked, the last player withdrew his right hand to be the Knocker. The Knocker said to the owner of the top fist, "What you got there?"

Answer   Club fist.

Knocker   Take it off or knock it off?

Answer   Take it off (and removed it) *or* Knock it off (the knocker then knocked it off).

Sometimes the knocking off became a tussle pulling the group about all over the room. A skilled Knocker learned to rap knuckles with his own knuckles in a quick, sharp rap to make the recipient turn loose in agony.

One by one the fists were eliminated until the bottom fist

was reached. Then followed the question–answer between the knocker and the bottom-fist owner:

Knocker What you got way down in there?
Answer Bread and cheese.
Knocker Where's my share?
Answer Cat's got it.
Knocker Where's the cat?
Answer In the woods.
Knocker Where's the woods?
Answer Fire burned 'em.
Knocker Where's the fire?
Answer Water quenched it.
Knocker Where's the water?
Answer Ox drank it.
Knocker Where's the ox?
Answer Butcher killed it.
Knocker Where's the butcher?
Answer Rope hung it.
Knocker Where's the rope?
Answer Rat gnawed it.
Knocker Where's the rat?
Answer Cat caught it.
Knocker Where's the cat?
Answer Hammer killed it.
Knocker Where's the hammer?
Answer Hidden behind the old church door. And the first one smiles or shows his teeth gets a hairpull, pinch, and slap.

Players sat or moved around. Boredom made them do tricks to entice other players to laugh. A player would grunt like a hog, walk spread-legged like a cow, walk backwards on all fours, distort his face and body in any grotesque way he could devise. Tickling was "not fair." Boredom could cause an older player, one fleet of foot, to end the game by deliberately laughing, then running with the pack pursuing.

CRACK THE WHIP

Four to twenty players formed a line, locking wrists. The two largest, strongest players took positions: one as head or whip cracker; the other next to the end or tail. The other players were arranged according to size and speed, with the smaller, slower players near the cracker and the larger, faster players toward the tail. The tail was a small, fleet child who, when thrown off his feet by the speed of the line, was light enough to fly through the air supported by the sturdy player next to him. The whip cracker ran carrying the line with him, describing an arc, reversing the arc, creating the movement of a black-snake whip, and finally led the line in a long convex curve, followed by a short concave curve, thus throwing the tail of the line into a speed swift enough to break the line or to send the players rolling on the ground or into a barbed wire fence or, if the line held, to give the tail-player a ride through the air and safe landing (depending upon his own agility and skill and that of his supporter).

DOODLEBUG

The game was played by one child and one doodlebug (a dark brown bug the size of a bumblebee, with pincers; it lived in a hole in the ground). The child stuck a straw or twig down the hole and called:

> Doodle bug, doodle bug, fly away home
> Your house is on fire and your children all gone
> Doodle bug, doodle bug, doodle bug, doodle bug,
> Doodle bug, doodle bug, doodle bug.

The child continued to call until the bug caught hold of the straw with his pincers. He then pulled the bug to the surface where the game became a contest to see how soon the bug would release his grasp and crawl back into his hole. After he had had time to crawl to the bottom, the game began again.

DRAMATIC PLAY

Dolls Rag dolls ten to fifteen inches tall were made of unbleached muslin, stuffed with cotton. The eyes were black shoe-buttons, the nose and mouth drawn with lead pencil or ink. Grandma made the dolls and also made sets of clothes for the dolls: drawers, underskirts, chemises, and dresses (or pants). Underskirts and chemises had lace edging.

Dolls from five to eight inches tall, with china heads and hands and cloth bodies filled with sawdust, were Christmas presents, found on Christmas morning staring out of stocking tops. The china dolls arrived with carefully made wardrobes — homemade.

Dolls made of cobs were temporary dolls made hastily by pinning a piece of cloth around the cob and making a paper hat or bonnet to pin on the top.

Paper dolls were cut from the pages of the Sears and Roebuck catalogue, or were cut free-hand out of folded paper. The paper could be folded to cut one doll at a time or a string of several dolls with hands joined. Paper-doll furniture often was cut out: stoves, chairs, and beds. Each child had a lidless wooden box about two feet by one foot by one foot (kept under the bed) in which playthings were stored. Doll furniture was made from shoe boxes, match boxes (five by two and one-half by one and one-half inches), and a few cigar boxes and spools. The cardboard boxes were cut and contrived into shapes of tables, chairs, and beds held together with flour paste. A bit of tinfoil from chewing gum made a mirror. A set of tiny tin dishes (a Christmas stocking present) gayly painted, probably came from Sears and Roebuck.

Playing with rag dolls differed from play with the china-headed dolls and paper dolls. Rag dolls were the children, and the players were parents. Sometimes Little Brother was Papa and Dorothy was Mama and the collection of rag dolls was one family of children: punished for disobedience and loved and rewarded with candy, trips to Point, and story-telling and story-reading. Or on another afternoon, Little Brother could be Papa for one family of dolls living in one corner of the room, and Dorothy the Mama of another family living in another corner. This situation called for visits between families or for community gatherings like picnics, fish-fries, funerals, box suppers, and singing school, all acted out by moving the dolls about the room.

Play with both the china-headed dolls and the paper dolls followed the same pattern but the dolls were puppets moved about and voiced, omnipotently producing wishful dramas of living in great houses with many rooms or "Going Out West" in wagon trains. The wagon was made of a shoe box with spool wheels fastened to twig axles sewed to the bottom of the box, and with willow twigs as staves to hold up the cover—a piece of old sheet. The dolls were placed in two or three wagons pulled by strings around the house from room to room. In good weather the back and front galleries were roads west.

Funerals The funeral ceremony was always the same; corpses were: dolls—buried and later dug up—or dead baby chickens, dead baby field mice, or dead kittens, all buried permanently in cardboard boxes lined with cloth and covered with brown wrapping paper (to simulate wood) pasted on with flour paste. The graveyard was in the peach orchard north of the house. Tombstones were dried, carved mud, pieces of brick, or carefully chosen rocks.

Going Out West "Let's play 'Going out West'" invited the dramatization described for "Dolls" or another play entirely: Two armless chairs were placed touching and facing each other. An old quilt or sheet was thrown over the chairs to make a covered wagon. Two children sitting on the chairs, under the covering, pretended to be travelers going "West," and carried on conversations about Indians, lame horses, broken wagon axles, or about a shortage of food supplies which led to Little Brother's climbing down, taking the shotgun (broom), and going into the forest (another room) to shoot and bring back squirrels or rabbits (door-stops—made of brickbats covered with cloth).

Playhouse "Let's make a 'playhouse,'" when children played indoors, led to the creation of a tent-house by placing two chairs back to back about three feet apart, placing the broom across the chairs as a roof-pole-ridge, and draping the chair-broom frame with an old quilt or sheet. Inside two children pretended to live, acting out the daily activities of a household: one the father, the other the mother; rag dolls were children.

Outdoors, "Let's play house" led to a grove of pin oak trees in the pasture beyond the barn beyond the pool. There, brooms, made of weeds bunched together and bound with string, swept spaces clear for house space divided into rooms defined by dead tree limbs laid in careful diagrams. Each player had a playhouse of many rooms. A playhouse in its entirety was defined by trees standing in strategic positions. The houses were from fifty feet to fifty yards apart. Logs and stumps were furniture. Pieces of bark and bits of broken dishes (carefully garnered, saved, and transported in apron pockets) made household utensils. Each player was the head of a household with imaginary spouse and imaginary children. Visits between families constituted most of the drama, which never drifted too far from the verge of reality to preclude awareness of the possibility—even the probability—of a real snake intruding into the imaginary homes. Equipment in each household included a snake-club made of a tree limb (green, not dead) with a knot on the end; and when a snake (blue racer or black coach-whip) invaded a household, the cry "Snake" brought all householders running with their clubs to kill the snake, which usually escaped into the underbrush. There was always the possibility of a copperhead, a ground rattler, or a cottonmouth.

This same drama took place in playhouses under the hackberry trees across the road in front of the house—the road bordering the Calloway farm. There, the playhouse diagrams (because of the lack of tree limbs) were lines carved with sticks in the sand.

Riding Horses The horse was a broom, with the broom-part the horse's head, and the bridle a piece of string or old shoelace. If not a broom, then the horse was a tree limb with a brown paper sack blown up and tied over the end of the stick for the horse's head. The player, astride, galloped, cantered or single-footed, trotted or walked going to Point, to mill, to the sawmill, to Flats Schoolhouse, to the river. The horses were fed, hobbled to graze, put into stables, and finally turned into pasture when the game ended.

School Playing school might be a session in which one player was teacher and the others pupils and the drama the routine recitation of spelling and reading. Or the play was imitation of a Friday afternoon "program" where the teacher called on individual children to stand before the class and recite a verse or sing a song. When the game was played in the house or on the front or back gallery—in earshot of grown-ups—the verses recited were those actually recited in school:

1. *Roses are red*
   Violets are blue
   Sugar is sweet
   And so are you.

2. *Roses on my shoulders*
   Slippers on my feet

I'm my Mama's darling
Don't you think I'm sweet?

3.   *As sure as the vine*
      Grows round the stump
      You are my darling sugar lump.

When the play setting was a safe distance from adult ears — in the hackberry grove or under the pin oaks in the pasture beyond the barn — the recitations were:

4.   *Climbed a hickory*
      Shinned a pine
      Tore my britches
      Right behind.

5.   *As sure as the vine*
      Grows round the rafter
      You are the girl
      That I am after.

6.   *Had a dog and his name was Rover*
      When he died, he died all over
      Except his tail and it turned over.

7.   *Had a mule and his name was Jack*
      Rode his tail to save his back.

8.   *Here I stand on two little chips*
      Come and kiss my sweet little lips.

9.   *Here I stand all ragged and dirty*
      If you come kiss me, I'll run like a turkey.

10.   *I know somethin' I'm notta gonna tell*
      Three little niggers in a peanut shell
      One can read and one can write
      And one can smoke his daddy's pipe.

11.   *I went down to my pea patch*
      To see if my old hen had hatched
      She'd hatched one chicken and the peas was green
      A yellow gal a pickin' on a tambourine.

12. *I went to the river and I couldn't get across*
I paid five dollars for an old gray horse
I lost my money cause the old hoss died
Might have got across if I'd half tried.

13. *Monkey sittin' on the end of a rail*
Pickin' his teeth with the end of his tail.

14. *Mulberry leaves and calico sleeves*
All the pretty girls are hard to please.

15. *My nose itches*
I smell peaches
Yonder comes Johnny
With a hole in his britches.

16. *Possum up a gum stump*
Coony up a hollow
Pretty gal at our house
Fat as she can wallow.

17. *The boy stood on the burning deck*
Eating taters by the peck
A spark flew up and hit him on the chin
And oh how he dropped that tater skin.

18. *The boy stood on the burning deck*
His feet were full of blisters
The flames flew up and burnt his pants
So he had to wear his sister's.

19. *Mary had a little lamb*
Its fleece was white as butter
When Mary turned a summerset
The lamb he couldn't cut her.

DROP THE HANDKERCHIEF

Players formed a ring, then dropped hands and stood while "It" (with a handkerchief) ran around the outside of the ring until he decided to drop the handkerchief behind a player. Each player, by rule, faced the circle but kept his eyes on the ground, glancing sidewise, alert to see any movement indicating that "It" was dropping the handkerchief behind him so he would be ready to swing into action: snatch the handkerchief and be off in pursuit in one movement. *If* he could tag "It" before "It" could run around the outside of the circle and return to the vacated position, then "It" lost his position as dropper and took his place in the circle.

Any variations from these rules were agreed upon before a game began. "It" could be allowed to run around the circle three times before he dropped the handkerchief or once or as many times as he wished. After dropping the handkerchief, he could be allowed one time around, twice around, etc. Cutting through or in and out of the circle could be allowed. A legislative session before the game established the laws for the game for the day. Sometimes laws differed for younger players less fleet of foot and for older, hardier players intent on proving their stamina or prowess.

The game was always played outdoors, at Sunday school picnics, fish-fries, or at home when families came visiting and the children had opportunity for play—threshing time, for example.

FISHING

The fishing rod was cane from the canebrake, four feet long. A piece of twine three or four feet long was tied to one end of the pole and a bent pin for a hook tied to the end of the twine. After rains, when the gulleys and branches held water for crawfish and furnished mud banks for the crawfish to hide in, children took a fishing pole and a syrup bucket apiece, and a pocketful of small pieces of meat (salt pork probably) for bait, and followed the small water courses looking for signs of crawfish. Discovering a good hole, they baited their hooks, threw them in, and pulled in their catches, careful each time to grasp the crawfish behind its pincers to take it off the hook and dump it in the bucket. The object of the game was to see who could catch a bucketful first. Sometimes the contest was so close that the crawfish had to be counted. Then the fishermen carried their buckets some little distance from the gulley or branch and, one bucket at a time, dumped the crawfish on the ground to count them, leaving the counted crawfish to find their awkward way back to water.

Watching the crawling crawfish was also part of the game. The larger the crawfish, the faster he could travel. So, in order to give the smaller ones a better chance, the children wiggled sticks before the pincers of the large ones. They stopped, grasped the sticks, held on. When the smaller ones had gained sufficient ground the children flung the sticks, flinging the big crawfish off. And so the race went on.

FLYING JENNY

The flying jenny was a seesaw plank with a strong cross piece (two-by-two board, two feet long) fastened about two feet from each end to act as handholds for the riders. The plank was center-anchored to a sturdy post or stump set deep in the ground. To anchor the plank, a hole was bored in the plank and another in the center of the flat top of the stump or post. A bolt, dropped through the plank hole into the post hole, allowed the plank to revolve like a merry-go-round. Three players were needed; two riders and a pusher.

There was a flying jenny on the playground at Woosley School where the Sunday school and Sunday school picnics were held.

On the farm, in the oak grove beyond the barn, the sorghum mill for grinding the sorghum and ribbon cane for syrup-making was used as a substitute flying jenny and was called that by the children. A child climbed from the top of a keg onto the end of the rotating arm (to which the horses were hitched at syrup-making time) and clung there, while all the others pushed hard to make the heavy arm swing into motion and move into its big circle.

FOOTRACES

One for the money
Two for the show
Three to make ready
And four to go.

On "go" the racers shot forth, whatever or wherever the race. Races could be running, hopping, skipping, or walking races from anyplace to anyplace — against each other or against the elements, or both. When summer wind clouds blew near, bringing rain, the children raced down the road into the wind to see how far they could go before the first drop of rain touched them. Honor-bound to stop on the first drop, the winner declared his own victory. They all then stood in the middle of the dusty road waiting for the rain to drench their clothes, their bodies, to trickle down their foreheads, drip off the tips of their noses and turn the dust into mud around their bare feet.

With mud mushing up between their toes, they walked home slowly, stopping to create little dams in the wheel ruts or to smear brown mud over their arms and legs and be Indians for a little while until the rain washed them into white children again.

When summer whirlwinds were sighted following the road as they sometimes did (though more often they careened off across the cornfields and pastures), the children raced to meet the whirlwind; they won by getting eyes full of sand and then made their blinking way home to Grandma, who got out her flaxseed jar and put a flaxseed in each dusty eye. The flaxseed chased the dirt out, so Grandma said; and in short time she wiped away flaxseed, dirt, and all with a clean handkerchief.

Hopping was reserved to short races: from the front step to the gate; from the back steps to the woodpile; or if the hopping race was from .the house to the barn, the hoppers were allowed one put-down or two put-downs on the way.

FORFEITS

Though paying forfeits was a part of other games, a game by that name was played at home. One player sat in a chair, eyes closed. Another player standing behind the chair held an object (belonging to the sitter—a doll, a shoe, a ribbon, a stocking) over the sitter's head saying: "Heavy, heavy, hangs over your head.

The sitter asked, "Fine or superfine?" ("Fine" meant ordinary or utilitarian: shoe, stocking, handkerchief. "Superfine" meant a ring, hair ribbon, or a pin.)

The standing player answered either "fine" or "superfine." The sitter then asked, "What must I do to redeem it?" The order would be: to sing a song, gather the eggs, catch a rooster. After payment, the redeemer received the forfeit—sometimes very disappointing.

FROG IN THE MIDDLE

Players formed a circle, with Frog squatting in the middle, and sang.

On the last two lines a chosen player left the circle and (with or without stick in hand) went to the middle, pulled Frog to his feet, turned him around three times, pushed him to squatting position again, and returned to his circle position. All players then chanted,

"Froggie, Froggie, Froggie, Froggie" as they darted in one, two, or three at a time from various directions to touch him before he could touch them. The touch often became a slap from a player approaching Frog from the rear while his attention was centered on a frontal attack. Frog was required to remain in squatting position. When he succeeded in tagging a player first, the two changed places and the game went on. The game was played mostly at community gatherings.

Frog in the middle
Can't get out
Take a stick
And stir him about.

GOING OUT WEST

Players sat in a circle. One player, as leader, said, "I'm going out west and I'm going to take a washtub." The next player said, "I'm going out west and I'm going to take a washtub and a frying pan." The third player said, "I'm going out west and I'm going to take a washtub, a frying pan, and a lantern." And so on around the circle. Any player who failed to repeat all items in order was required to forfeit some possession—a doll, a shoe, a hair ribbon, to be redeemed later. Those paying forfeits were sent from the room while the group decided what the payment was to be: "stand on your head," "run around the house five times," "kiss the cat," "bring in five loads of stovewood." More often played at community gatherings, the game was occasionally a family game with Grandma participating.

Going Out West and *Going to Dallas* were names given to dramatic play when Dorothy and Little Brother pretended to go on a trip. To make a covered wagon they spread an old quilt over two chairs which faced and touched each other. Dorothy and Little Brother rode in the wagon taking with them all their play-things. Because the wagon was crowded the playthings fell out and Little Brother who was the driver often shouted "Whoa!" to retrieve the lost belongings. He also shouted "Whoa!" pretending a wheel had broken or that the horses were running away or when night fell and they stopped to camp. Then, to make a tent, the two chairs—still facing—were turned down on the floor so that the chair backs made a tent roof when the old quilt was thrown over the chairs.

They also played *Going Out West* by pulling covered wagons made of shoeboxes and covered with old handkerchiefs or white rags. Dorothy and Little Brother were the horses and pulled the wagons by strings attached.

GOING TO MILL

Two players needed paper, pencil, and a small object such as a thimble, bean, or pebble (called a "taw") to hide in the hand. A diagram was drawn on which each player's progress was marked in miles to and from the mill. One player, holding the taw in his hands behind his back, brought forth clenched hands for the

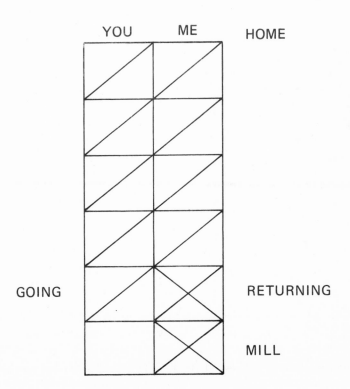

opponent to guess the hand that held the taw. If successful, he marked one mile on his journey, took the taw, and hid it in a hand for the first player to guess. The miles marked going to mill were drawn diagonally across the squares from left lower corner to right upper corner. Going home, the miles intersected those lines (from left upper corner to lower right). This was a wintertime, rainy-day indoor game. Grandma sometimes played too.

GREEN GRAVEL

Green gravel, green gravel
The grass is so green
The fairest young maiden
That ever was seen
I'll wash you in new milk
And dress you in silk
And write down your name
With a gold pen and ink.
Oh Mary, Oh Mary
Your true love is dead
He sent me a letter
To cut off your head.

Players, holding hands and marching in a circle, sang the song while one player stood in the middle. When the singers reached "Oh Mary," the circle stopped marching, the center player chose and approached a player in the circle and stood facing her as the song was completed. Then the two exchanged places and the chosen "Mary" took her place in the center of the circle as the song and march began again. Little girls played the game at community gatherings.

HAND AND KNEE RHYMES AND PLAY

1. *Chin chopper*
    Mouth eater
    Nose dropper
    Eye winker
    Tom tinker
    Chin chopper chin
    Chin chopper chin.

    The adult, holding a child on his lap, touched the chin, mouth, nose, eye, forehead, then chucked the child under the chin.

2. *Goosie, goosie gander*
    Say goose—turn 'em loose
    Say gander—pull 'em way out yander.

    The adult, holding the child's ears, first turned them loose, then pretended to pull them out—extending his hands either side of the child's head.

3. *Knock at the door*
    Peep in
    Lift up the latch
    And walk in.

    The adult gently tapped the child on the forehead, lifted his eyelid and looked into his eye, flipped the child's nose-tip with a finger, and then stuck his finger in the child's mouth.

4. *Little rooster lived up here* [forehead]
    Little hen lived down here [chin]
    Little rooster came down to see the little hen [forefinger
        was moved from forehead, down the bridge of the nose,
        across the lips to the chin]
    And when he went back home [finger was moved across
        the lips toward the nose]
    Up jumped a rabbit [on *up* the finger caught the nose-tip
        and gave it a gentle flip].

5.   *These are mother's knives and forks*
      This is mother's table
      This is sister's looking glass
      And this is baby's cradle.

      This is father's hayrake
      This is mother's table
      This is sister's looking glass
      And this is baby's cradle.

The adult or child with hands back to back, interlocked his fingers for "knives and forks" or "hayrake." With fingers still interlocked the palms were turned inward making a double fist on "table." On "looking glass" the two forefingers were extracted from the fist with fingertips touching. On "cradle," the two little fingers were extracted from the first with fingertips touching.

6.   *This is the church*
      This is the steeple
      Open the door
      And out come all the people

The adult or child interlocked fingers and closed his hands to made a double fist (church). On "steeple," the two forefingers were extracted from the fist and pointed, with fingertips touching. On "open the door" the hands were reversed with palms out—fingers still interlocked. On "out" the fingers were released and the fingers were moved across the lap or table (people walking).

7.   *This little pig say I gonna steal some wheat*
      This little pig say where you gonna get it?
      This little pig say out of master's barn
      This little pig say I go tell
      This little pig say week, week, week
      Can't get through the crack in the fence.

Counting a baby's toes or fingers, beginning with the thumb or the big toe.

8.   *Trotty, trotty, gallopy trot*
       Sold my buttermilk every drop
       Going home, going home, going home
       Going home, going home, going home
       Going home.

The adult trotted a child on his knees, trotting up and down (heels going down on "trot" and "ty") through the first two lines; then changed to a side-to-side movement on "going home" and continued (like a gentle gallop) to the last "going home," when he spread his knees, allowing the child to drop between them (but catching the child before he hit the floor).

HANDKERCHIEF BALLOON

Materials needed were a man's handkerchief or a square rag of similar size, four pieces of string some twelve inches long, and a rough rock the size of a hen's egg but of irregular shape.

A string was tied to each corner of the handkerchief. The four strings were brought together and tied around the rock (ballast for the balloon).

The strings and handkerchief were twisted and wound around the rock. The rock was thrown into the air. The string and handkerchief unwound and the handkerchief ballooned into an umbrella to float with the breeze and descend to earth gradually.

HIDE AND SEEK

Any number of players could play indoors or out, though outdoors was preferred and indoors often forbidden. On cold, rainy days when big sisters were in school, Little Brother and Dorothy played the game in the house, taking turns hiding from each other: under a bed; behind Grandma's chair (with Grandma sitting in it); under Mama's apron as she stood working in the kitchen.

On summer evenings after supper (with dishes done) the three sisters and Little Brother played in the front and back yards, hiding in the chimney corner, behind or in the smokehouse; in the closet (privy) — but *not* behind it; behind the stormhouse, the big hackberry, the woodpile, Papa (sitting on the steps); under the washpot or a tub (turned bottom-side-up) or under Grandma's full, spread skirt as she sat in a chair on the back porch.

At fish-fries on Sabine River, at day's end with the fishing over, the food eaten and the picnic boxes and baskets packed for home-going, all family members except babes in arms played "Hide and Seek" ranging over a wide area extending into the darkening woods where only the men and big boys dared go. Small children hid close to home base and were allowed "in free" while the adult hunters searched the farther hiding places for big game.

To begin the game, "It" was selected by formula or volunteered. Then with eyes shut and facing home base (a tree, stump, house corner, post), he counted to one hundred or two hundred by fives or by tens (as previously agreed), while the others ran and hid in individual hiding places. Also previously agreed upon were the geographic limitations of the hiding area.

The counting done, "It" called:

Bushel of wheat
And a bushel of rye
All not hid, holler I.

He listened. If a player called "I," "It" covered his eyes again and counted to one hundred by fives. Then he called:

Bushel of wheat
And a bushel of clover
All not hid
Can't hide over.
All within ten feet of my base
Are caught
Ready or not, here I come
Both eyes open.

He then hunted them down and raced them to home base. Cautiously reconnoitering the area near home base, alert to possible nearby hiders, "It" gradually widened his operation, spending his attention on the probable hiding places and trying to guess who might be hiding where. If a hider believed his discovery to be imminent, he might decide against waiting to be spied and instead, make advantage by a dash for home. When a player won the race, he patted home base three times saying,

"One, two, three, in free." When "It" won the race, he patted home base three times and said, "One, two, three, you're 'It'" (if the player was the first one caught) or "You're out" (for later players).

The hunt continued until all players were either "in free" or "caught." Occasionally when a player was too well hidden, "It" gave up and called out, "All out in free." The game was over. The first player caught became "It" for a new game.

HOOPROLLING

Hoops (wooden and metal hoops from barrels, wire hoops, metal baby buggy rims, wagon wheel and buggy wheel rims) were rolled by hand about the yard, down the paths leading to the barn and fields, and in the road in front of the house.

Hoop contests — not races — were held to see which hooproller could keep his hoop upright and within a path the greatest distance down a road.

Little Brother was enticed to curl his body inside a hoop for a hoop ride while one of his sisters rolled the hoop. The rides were short and disastrous, for Little Brother couldn't stay in the hoop, the hoop could not be guided, and Little Brother often landed in a briar patch, a barbed wire fence, a chicken trough, or a mud puddle, crying for Mama.

Rolling in barrels was more successful. The rider curled his body inside the barrel, braced himself by pushing his back against the barrel while it spun over and over as a playmate rolled the barrel down a slight incline. The favorite place for barrel rides was on the grassy bank of the branch south of the Miss Gussie house. Sometimes a rock or clod deflected the barrel from its course and sent it careening into a mud or water hole.

That same grassy bank was the favorite place for springtime grass-rolling. The three sisters and Little Brother simply lay down at the top of the rise and allowed their bodies to roll over and over until the water's edge approached, then clutched wildly for tufts of grass to break their speed and stop them.

HOPSCOTCH

The hopscotch diagram was carved with a stick on the ground. An angular flat stone chosen for hand size was the "taw" tossed onto the diagram beds. Two or more players played.

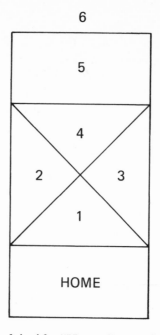

The first player stood inside "Home," tossed the taw into Number 1, hopped into Number 1, picked up the taw, hopped backward to Home. Next, the taw was tossed into Number 2, the player hopped into Number 1, then into Number 2, picked up the taw, and hopped backward into Number 1 and backward into Home. Next, the taw was tossed into Number 3, the player hopped into Number 1, jumped with left foot landing in Number 2 and right foot landing in Number 3, picked up the taw, hopped backward to Home. The player continued, hopping into Numbers 4 and 5, then backward, and then stepping into Number 6, turning around, and returning to Home, thus completing the game.

Rules required that neither the taw nor a player's foot should touch a line. In either case, the player relinquished play to another playmate.

On the moves that required hopping, if the hopper's lifted foot touched the ground, he relinquished his turn.

Each player who did not execute the entire routine without missing had to start from Home on his second turn. Small children were allowed (on second turn) to start from the last base executed correctly. Thus the winning player was the one who returned Home first.

HULL GULL

Two or more children, preferably more, played with corn grains, dried peas or beans, acorns, or pebbles, each player holding the same number at the start of the game. Players, if two, sat facing —if more, sat in a circle—each with his holdings in his pocket or lap or on the ground between his legs so arranged for secret maneuvering.

The first player, with closed hand holding one, two, three, or no objects, extended his fist to the second player, who responded, "Hull Gull."

The first responded, "Hand full."

The second asked, "How many?"

The first answered, "Guess."

If the second guessed correctly, he won all in the hand and became the caller, holding his fist to the third player. If he guessed incorrectly, he paid the first player the number guessed, and the first player remained the caller, holding out his closed hand again for the second player to guess. A player remained in the game until he lost all his holdings. The game ended when one player had won all the beans, peas, corn, or pebbles.

"IT" RITUALS AND RHYMES

Order of play and play roles, sometimes established on a voluntary basis, were more often determined by chance, chicanery, or prowess. An older player wishing to display bravery, stamina, or altruism volunteered for an onerous role and thereby assumed the leadership of a group, claiming the privilege of making other decisions for the group: rules for the game, geographic limitations of play, handicaps in favor of smaller players, and length of play time if a specific game did not include a formal ending. Under such leadership, one team sometimes granted an opposing team first go in a game. More often trick or prowess, masquerading as chance, determined roles and order of play. A player wanting to start a game shouted, "Let's play 'Hide and Seek.' Not 'It!'" Nearby players, in turn, shouted "Not 'It'" until the last slow arrival's "Not 'It'" forced him into the role. Or a player shouted, "Let's play 'Hide and Seek!' Last to the gate is 'It!'"

Drawing straws (broom straws when the game was indoors, or sticks when the game was outdoors) was ostensibly chance. But the player holding the straws or sticks could arrange them to confuse the chooser, especially the younger choosers. They could be arranged according to length with the shortest appearing to be the longest and the longest the shortest.

Crafty counters could manipulate O–U–T rituals by premeditated arithmetical maneuvering and thus predetermine the player on whom the last count would fall.

Rhymes for choosing game positions or choice of candy or hair ribbons to wear were:

Eeny, meeny, miny moe
Catch a nigger by the toe
If he hollers make him pay
Fifty dollars every day.

Tic tac toe
Round I go
If I miss
I'll take this.

JACKSTONES

Five small rocks the size of a sparrow's egg but irregular in shape (not smooth) were carefully chosen and kept in the apron pocket for the game, played indoors on the floor or outdoors on the ground in the shade of the hackberry. Two or more players could play this rock-juggling game, which began with one player holding the five stones cupped in the palm of the right hand. He tossed them into the air, then, fingers slightly spread, turned the hand over to catch the five or as many as possible—on the back of the hand, encouraging them to lodge in the finger crevices. The hand holding the caught stones tossed them into the air and caught them in the palm. Any stones lying on the ground were scooped up while the player tossed one stone (taw) into the air and caught it (using the right hand only).

The next moves were called Onesies, Twosies, Threesies and Foursies. These moves each began with the stones being tossed into the ground in a broadcasting motion so that they would scatter and no stones would touch. The player then picked up one stone to use as Taw (choosing it carefully, it would be the stone lying closest to another stone). The taw was tossed into the air (right hand), one stone picked up from the ground (right hand), taw caught (right hand). The stone picked up was deposited in the lap. The taw was tossed up again, another stone picked up from the ground, the taw caught, and the stone deposited in the lap. Thus each of the four stones on the ground was picked up and Onesies were accomplished.

On Twosies, the stones were scattered and picked up two at a time, the hand making a sweeping motion to do so. In Threesies, three were picked up, then one. And in Foursies, the stones were thrown, in a way to make them bunch, and were picked up in one move.

Rules required that the hand must pick up the stones on the ground without touching any stone not included in the move. For example, on Onesies, the hand picking up one stone from the ground must not touch another stone on the ground. Violating the rule meant relinquishing play to the next player. To miss a catch or a pick up also meant relinquishing play.

When the second player's turn was relinquished (back to the first player) the first player continued with the game from the last move of his previous play. After Onesies, Twosies, Threesies, and Foursies, came Over the Stile, Cows Through the Gate, Horses in the Stable, Pigs in the Pen, Kittens in the Well (all of which required both hands, with the right hand juggling and the left hand forming the metaphors).

For Over the Stile, the left hand was placed edgewise on the ground, with fingers close together—little finger on the earth and thumb on the top, to form a barrier. The player then scattered the stones to the right of the "stile," chose a taw, juggled it, lifting each of the four remaining stones over the stile, one at a time; next, two at a time, three, and finally four at once. (Each time, the bunched stones were picked up in the last act of the figure.)

For Cows Through the Gate, the left hand with thumb and bunched fingers formed an arch. The player followed the play pattern of Over the Stile, this time, pushing the stones under the arch.

For Horses in the Stable, the fingers and thumb of the left hand were spread and the spread hand placed with fingertips—but not the palm—touching the ground, making four openings: stables. The player then pushed one stone into each opening.

Pigs in the Pen was played exactly as Cows Through the Gate.

In Kittens in the Well, the left thumb and forefinger formed a circle with the other fingers forming a semi-cylindrical receptacle into which to drop the stones (kittens) one, two, three, and four at a time.

With the player over the stile, the cows through the gate, the horses stabled, the pigs penned, and the kittens all drowned in the well, the game was over.

Dorothy learned the game from her sisters, who had learned the game at school. She seldom played the game with them, however. She and Polly Malloy played together and when no playmate was available Dorothy played alone, since Little Brother was too young for the skills involved.

JUMPING ROPE

Rope jumping was not an activity of children only. At community gatherings grown men (not women) and adolescent girls in long skirts jumped in "hot" marathons, with bystanders counting to five hundred and more as the rope, turned by the strongest men, whizzed round and round, slapping little dust clouds under the men's feet alternately touching the ground so fast that their crouched bodies seemed suspended in air. And when an agile big girl, long-skirted and ruffled, ran to join a jumping beau, the rope throwers played tricks with the rope to make it cut the girl's skirt as she ran in or out and throw her skirt over her head showing her ruffled underskirts and tucked, lacy drawers.

Children at community gatherings formed themselves into rope-jumping groups, the smaller ones usually jumping the single, short rope (calf rope) thrown by the jumper. The jumper often invited a playmate to "jump in" and the two, facing, jumped the same rope, which had to be thrown higher and wider to clear the second jumper. The rope-thrower gave the orders for jumping: both feet, feet alternating or hopping on one foot; and "high water," "low water," "pepper," "hot pepper." This double-jumper arrangement was more successful when the rope-thrower was taller than the playmate. Otherwise the stinging rope too often caught the playmate on the back of the head or neck, leaving a welt or lump not soon forgiven. When two players wanted to use a long rope, one end of the rope was tied to a post or tree (necessitating only one thrower).

A jumper prided himself on his speed, stamina, and ability to run into a turning rope, either "front door" or "back door," without "catching flies." Criteria for speed, stamina, and skill were established by grown-ups for children, whose ambition was to grow up to take part in "hot" marathons at Sunday school picnics.

KING KING CALICO

One player, the catcher, was chosen or volunteered to be "King." Two leaders then chose the players into two groups, each trying to select the fleetest runners. Two parallel lines were drawn some forty feet apart; the space between was forbidden ground belonging to the King, and safety zones lay behind those lines. The game began when each leader had arranged his players in a row behind their safety line, the two groups facing. One group chanted:

> King, King Calico
> You may come
> And I may go.

On "go," all players ran across the King's territory trying to reach the opposite safety zone. The King caught the players one by one. He seized a player by the arm or clothing and tried to hold him while he patted his head three times with the other hand. A player thus caught became a King's man and assisted in catching the other players on the next call. The groups took turns calling. When all players in one group were caught, the game was over. The first player caught became King in the next game.

"King King Calico" could include any number of players of various ages and was a favorite game for community gatherings — picnics, fish-fries, or threshing time.

KITE FLYING

Kites were homemade with adult help. The kite frame was made of small, slender tree limbs or willow fronds, of lightweight laths or old windowshade slats to form a cross two to three feet tall by eighteen inches to two feet across, fastened together with twine criss-crossing. To complete the frame, heavy twine was fastened to the tip of a lath, stretched to the adjacent tip, fastened by looping around, then on to the next, to the next, and back to the first lath.

On the completed frame of wood and string, newspaper or brown wrapping paper was pasted with flour paste. A tail was made of strips of bright-colored rags from old clothing tied together, with the heaviest piece toward the end of the tail. The length and weight of the tail had to be determined by trial and error. Too much ballast meant the flyer could not get his kite off the ground and too little sent a crazy kite careening uncontrolled and falling into a treetop or pond.

The flying string (a ball of string) was attached to a strong harness. The harness was formed by tying short strings to the top tip and to the two wing tips and bringing the three strings together at the center of the cross, then tying them loosely enough to allow attaching the flying string some six inches or more from the body of the kite.

The kites were flown most successfully in the north pasture, which allowed open sky for maneuvering, ample running space, and sloping terrain so that a flyer, running uphill into the breeze, got his kite into the air with little effort.

Kite flying in the road was less satisfactory unless the breeze was strong and steady. A slight gust (with little space for maneuvering) could send the kite diving into a treetop or telephone wire.

LEAPFROG

This was considered a boys' game which little girls were allowed to play in girls' groups (when no boys were in sight) but never, never in mixed groups. However, at community gatherings, when the evening shadows gathered, rowdy daring big girls joined the boys in games of "Leapfrog" on the far side of the schoolhouse while the grown-ups sat preoccupied with adult talk on the other side.

Two or more could play the game—the more the better. Players arranged themselves in a row, one behind the other, Indian file, about six feet apart. Each player except the one at the end of the line leaned forward, placing his palms or hands on the ground to brace himself. The players formed a row of bent bodies. The rear player leaped over the stooped player immediately in front of him, placing his hands on the other player's back to brace himself and give himself momentum for the next leap over the next player. On he went, leaping over the line of players until he reached the head of the line, whereupon he bent over to take his place as a hurdle.

As soon as the first leaper cleared one player, creating a new rear man, the new rear man began leaping up the line. Soon the entire line of players was in constant endless motion, leaping faster and faster until they piled into a laughing, scrambling pile of bodies.

Big boys and men braced their bent bodies by placing their hands on their knees and spreading their legs twenty inches apart. Big boys and men sometimes made a rule that leapers must hurdle a body without touching it.

LEMONADE

Girls and boys played "Lemonade" in groups of six to twelve on the banks of Sabine, on the Woosley Schoolhouse playground, or under the hackberries across the road from the farm. Two self-appointed leaders—older players—chose the remaining players into two groups. Each leader led the group to a home base established by drawing a line in the dirt with a stick or finger. The home bases were parallel lines about forty feet apart. The space between was the ground for a chase—a later part of the game.

By common agreement or ritual one group went first. That group, whispering together, agreed upon some action to pantomime. Then, advancing toward the opposing group, they called:

> *Here we come.*

Group 2   *Where you from?*
Group 1   *New York.*
Group 2   *What's your trade?*
Group 1   *Lemonade.*
Group 2   *Go to work and show us some.*

Each individual in Group 1 then acted out his own interpretation of the specific work: churning, hoeing corn, chopping wood, carrying stovewood, picking peaches, washing clothes. Group 2 was allowed three guesses. When a member of group 2 called out the right answer, then Group 1 ran for home with Group 2 in pursuit. Any player tagged joined the pursuing group, which returned to its home base, whispered together, and approached Group 1 with a pantomime.

When all three guesses were wrong, the pantomiming group returned to home base, decided on another pantomime, and approached the opponents again.

Skillful players chose motions allowing many interpretations. For example, a stirring motion with the hand and arm could be mixing a cake, or corn bread, or making soap, or stirring clothes boiling in the big black pot. Younger players were instructed by older groupmates to make ambiguous motions to mislead the guessers.

MARBLES

Each child kept his marbles in a cloth sack (smoking tobacco sack) with a drawstring tied, sometimes in a hard knot. Marbles were glass or clay. There were two kinds of glass marbles: solid color glass in red, blue, yellow, and green; and "immies" (imitation agate), variegated swirls of rainbow colors. Then there were "aggies" (real agate), the choicest of all marbles. "Immies" were second choice, and the dun-colored clay ones, "commonies," least prized. "Keepsie" was forbidden by parents but children pretended to play for keeps, paying marble debts with "commonies" as games progressed and returning their winnings to the original owners at the end of playtime.

Two different games were played. In the simplest, one hole was dug with fingers, an inch deep and large enough to hold one marble from each player in the game (usually "commonies"). With a stick or finger, a circle was drawn on the ground about three feet in diameter with the hole "pot" in the center. Each player chose a "taw" from his own marbles to shoot with—chosen for size to fit his hand. The first player, from back of the circle line, shot his marble for the pot, holding the marble between forefinger and thumb and propelling it with a flick of the thumb. If he succeeded, he took all the marbles in the pot. If not (and usually he did not) the next player shot either for the pot or for the first player's marble on the field. If he hit the field marble, he took it, then had another shot for the pot. Successful, he took the pot and that game ended regardless of how many players were to follow. A new game started with all players contributing one marble to the pot. A player unsuccessful at hitting the field marble or the pot left his marble on the field and the next player took his turn.

Rules required that the marble shooter's hand must not touch the circle line as he shot. Rules could allow "spanning," which meant that when a shooter hit a marble on the field, he could place his thumb on the spot where the struck marble stopped, describe (with his fingers) a circle in the dirt, then shoot from any point on that circle.

A more complicated game included five holes: four dug at corners of a three foot square with the pot in the center. Players shot from hole to hole ("spanning" allowed on each hole) through the four holes and then for the pot. Shooting for field marbles was allowed all along the way, and a game with four or five players beginning the game usually ended as a contest between two. When the field held a taw from each player in the game, a shooter was allowed to try to clear the field, then shoot for the pot without shooting the four holes first. That decision required a very confident player gambling for high stakes on his own skill and luck—luck, because a pebble or minute uneven place on the ground could deflect his marble.

The marble games played on the home ground were modifications of the games of older boys and girls playing on school yards and at community gatherings.

MARCHING ROUND THE LEVEE

We're marching round the Levee
We're marching round the Levee
We're marching round the Levee
For we have gained the day.

Go forth and choose your lover
Go forth and choose your lover
Go forth and choose your lover
For we have gained the day.

I measure my love to show you
I measure my love to show you
I measure my love to show you
For we have gained the day.

I kneel because I love you
I kneel because I love you
I kneel because I love you
For we have gained the day.

Goodbye I hate to leave you
Goodbye I hate to leave you
Goodbye I hate to leave you
For we have gained the day.

Players, with hands joined, marched counterclockwise in a circle, singing; while "It" stood in the center. On "Go forth," "It" marched around the circle clockwise until the stanza ended.

On "day," at end of second stanza, "It" took the hand of the child nearest him in the circle and led the partner to the center of the ring. The two stood facing holding hands—right hand in right hand and left hand in left hand, so that the arms were crossed.

During the third stanza, the two seesawed their arms back and forth "measuring" their love. In the fourth stanza, "It" knelt before his partner, holding the partner's right hand in his right hand.

During the "Goodbye" stanza, the two stood shaking hands—left hand in right hand and right hand in left hand—until the last line was reached. "It" then left his chosen partner, joined the circle, and the game started from the beginning with a new "It" in the center.

Girls and boys from four and five years old to twelve and fourteen played "Marching Round the Levee" at community gatherings.

MUMBLEPEG

The game, played with a two-bladed pocketknife (both blades opening from the same end of the knife), was a game for spring or fall weather. Winter was too cold for sitting on the ground and in summer the ground was too dry. Moist soil, neither too wet nor too dry, was a necessity, as was a grassy turf where the grass was not too high. Bermuda grass was best with its intricate web of roots to hold the knife blade upright once it stuck. Two or three well-matched players—not more than three—made for a good game.

Each player owned his own mumblepeg knife, a Christmas or birthday present, likely, and chosen for that purpose; the weight, size, shape, and length of the handle were important in proportion to the lengths of the two blades, and the ratio of the lengths of the two blades was equally important. Each player played with his own knife, with which he had practiced long hours at every opportunity, for the game was long and depended on skill (more than luck) learned by watching and copying skilled players.

The game started with the easiest of all the tricks of skill and ended many plays later with the losers "rooting the peg." First play: the player held the knife (with the long blade open) by the tip of the blade between his thumb and forefinger; flipped it outward from him to make the blade stick into the ground upright (rule: when the knife slanted, the slant must allow the thrower's finger to pass between the knife handle and the earth; otherwise the thrower lost his turn to another player). The player flipped the knife thus three times.

Second play: a fist was made, first of the right hand; the open knife, placed across the fist (palm up) with the blade thumbward, rested in the trough made where the fingers clenched the palm. The fist then described a half-circle in the air counterclockwise, carrying the knife with it, giving the knife momentum on the downward movement, to plunge blade first into the ground. This move was repeated with the left hand.

Third play: the open knife was held on the palm of the outstretched right hand, blade pointing away from the body. The hand and arm then moved swiftly upward, describing an arc declining toward the body to make the knife describe a half-circle toward the body with momentum to plunge into the ground. The player usually stood on his knees, prepared, if necessary, to move backward from the descending knife. This move was repeated with the left hand.

Fourth play: the open knife was held on the hand as in the third move except that the back of the hand instead of the palm held the knife. The movements of the third move were duplicated.

Fifth play (called "breaking the chicken's neck"): the knife was held horizontally with its blade secured and balanced by the forefinger and middle finger of the left hand (on top of the forefinger and under the middle finger). The right forefinger struck the knife handle quickly, dislodging it, making it flip to describe a half-circle clockwise and plunge into the ground.

Sixth play: the knife was held in the right hand with the blade pointing down. The forefinger of the right hand pressed on the end of the handle and the handle secured between thumb and the other three. The point of the blade was poised on the tip of the thumb and forefinger (pinched together) of the left hand. The knife was then flipped by the right forefinger outward to describe a half-circle and plunge into the ground. Next the thumb and middle finger (left hand) formed a tip on which to poise the blade for another flip and plunge. Next, the thumb and ring finger and last the thumb and little finger.

Seventh play: the blade tip was poised on the back of the left hand, flipped, and plunged into the ground; then, in turn, it was poised on the wrist, on the elbow, on the shoulder, on the chest, on the top of the head.

Eighth play: the arms were crossed (right arm inside) so that each hand could grasp the tip of an ear. The right hand held the knife blade by the point and from the ear flipped the knife outward to stick in the ground. Then changing arms and hands the move was repeated.

Ninth play: by the thumb and forefinger the knife was held, handle down, by the blade tip, with the blade tip touching the chin; then it was flung out by a head and body movement carrying the knife into a counterclockwise half-circle; next it was released, point downward, to plunge into the earth. The play was repeated with the knife tip held, in turn, to the mouth, the nose, each eye, and the forehead.

Tenth play: the knife tip was held by the right hand (thumb and forefinger) and the knife thrown over the left shoulder to stick in the earth behind the thrower. This move was repeated with the left hand over the right shoulder.

Eleventh play (called "bucket in the well"): a circle was formed with the thumb and forefinger of the left hand, and the knife handle was held (blade down) by the right thumb and forefinger and dropped through the circle (or hole). Then the thumb and middle finger formed a second "well" to drop the "bucket" into, then the thumb and ring finger, and last, thumb and little finger.

Twelfth play: the shorter blade was half opened to form a right angle with the long blade. The knife was then placed on the ground, blades down, and pushed gently until the blade tips sank into the earth and anchored the knife to stand alone. The player, kneeling, gave the knife handle a whack upward and forward, sending the knife rotating through the air to land—and with good luck and skill—to stick into the ground, handle up, some ten to fifteen feet distant.

The first player to accomplish all twelve plays was the winner. He would then rule that all losers must "root the peg" or he could allow the other players to play the game out until only one peg rooter remained. A small, sturdy stick or twig was driven into the ground (with a knife handle as a hammer) so far that the rooter (required to remove it with his teeth—his hands behind him) got a mouthful of dirt in the process.

NEEDLE AND I

Needle and I
Come passing by
The thread keeps rolling through
Many a beau have I let go
But now I have caught you.

or

Many a lass have I let pass
But now I have caught you.

This singing game was played indoors or outdoors at community gatherings by children, boys and girls in their teens, and sometimes by young adults, usually playing in age groups with the little ones imitating their elders.

Two leaders (a boy and a girl, when teenagers or young adults played) whispered together, each deciding on a gift to offer the players: one might choose a gold locket, the other, a silver bracelet; or one a silver watch, the other a gold ring; or one an opal ring, the other a ruby stickpin.

The leaders then faced each other, joined hands, raised them to form an arch as in "London Bridge." The other players, singing, marched under the arch. On the word "you," the arched hands were lowered imprisoning "you." One of the two leaders whispered:

"Which had you rather have?
A diamond ring or a ruby broach?"

The imprisoned player whispered his choice and was ordered to take his place behind the leader whose gift he chose.

The players marched and sang until all players were lined up behind the two leaders.

A line was then scratched on the ground between the two leaders preparing for a tug of war. The two leaders joined arms (each grasping the wrists of the other, to make a double hold). Each player behind the leader put his arms around the player in front of him and grasped his own wrists in a double lock.

The leaders braced their feet. The followers pulled. The game ended in a pile of joyful boys and girls on one side of the line or the other. The joyful girls pretended to need help in getting to their feet and the joyful boys were glad to give them more help than they needed including a kiss when the night was dark.

NOISEMAKERS

Blowing leaves A slender, slick leaf (from a pear tree, for example) was held flat between the little fingers with the palms almost touching (hands were held as in prayer or suppliance). The leaf holder blew his breath through the opening at his thumb-knuckles, making the leaf vibrate; the harder he blew, the higher the pitch.

Popping paper sacks The top of the paper sack was gathered by the left hand closing it. The right hand, poking the forefinger into the closed sack, made a small opening. The popper blew his breath into the bag, filled it with air, closed it by clenching his left fist, struck it with his right fist. The game was to approach a playmate from the rear, pop the sack, and laugh when he jumped and ran.

Playing a comb A comb with tissue paper stretched over the teeth was played like a harmonica. Holding it between the lips and teeth, the player hummed a tune and the sound emitted through the comb teeth turned the human voice into a strange musical instrument.

ONE-EYED CAT

The game was called "One-Eyed Cat," "Two-Eyed Cat," or "Three-Eyed Cat," depending on the number and skill of players available. It was played with a ball (described in "Anty Over") and a bat (a tree limb, chosen and cut to resemble a baseball bat). The players first decided on the number of bases: home base and one more meant "One-Eyed Cat." (Cat eyes were bases other than home base.) Two leaders then chose teams from available players, after which they decided which team would be "in town" (up to bat) first and which "in the country" (in the field). To decide this matter, one leader grasped the bat close to the smaller end and tossed it to the opposing leader, who caught it as best he could, grasping it tightly. The first leader then grasped the bat with his right hand, above the hand of his opponent. The second leader in turn grasped the bat with his left hand above the grasp of the first leader. Thus alternating grasp above grasp the leaders approached the end of the bat close enough that one of the two could extend his thumb over the end of the bat and shout "No inch of crow picks" before his opponent shouted "Inch of crow picks." That accomplished, his team went to bat first. If, however, the opponent cried "Inch of crow picks" first, the opponent was allowed to grasp the end of the bat with his thumb and fingers and toss it over his head to land twelve feet away (determined by stepping off the space). If he succeeded, his team was "in town" first. Arguments over the measurement and also over "crow picks" often held up the game.

Two or four players played "One-Eyed Cat." When two played, the batter tried to hit the ball so that he could run to the base and home before the pitcher could hit him (by throwing) with the ball or could throw the ball between the runner and home base (the rule was decided before the game started).

When four players played, the field players usually played the positions of pitcher and fielder (no catcher). And the rule for putting a runner out was usually by tagging him with the ball. The batter was always out when his ball was caught. Younger players were sometimes allowed to catch the ball on one bounce.

Bases were large rocks, pieces of bark or an old sock or cap.

Rules for playing "Cat" were the subject of lengthy discussion and sometimes debate before a game could start. Score was kept by scratches in the dirt with stick or finger, and the game continued until the players grew tired or were called away by parents.

The best place for playing was in the north pasture when six or eight players were available. The road in front of the house was more often the playground in winter, summer, spring, or fall.

PACKSADDLE

A packsaddle was made by two players to carry a third (smaller) player. Each packsaddler grasped his own left wrist with his own right hand. The two faced; then, each with his left hand grasped the right wrist of his partner. The four hands thus formed a square.

Kneeling or squatting, the packsaddlers allowed the rider to mount (sit), then stood and carried the rider to some designation.

The packsaddle was useful to carry an injured playmate to safety or help. At community gatherings packsaddle races were held with teenage boys and girls—and sometimes young men and women—carrying smaller players as riders in races of one hundred yards or more. A packsaddle race was no easy ride for the rider, who learned by experience to cling to the saddlers. In the excitement of the race, the saddlers gave him a bronco busting ride at best and, at worst, let the saddle disintegrate from under him.

PAPER FOLDING AND CUTTING

Boats, hats, boxes, baskets, and windmills were made from folding a square of newspaper or school tablet paper. A six-inch square was the right size for a boat or a windmill, and a fifteen-inch square for a hat.

Stars, snowflakes, diamonds, hearts, lace, and boys and girls were cut from folded paper, and paper chains were made from strips of paper (old *Christian Observers*) one inch wide by six inches long pasted with flour paste. Because scissors were considered dangerous, Grandma supervised all paper-cutting. Paper boats were put afloat on rivulets made by spring and summer rains, and were followed by the child downstream as they made their way toward a branch, then on into the pool or toward Shuffle Creek. The boat follower's job was to disentangle them when they were caught in debris and to steer them where the rivulet forked. When water was flowing fast, the boat could capsize, become waterlogged, and sink helpless and permanently lost with its cargo of pebbles, acorns, and sticks. But the boat watcher carried spare boats in his pocket to launch in such an emergency, when he salvaged the sunken cargo if he could or foraged for new cargo in nearby territory.

Windmills were pinned to a stick, and the stick was held in the hand of a player running into the wind.

Paper hats were worn by soldiers mounted on broom or stick horses parading around the yard. They were also a part of a costume when players dressed up in grown-up clothing.

Rows and rows of boys joined hand to hand, and rows and rows of girls were cut from folded strips of the *Christian Observer* and pasted for decorations on windowpanes and walls, along with the linked diamonds and hearts. Lonely white stars and snow-flakes were pasted on doors and windows in long December days before Christmas.

PEEP-EYE

This game of Hide and Seek was played by an adult or an older child with an infant from six months to three or four years old. With a baby, the adult facing a baby (across the room on a pallet on the floor or on another person's lap) covered his own eyes saying, "Where is baby?" or "Where is Little Brother? I don't see him anywhere." Then uncovering one eye, the older player said, "Peep-Eye. *There* he is!" The child laughed.

Over and over, again and again, this ritual could continue indefinitely. After the form was well established, a baby one year old participated by hiding his own eyes. The older player then said, "Where is baby? I don't see him anywhere." The baby un-covered one eye and laughed.

Since the baby never wanted to stop, the older player could force the baby into more active participation by stopping the game after three or four repeats. The baby then was forced to take the initiative for the game to go on. Lacking verbal ability, he made sounds copying the inflections of the older player. The older player could lengthen the formula: "Peep-Eye. Where is baby? I don't see him anywhere," adding: "I wonder if he has gone away. Papa, have you seen baby? Do you think he may have gone to the kitchen? I'm afraid he'll *never* come back."

The monologue eventually was interrupted by the child's

uncovering one eye. The older the child and the longer he had been playing the game, the longer he kept his eyes covered.

When the older player's interest in the game was exhausted, he could say: "*There* he is. I'm so glad he has come back," then pick up the baby, kiss him and hug him, and say: "He has been gone so long, I'm sure he is thirsty. He needs a drink of water," meanwhile carrying the child to the back gallery for a drink. To divert him further, the older player could continue: "Now, I'm sure he is hungry. He has been gone so long. He needs a cookie." As the baby learned to talk, he first copied the words of the older player. The older player could encourage him to be inventive by varying the formula a little each time the game was played. To "Where *has* he gone?" he could add, "I wonder if he has gone to the sorghum mill" or "I think he may have gone to Mrs. Malloy's house to play with her guineas: put-track! put-tract! put-track!" (or "to Mrs. Hughey's to play with her ducks: quack, quack, quack!" or "to Mr. Calloway's to ride his donkey: honk-hee-honk-hee honk!" or "to the henhouse to count the little chickens: peep, peep, peep!") and on and on.

When a baby cried from a minor injury—a stumped toe, a mashed finger, or an ant sting—his attention could be diverted by saying, "Peep-eye. Don't cry. Sister loves the baby," and thus lead him into a game of "Peep-Eye."

PIGGYBACK

The small child rode the back of an older child or adult, straddling his hips and holding on with his hand over the shoulders or clinging to clothing. When the summer earth was too hot or when sandburs were too thick for bare feet, the shoeless child was offered a piggyback by a shod elder (playmate or grown-up).

Another method of transportation for barefoot children was to sit astride an elder's neck with hands locked around the elder's forehead. Occasionally, for short trips, a child sat on an elder's head, one foot on each of the elder's shoulders, with the elder holding his hands

When a grown man needed to carry two children, he set one on each shoulder, four legs dangling over his chest; he then pinned the legs down safely with his arms and the children put their arms around his head or clung to his hair.

PUSSY WANTS A CORNER

Indoors, the corners of the room were bases for four players, plus "It" (roving Pussy) trying to steal a corner. Outdoors, trees properly located made the bases, or stones or circles scratched in the dirt by finger or stick. The game was always adapted to suit the number of available players and the terrain.

Pussy approached a player standing in a corner and said, "Pussy wants a corner," and received the answer, "Go to the next neighbor." Pussy approached the child in an adjacent corner to repeat the question and receive the same answer. Meanwhile the other three players were busy signaling, preparing and agreeing for two to exchange corners. At the same time Pussy, knowing what was underway but pretending not to know, was tense, alert, and ready to dash for a vacant corner. If he was successful, the displaced player became Pussy and the game went on.

The game formula was varied by players calling, "Meow, Meow" and "Poor Pussy" to distract Pussy's attention.

RED ROVER

Two self-appointed leaders chose the players for two teams, who faced each other, each team standing behind a line scratched on the ground. The two parallel lines were about forty yards apart. The leaders then scratched a third parallel line midway between the two team lines.

The challenging team and their leader (the swiftest player, usually) decided on the member of the opposing team to be challenged. The challengers then called, "Red Rover, Red Rover, we dare Earl to come over." On "over," Earl left his home line, running toward the center line. The challenging leader left his home line on "over" and tried to tag Earl (three pats on the back) before he could reach the center line and return to his home base. A tagged player was required to join the opposing team, and the challenging team then issued another dare for another player. When a challenged player reached home base safely, his team then became the challengers.

As the game proceeded and the losing side had been reduced to the slower, younger players, the challenging team chose a player to match the skill of the challenged player and sent him out on the field.

RHYMES FOR MANY REASONS

1. *Amen, Brother Ben*
   Shot a goose and killed a hen.

   A mock prayer used in play for grace at table, funerals, church.

2. *Now I lay me down to sleep*
   I pray the Lord my soul to keep
   If I should die before I wake
   I pray the Lord my soul to take.

   Prayer said at bedtime, after the child was in bed.

3. *Goodnight, sleep tight*
   Wake up bright
   In the morning light
   And do what's right
   With all your might.

   Said in fun when a child bade another goodnight.

4. *H-U, huckle*
   B-U, buckle
   H-I, hi
   H-U, huckle
   B-U, buckle
   Berry pie

   Mock spelling.

5. *T-U, turkey*
   T-Y, tie
   T-U, turkey
   Buzzard's eye

   T-U, turkey
   T-Y, ting
   T-U, turkey
   Buzzard's wing

6. *Tattle tale, tattle tale*
   Hangin' on a cow's tail.

   For taunting an informer.

7. *Ask me no questions*
   I'll tell you no lies

Shut your mouth
And you'll catch no flies.

For taunting a child questioner; "Shut your mouth" was forbidden.

8.   *Mary's mad and I'm glad*
     And I know what will please her
     A bottle of wine to make her shine
     And a sweet little boy to squeeze her.

For teasing—outside of adult earshot.

9.   *Goody, goody gout*
     Your shirttail's out
     Goody, goody gin
     You can't get it in.

For teasing any child whose underwear was showing—underskirt, drawers, or shirttail.

10. First player   *What's your name?*
     Second player   *Puddin' Tame.*
     First player   *Where do you live?*
     Second player   *Down the lane.*

11. Child speaking   *Grandma Gray*
                                 Can I go play?

     Grandma Gray replying   *No, child*
                             It's too late in the day.

                             Grandma Gray
                             Can I go play?

                             Yes, child, yes
                             Just run away.

A dialogue carried on with Grandma for fun.

12. *It's Judah this and Judah that*
     And Judah skin the old gray cat
     The same old thing every day
     I never, never can go play.

A complaint, mumbled under the breath when the child was required to do too many chores.

13.   *If this book should chance to roam*
      Box its ears and send it home.

A flyleaf rhyme written in school textbooks.

14.   *April fool is gone and past*
      And you're the biggest fool at last.

When a child tried to trick another, he answered with this rhyme.

RING AROUND THE ROSIE

> *Ring around the rosie*
> *Pocket full of posie*
> *Last one squats*
> *Will be old Josie*

Very small children played this circle game with "Josie" in the center of the circle as the players joined hands, sang, and marched. When the word "Josie" was reached, they all popped down sitting on their heels, and the last one down took Josie's place in the center of the ring.

ROCK SKIPPING

Skipping rocks on water was a pastime of children and grown men. When neighbor families came for a Sunday afternoon visit, the women sat on the shady back gallery, the babies lay sleeping on quilt pallets nearby, the men took a walk over the farm to look over the crops, and the children followed the men. When the men sat down on a log in oak tree shade behind the barn, the children searched for rocks for rock skipping on the pool water nearby. Flat rocks with rounded edges were best (jagged or angular edges caught in the water and pulled the rock under) and they had to be of proper size to be held by the thumb and forefinger, secured underneath by the other three fingers.

When the skippers had their pockets full of skipping rocks, they congregated on one side of the pool for a skipping contest, and many times the men joined them.

To make a rock skip, the arm and hand were held so that the flatness of the rock was parallel with the water's surface. Then the body was bent to the right as the right arm, moving from the shoulder socket, flung the rock bouncing over the water's surface.

The skipper's object was to make his rock skip as many times as possible before it sank or to make it bounce with enough force to land on the far bank of the pool. Only men and big boys could produce the force for a bank landing. Children, in their agonized efforts to copy the men, sometimes threw themselves along with their rocks into the pool and either came wading ashore or, if they lost their balance in the water, were brought ashore, coughing and choking, by one of the men. In either case they emerged surrounded by a chorus of loud, humiliating laughter that prompted them to many private-practice, rock-skipping sessions before performing again with their elders.

ROOSTER FIGHTS

This game was a springtime game played on a Sunday afternoon walk in the woods and pastures when the wild violets were blooming. The players first gathered a fistful of violets each, then sat beside a branch or rivulet, dipping the violets in the water to keep them from wilting while they played their game, which continued until one player had no violets left.

Two players, each holding a violet by its stem, hooked the violet blossoms, then jerked. The owner of the decapitated violet was the loser. In gathering violets, the players searched for blossoms with sturdy hooked stems. As they played, they developed skill in hooking and jerking.

RUN, SHEEP, RUN

The players were a shepherd, a wolf ("It"), and any number of sheep. The game was played most successfully at twilight, in a large outdoor area with many good hiding places—trees, bushes, buildings.

The Wolf scratched a circle on the ground some six feet in diameter (the den), usually near a tree, bush, or corner of a building. The Shepherd drew another circle near another tree or bush (the fold) before he led his sheep off into the distance in and out and round about while the Wolf stayed at his den. The Shepherd hid his sheep, each one in a separate hiding place, and returned to the Wolf's den by a devious route.

The Wolf started his search for the sheep with the Shepherd following him, calling signals to the hidden sheep to let them know the Wolf's position. "Hot" and "cold" accompanied by other word or sound signals previously agreed upon told a sheep whether it was safe for him to run for the fold or whether he was in danger of being discovered and should be prepared to run for the fold.

When the Wolf spied a sheep, he called the sheep's name and pursued him as the sheep ran for the fold. If the Wolf was successful, the sheep went into the Wolf's den and the Wolf went searching for more sheep with the Shepherd following.

At this point the game became more complicated. A sheep in the Wolf's den could be liberated by another sheep who crept from his hiding place, tagged the prisoner, and ran with the liberated sheep back to a hiding place or safe to the fold. That could be accomplished by fleet sheep interpreting the Shepherd's signals correctly.

A sheep who had successfully raced the Wolf to the sheepfold then followed the Shepherd, who followed the foraging Wolf.

When the Wolf caught all the sheep and had all the sheep in his den at one time the game was over. Seldom did this happen. More often, the game went on and on with sheep caught, liberated, caught, and liberated again until the players grew tired or black night or parents stopped the game.

SEESAW

The seesaw was a plank, supported on a fulcrum: a carpenter's horse, a log, a stump, or the wagon tongue propped up on a keg. The best plank for a seesaw was ten to twelve feet long, at least an inch thick, and six to eight inches wide. When the plank was twelve inches wide, the seesawers rode sidesaddle. The seesaw plank was always borrowed from a pile of lumber destined to go eventually into a barn, shed, crib, house, stormhouse, or smokehouse. A plank of ideal proportions was seldom available and the seesawers adjusted their seesaw and seesawing techniques to fit the available materials.

When two seesawers were of the same weight (which they seldom were), the plank was always centered on the fulcrum and the two sat on the ends of the plank equidistant from the fulcrum. Otherwise, the heavier player could slide forward toward the fulcrum, allowing his playmate extra board for ballast. Or the board itself could be moved on the fulcrum to allow more board to the lighter player. Or, if a baby or very small child was available, he was taken on for ballast and balance.

Sometimes an agile third player waiting his turn on the seesaw stood on the plank with one foot on either side of the fulcrum and, shifting his weight from one foot to the other, speeded up the seesawing process.

A beginner at seesawing learned how to put his heels close together under the plank to push himself and the plank into the air and, by painful experience, how to spread his legs while coming down so that his heels would not be caught between the plank and ground.

He also learned from painful experience what happened when the seesawer at the other end jumped off without warning (from anger or ignorance — the results were the same). The ignorant jumper was punished by ostracism for a time or was rewarded with a return bump or two — and thereby learned from the bottom up. When anger motivated the jumper (or the injured player thought so), the jumper could expect vengeance whether or not the injured said, "I'll get even with you."

The unfinished seesaw planks were full of splinters, and picking splinters out of feet and legs was a regular aftermath of seesawing sessions. When the seesaw was in the back yard under the hackberry tree, the children remembered to go immediately to the sewing basket for a needle to remove the splinters. When the seesaw was in the barn lot or beyond, the splinters were often forgotten in the zest for other games. Splinters left in the flesh for a day festered and required attention from Mama, Grandma, or Papa, who preferred to use the tip of the small blade of his pocketknife to remove splinters. The wound was then wiped with turpentine or the foot was soaked in a pan of coal oil.

SHADOW FIGURES

Moving shadow figures were created by manipulating the hands and fingers between the lamplight and the wall, sometimes with a bedsheet fastened against the wall to make the shadows more distinct. The actors were older children or adults entertaining younger children with improvised dramatizations.

The characters created were a goose, a fox, and a donkey. The goose was made with one hand by folding the ring finger over the middle finger and propping the little finger tip on the knuckle of the ring finger so that a hole represented the goose's eye. The forefinger and the middle finger together operated as the goose's upper beak and the thumb as the lower beak.

A fox was made with one hand simply by holding the thumb extended as the fox's pointed ears, holding the forefinger, middle finger and ring finger together to operate as the fox's nose and upper lip, and allowing the little finger to move up and down as the fox's lower lip. An agile actor could make the fox's nose (middle finger) tremble as if sniffing food.

Two hands were used to make the donkey's head. The forefinger and middle finger of the right hand (the thumb clung to the hand) were separated and extended for the donkey's ears. The left hand, making a fist, grasped the ring finger and little finger of the right hand to form the head of the donkey.

Since the goose and the fox required only one hand, one actor could operate two characters. Usually, however, two actors played the parts. The actor acting the donkey could be nothing but a donkey; and since the donkey's actions were limited to the movement of his ears and his head, the actor's ingenuity was taxed to make him a believable talking donkey.

The actors operated their shadow figures as puppets, hiding their own bodies behind a table, a chair, or a bed, the shadow of which formed a stage.

One favorite dramatization presented the goose busily eating corn (real corn picked up and apparently swallowed as the goose lifted its beak). The fox approached, nose quivering; talked to himself about deferring the slaughter until the goose was fat; crept closer and closer until he was ready to pounce upon the unsuspecting goose. Startled by the donkey's bray (off stage), the wolf stopped. The goose stopped eating, turned, saw the wolf, said "Dear Me" or "Mercy me," and raced off quack quacking. Soon the donkey appeared, braying loudly. As the donkey advanced, the fox closed his mouth, skulked, and crept backward. The donkey stopped braying and said, "What are you doing here?" The fox lied, quivering his nose and bowing obsequiously, saying (perhaps), "I came to visit my cousin who lives over yonder."

To that the donkey would reply, "Very well, I'll trot along with you. I'd like to meet your cousin." The fox, caught in his lie, might reply, "Oh, no! He is not at home."

Donkey How do you know?
Fox The goose told me.
Donkey Where did the goose say your cousin has gone?
Fox The goose failed to tell me.
Donkey Come, let's go find the goose and ask her.
Fox No, no. Thank you kindly. I must go home. I have the stomachache.

Donkey   Let me go with you. I'll give you a dose of castor oil.
That will cure your stomachache.
Fox   No! No! My stomachache is gone but I have a chill.
Donkey   Then I'll give you three tablespoonfuls of Groves Chill
Tonic, two capsules of quinine, and a big dose of calomel.
Fox   No! No! Mercy no! [retreating from sight saying over and
over in quivering voice] No! No! Mercy no!
Donkey   [calling after him] When you get well and come again,
I'll be waiting for you. I want to meet that cousin of yours.

The improvised plays always presented the fox as the villain,
the goose as the intended victim, and the donkey as the savior.
The dialogue differed in every play. The actors prided themselves
on their originality. Sometimes the goose and fox carried on a
lengthy conversation, with the fox snapping at the retreating,
pleading goose.

When small children played with shadow figures in imitation
of their elders, their plays were truncated versions of the plays
they had seen and heard. They did not parrot the dialogue,
however, but exercised their own originality by having the fox
say, for example, "I have a stomachache. Get out of my way. I
am going to throw up," or "I've got to go home because I've got
the measles."

Shadow plays were winter evening diversions for Friday night
when no school lessons had to be learned for the morrow and
Saturday night while the children were having their turns at the
weekly bath. On a cool rainy evening in summer, spring, or fall,
a shadow play sometimes developed spontaneously.

A daytime imitation of the shadow puppets was contrived
with hand puppets made of a man's pocket handkerchief or a
square of cloth torn from an old sheet. A corner of the square
was tied into a knot. The child stuck his forefinger into the knot
so that the folds of the knot were over his fingernail. The flat side
of the knot was the face of the puppet. Eyes, nose, and mouth
were drawn on with a pencil. The corner of the cloth square
protruding from the puppet's head could be bent and turned in
different directions to simulate different kinds of hats. Sometimes
a bird feather (or feathers), a flower, or a blade of grass was
stuck into the knot.

As with shadow figures, the actors hid themselves behind a

bed or table, held their hand puppets above the bed or table stage, and made them talk. The characters were people and animals.

SIGNS AND SIGNALS

In situations where children were forbidden to talk, they communicated with signs and signals. Sticking the tongue out (and sticking the chin out at the same time) at another child was a silent way of doing battle. The act could initiate a battle or be retaliation—and often the two were inseparable.

A child at supper table, suddenly remembering some unfair play of a sister or brother during the day, caught his adversary's eye and stuck his tongue out while his parents' attention was elsewhere. To express extraordinary anger, he squinted his eyes, wrinkled his nose, and jutted his chin out as far as possible while sticking his tongue out and wiggling it sideways. The adversary replied, trying to outdo the contortions of his challenger, or shrugged his shoulders and wrinkled his nose, meaning "I'll get even with you later." "Getting even" later could be leading the playmate into a sandbur patch, dumping him on the seesaw, or barring him from a game. "Making faces" was a kind of game. At supper table, where children were not allowed to sing, whistle, laugh, or talk except with permission, a child who felt safe from adult scrutiny puffed out his cheeks, pulled his lower eyelids down, wrinkled his nose, and moved it up and down, to entice the children across the table to laugh—and be scolded for it.

"Making faces" and sticking the tongue out were directed at adults as well as children, but with an important difference. The child faced his child adversary but not his adult adversary. He made faces and stuck out his tongue "behind his Papa's back" or "Mama's back" either in anger (sticking the tongue out) or in derision (making a face).

One child could "shame" another ("to shame" meant to embarrass) by moving his right forefinger over his left forefinger in a stroking movement (like whittling). The shamed child retaliated either by sticking out his tongue or "getting even" later.

Walking "prissy" was another way of expressing defiance, derision, protest, or bravado. Walking "prissy" meant to prance or swagger, moving fast and swinging the buttocks from side to side in an exaggerated way. When directed at another child, the protester made sure the other child was aware of his protest.

When directed at an adult, the adult was not looking—or so the child hoped.

SKIN THE CAT

A sturdy tree limb in horizontal or near-horizontal position, the right size for a child's hand-hold (say, four or five feet from the ground) was the usual equipment for skinning cats. Sometimes a horizontal bar was contrived by propping an old rake handle or hoe handle in the forks of two adjacent trees or saplings.

With practice the cat-skinner acquired the necessary nimbleness to skin cats three ways: (1) He grasped the bar with both hands, next he flung one leg followed by the other forward, up and through the opening made between his head and the bar, turned the bar loose, and landed on his feet. (2) He went through the movement described above but instead of dropping to the ground, he reversed the movement and landed in his original position. That double cat-skinning depended on the agility and strength of the twisted wrists. (3) He sat on the bar, holding the bar on either side of his body, threw his head back to unbalance his body, flung his legs after his head, and landed on his feet. That was called "Skinning the cat backwards."

There were hazards in cat-skinning, whether the bar was a limb or a hoe handle. A limb small enough for a child's hand could bend too much or crack and dump the cat-skinner on his head. The hoe handle, never securely fastened, could slip out of the tree fork, dumping him and whacking him simultaneously.

SKIPPING

The simplest skipping step (the sliding hop forward first on one foot then the other) had its variations and various uses. In skipping races, the arms with elbows bent, moved as in running, to propel the body forward forcing longer strides and slides. Skipping races were sometimes endurance tests instead of speed tests, to see who could skip around the yard the longest.

Skipping into the wind, the skipper held his arms out like wings, bent his hop-sliding leg to propel his body upward as well as forward in long, high skipping leaps.

In prissy skipping, the skipper made short skips, throwing the buttocks from side to side in swaggering jerks usually in rhythm with a rhyme, like:

Brother's mad and I am glad
And I know what will please him
A bottle of wine to make him shine
And a sweet little girl to squeeze him.

Another skipping step required outstretched arms for balance. The feet moved forward one behind the other. First, the right foot stepped forward carrying the weight of the body; then the weight shifted to the left foot on a sliding hop which sent the right foot forward again to regain balance.

A skipper chose his skipping ground carefully: the clean swept yard or the sandy road, free from sandburs, chicken doings, and horse and cow manure.

SLINGSHOTS

The simplest slingshot was a long, green willow twig performing as a catapult with a mud or clay ball (ammunition) stuck on one end. The twig was held by the other end; and the whole arm (swinging from the shoulder) and the twig acted as the catapult to sling the clay or mudball with great force at some target. The catapulter fixed his eye on his target—a knothole on the side of the barn, a fence post, or a tree trunk—and let go at it. Each player collected a pile of clay balls about two inches in diameter; each fired away at the target agreed upon and kept account of his own hits and misses. The player with the greatest number of hits in ten shots (or the number agreed upon) was winner.

A slightly more complicated slingshot was made of a piece of an old leather shoe-tongue (an oval about three inches long and two inches across) and two pieces of string or boot laces, each about fifteen inches long. A nail was used to punch a hole in each end of the leather oval, about one-third of an inch from the edge, and a string was attached to each end by drawing it through the hole and tying it in a hard knot. Small stones and acorns were ammunition. The loose ends of the two strings were held fast in the right hand, one between the thumb tip and forefinger tip and the other between the ring and middle fingers. The leather oval was thereby folded into a pocket to hold the ammunition, placed and held there by the left hand until the player, using his arms and the string as a catapult, started his swing creating the pull to hold the stone or acorn in place. With his eye on his target—knothole, fence post, barn, stump—the catapulter swung his arm and sling counterclockwise in an overhand throw, releasing one string — and thereby the ammunition — as he brought his arm forward.

The most complicated slingshot (made of a forked limb about six or eight inches long, shoelaces, and an old leather shoe-tongue) required adult help in the making. A limb of the right size was a half inch in diameter and forked symmetrically. The limb was cut so that the two forks (about three inches long) formed part of the catapult and the limb itself made the handle. Finding the right tree limb entailed a long search sometimes. Once the forked limb was cut and the forks notched for fastening the shoelaces, a child could complete the sling. A piece of shoe-lace about six inches long was attached to the notched end of each fork. The other end of one piece was attached to one end of shoe-tongue pocket. This slingshot operated in the same way as the string and leather sling.

SMOKING AND DIPPING

Smoking tobacco and dipping snuff were two adult activities imitated by children (without adult approval). Children made their own corncob pipes, and in place of tobacco, coffee grounds, dried mullein leaves (crushed), and dried corn silks (crushed) were smoked. Imitation cigarettes were pieces of grapevine, pieces of an old buggy whip handle, and coffee grounds rolled in cornshuck. Imitation snuff was coffee grounds dipped with a toothbrush made of a small feeder root from a redbud or elm tree. The root piece, about three inches long, was chewed at one end into a brush of fine, silken fibers, dipped into the coffee grounds, and then placed in the mouth at an angle, with the brush part in the cheek.

Coffee grounds were smuggled from the kitchen in snatched handfuls, wrapped in a piece of paper so folded as to open into a funnel at one end in imitation of a tobacco sack or Garrett snuffbox. Matches were stolen, three or four at a time.

Children learned where and how to look for redbud and elm roots; the distance from the tree trunk depended on the size of the tree; and scratching the soil with the big toenail discovered the ridges made by the feeder roots. A feeder root, discovered, was followed with the toe or pocketknife away from the tree until the roots were small enough for toothbrushes. The small roots were then dug out, cut, and cleaned of dirt by wiping them on leaves or grass.

To make a good corncob pipe, the artisan chose a dry corncob, cut a piece for the pipe bowl, reamed out the pith with a pocketknife — careful to leave sufficient pith to make a bottom for the bowl — and punctured one side of the bowl with the tip of the blade, reaming the hole the proper size for insertion of the pipe stem. Either before or after that operation, he made a trip to the canebrakes in the creek bottom to choose and cut a bamboo shoot the right size for the pipestem. Making the stem fit into the bowl satisfactorily came with practice. Meanwhile, the smoker held the stem in place with one hand and the bowl (which grew hotter and hotter) with the other. If the smoker smoked his "tobacco" down too close to the pith bottom of the bowl, he discovered his pipe on fire and rushed to the creek, branch, or pond to douse it.

Grapevine for cigarettes called for a trip to Shuffle Creek beyond the canebrakes. Children learned to choose old, dry vine ends sufficiently porous to allow the smoke to be sucked through into the mouth. An old buggy whip handle, it was discovered by trial, had the right degree of porousness for smoking and one old handle was cut into a dozen cigarettes. Grapevine cigarettes were easy to make and the smoke held a special fragrance, but the aftereffect was a sore tongue and mouth.

When neighbor boys and girls came visiting, smoking, dipping, and spitting sessions took place on the banks of Shuffle Creek or by the poolside behind the barn. Boys were better than girls at rolling cornshuck cigarettes, which they shared pridefully with the girls. The dippers allowed little dribbles of brown saliva to trickle from the corners of their mouths.

On a summer Sunday afternoon, under pretense of "taking a walk" (a permitted Sunday pastime), the children assembled their smoking supplies, then sat smoking and dipping in watchful silence, alert to the sound of adult footsteps and to sounds of spying Little Brother, who had been barred from the group because he was a tattletale.

STIFF STARCH

Two players faced and each held out his hands (fingers together and fingertips cupped) to form a hook of each hand. One player (overhanded, palms down) hooked his finger over his partner's fingers (palms up). The two stood toe to toe, leaned bodies backward as far as the arms could stretch, then stepped in mincing, tiptoe steps, keeping the toes together in the same spot to make an axis for their rotating bodies, rotating faster and faster until centrifugal force loosened their hands, flinging each sprawling on the ground, or until too dizzy to stand, they fell in a heap of laughter.

STILTS

Stilts were made for small children by adults (Papa, a hired hand, or a neighbor man). The two uprights were boards one inch by two inches by four feet, planed for safety from splinters. The base of the stirrup was a triangle—half of a four-inch-square board, one inch thick.

One foot from the bottom end of the upright, the triangle was nailed at a right angle to the flat side of the upright, centered, and with the hypotenuse underneath. A piece of leather about seven or eight inches long, usually harness reins, was firmly nailed or tacked along the hypotenuse, brought upward, stretched taut, and fastened to the upright about four or five inches above the stirrup base.

Adults or older children taught beginners to mount their stilts and to balance themselves, giving support from the rear as the stiltswalker walked forward. To mount without assistance, the child learned to stand bracing his back against a wall and bracing his stilts, one under each arm; to place one foot, then the other in a stirrup; and finally to hoist himself into the stirrup and push his body away from the wall into a walk.

When children developed enough skill on beginners stilts to walk, run, and hop, they wanted higher-stepping stilts and made them or tried to make them with stirrups two or three feet off the ground. These were mountable only from a stump, box, keg, or fence rail. The first child-made high-stepping stilts were never as sturdy as ones made by adults: the stirrup base, not firmly fastened to the upright, gave way under the walker's foot; or uprights poorly planed with a pocketknife instead of a carpenter's plane produced splinters to make stiltswalker's hands sore for days. When leather was not available for the stirrup, baling wire was substituted; and though baling wire was easy to manipulate to make the stilt, it rusted quickly and, sooner or later, always broke.

When a stirrup broke, the walker fell sprawling sideways, trapped by one stirrup and whacked by both uprights as he fell. He had to learn how to throw a broken stilt away from himself as he fell and how to disengage a foot from a stirrup in a stumbling fall.

Learning stiltsmaking and stiltswalking were both parts of one process. From his spills, the child learned — sometimes by asking for adult help — how to make nonspilling stilts as well as how to take the spills.

Racing, dancing (to singing), hopping, and jumping over logs or low bushes were favorite activities on stilts.

STRING GAMES

Among the favorite string figures were "Crow's Foot," "Double Crow's Foot," and "Cup and Saucer." A string about thirty-six inches long, ends tied together in a hard knot, was manipulated by the hands — and for certain figures, by the teeth — in a series of moves which created geometric patterns labeled with metaphoric names.

"Crow's Foot" and "Double Crow's Foot" could be performed by one player; but "Cup and Saucer" required another player's help in one of the series of moves. All three figures began in the same way: the hands were held about fourteen inches apart, palms facing, with the string looped around the four fingers of each hand (thumbs free) and pulled taut. The next move was also basic to the three figures: the right hand pulled the left-hand string up and over the middle and ring fingers to the palm side. The left hand duplicated the move on the right hand. From that point, the moves differed for the three figures.

On Sunday afternoons when neighbor families visited each other, children and adults (both men and women) together contrived string figures to display their dexterity.

SUMMERSETS (SOMERSAULTS)

Turning somersaults both forward and backward was a favored activity on grassy knolls or indoors on quilt pallets on the floor. Forward somersaults were turned from a standing position to standing position; or they might start from a sitting position, in which case the child, knees drawn to chest and held there, wrapped by his arms, head resting on his knees, pushed himself into a forward rolling ball and kept rolling.

Backward somersaults started from the same sitting position; the child, throwing his head backward and simultaneously pushing himself backward with his feet, executed a single somersault but no roll.

Occasionally children had somersault races outdoors, turning forward from a standing positon.

SWINGING

The rope swing suspended from the limb of the hackberry tree in the backyard was made of hemp rope about one inch in diameter. The limb from which the swing swung (about twelve feet from the ground) was about six to eight inches in diameter and chosen for its sturdy size and level horizontal position. The seat of the swing was a planed board four or five inches wide and eighteen inches long, with a triangular notch in the middle of each end. Each end of the rope—twenty-four and one-half feet long—was attached to a piece of harness trace-chain long enough to encircle the tree limb; and the trace-chains encircled the limb sixteen inches apart so that the hanging rope (with its notched seat in place) hung in parallel lines.

A swinger could swing himself without assistance if the distance of the swing seat from the ground was no more than the length of his legs from his knees to his heels. But if his heels could not touch the ground, he could not push backward with his toes with force enough to set the swing in motion and therefore needed help to start.

With a good start, a swinger could "pump" himself six or eight feet high by pushing his legs forward and pushing his body backward as the swing started its forward pendulum drive.

Attaining an elevation of six or eight feet, the swinger had two choices about what to do next. He could jump from the swing at the end of its forward movement and sail through the air describing an arc that landed him on his feet—he hoped—some ten feet beyond his jumping place. On the other hand, he could choose to climb to and stand on the swing seat, holding the rope at elbow level, and pump himself still higher with the added leverage of his entire body—as high, sometimes, as the limb from which the swing swung. Having gained additional height, he could then sit down again and jump into a higher, farther sail through the air.

"Push me" was the request for help in getting started. The complying playmate then stood behind the swinger (sitting in the immobile swing), grasped each end of the swing seat, pulled the swinger-and-swing backward several steps, ran forward, pushing the swing and swinger ahead of him, and released his hold only when the pendulum carried the swinger above his reach. Freed of his load, the pusher ran under the swinger and out of danger of being hit by the returning swing.

Two swingers standing, facing each other, pumping alternately, could go higher faster.

Small children whose feet could not touch the ground were given free rides by older playmates who "pushed" and "ran under" them. An older player sometimes gave a small child a free ride by allowing the child to sit facing him, astride his body, holding the rope, as the seated swinger propelled the swing. Babies, too young to hold the rope, were given free rides as they sat in the lap of an older swinger who encircled the rope and child with his arms while a third playmate pushed them into motion. Children took turns in the swing according to pre-agreement: the swinger was allowed twenty pumps (or more or less) and then either jumped or "let the cat die" before releasing the swing to a playmate.

A child playing alone could sit on the swing board, push with one foot to make the swing board go around in a circle to twist the rope, and then lift his feet from the ground to allow the unwinding rope to whirl him into dizzy stillness.

Swinging on grapevines, tree limbs, and saplings were activities that took place during Sunday afternoon walks through the woods and fields. Wild grapevines that grew along the banks of Shuffle Creek invited wild swinging matches that carried swingers —clinging with both hands to a hanging grapevine—out over the water, and with good luck, to the bank beyond. The vine could break or tear loose from its mooring and dump the swinger into the water. Or on a hot day the swinger could loosen his hold on the vine and, once in the water, stay to cool off.

Grapevine swinging was forbidden except with adult supervision, because quicksands and shifting creek bottoms following flood waters made Shuffle Creek water treacherous. The rule was obeyed because of fear of quicksand.

Tree limb swinging was also forbidden because of the danger of limbs breaking. The tree-limb swinger climbed the tree trunk of a large tree; then, straddling a high limb, worked his way out to smaller and smaller limbs until he could catch a slimmer limb on which to swing to the ground. Girls, forbidden to climb trees when boys were in the play group, disobeyed when parents were absent. And boys and girls both disobeyed the no-limb swinging rule, trusting their own ability to choose dependable limbs.

Elm saplings were among the best for swinging, though few saplings of any kind on the farm grew to trees without marks of a swinger. The sapling swinger, hoisted up the trunk by a playmate, rode it hand over hand to the end until it bent, taking him down to the ground. Then, holding the end firmly in both hands, he moved in a circle around the trunk in high bouncing leaps, making the sapling propel him upward in its attempt to spring upright again.

THIMBLE, THIMBLE

On a cold, rainy afternoon or evening, sitting with the children in a circle by the fire, Grandma Gray was a player in the game she had taught them; and it was her thimble.

Each player sat with hands held in his lap, palms together. One player walked around the circle with his palms together enclosing the thimble. As he approached each player, he said, "Hold fast all I give you." And wedging the hands of the seated player slightly open with his own slightly parted palms, he transferred the thimble or pretended to. The receiver's hands reclosed and the player dissembled possession whether or not he had actually received the thimble.

The thimble bearer repeated the ritual, "Hold fast all I give you," with every child in the circle, after which he called on a player and said, "Thimble, thimble, who's got the thimble?" When the answer was correct, the guesser became the next thimble bearer. When wrong, the thimble bearer said, "Rise up, Thimble."

The thimble possessor arose and became the thimble bearer for the next round.

The game was an outdoor pastime too, on a hot afternoon when sitting quietly in the shade was preferable to running on the sun-hot sand. When neighbor children came to play, boys and girls played the game together, substituting an acorn or a pebble for a thimble.

TICK TACK TOO

Two different games were called "Tick Tack Too." Both were played with pencil and paper, or slate: one, on a square diagram divided into nine small blank squares; and the other on a circle divided into quadrants and redivided to make eight segments, with a number, chosen at random, written in each segment. The first game was limited to two players. In the second, three or four players could play.

More often played indoors on rainy days with adults participating, both games were favored outdoor pastimes in quiet shade on a hot summer day.

In the first game each player, with his own mark—either an "X" or a "O"—placed his mark on a square, taking turns until all squares were marked. The player's object was to mark three adjacent blocks and meanwhile block his opponent from doing so. The first player with three marks in line won the round. Players agreed beforehand on an odd number of rounds for a game—from five to thirteen. When the number was five and one player had won three, he declared himself winner of the game and a new game began.

In the second game, a blindfolded player tapped with his pencil on the slate or paper with the segmented circle drawn on it and said:

Tick Tack Too
Round I go
If I miss
I'll take this.

On "this" he rested his pencil, took off his blindfold, and registered his score—the number in the segment indicated by the pencil. That number was then erased or crossed off and voided. If the pencil fell on a line, or a space voided, or outside the circle, the player won no points and lost his turn to the next player. He could continue to play, however, as long as he scored. The game ended when a player reached an agreed-upon score or when all numbers had been voided. In the latter case, the high score won.

TOP-SPINNING

Tops were homemade: cones were whittled from hardwood and grooved to hold the string wound around them. The best string for top-spinning was made of hard thread tightly twisted. The length of the string was in proportion to the size of the top: long enough to be wound spirally from the top's tip almost to the edge of the convex bulge of the top's top, with additional string held and anchored between the forefinger and middle finger by a button attached to the end of the string. A knot was tied in the other end of the string to anchor the string in winding. The top spindle was a nail, driven through the center of the cone and emerging through the apex, or inserted in a bored hole when the wood was too hard for nailing. The nail point was filed to a symmetrical spindle.

Once wound, the top was held with the entire hand, fingers spread and cupped around the top, with its flat surface against the palm directly below the forefinger and middle finger holding the anchored string. Standing with feet spread for balance, the top-spinner threw the wound top to the ground in an overhand movement, releasing it to unwind itself from the string and hit the ground with momentum to carry it into a long spin.

Top-spinners held contests to see whose top could spin the longest; they made their tops travel by flinging them at the ground at an angle and, in this fashion, held top races.

When neighbor families came to visit and big boys and men took to top-spinning, top-plugging was a favorite pastime. For top-plugging a circle was scratched on the ground — some two feet in diameter. The first spinner (determined by drawing straws or matches) threw down his top into the circle; the second spinner, in throwing down his top, tried to strike the first top at an angle to knock it out of the circle. Successful, he claimed the top. Unsuccessful, he left his top in the circle along with the first top. The third spinner either attempted to plug one of the two at an angle to make it leave the ring in such a way as to knock out the other top also, or he simply tried to plug and strike one top out of the circle and, if successful, claim the top and the right to plug the second in the ring.

If, in plugging, a spinner split a top (his own or the plugged top), he received all the tops in the ring as compensation; and if there were no other tops in the ring, the owner of the plugged top owed the plugger a top for immediate or future delivery. Splitting a top was a feat of strength and dexterity.

A child sometimes made his own top by driving a nail through a large spool (from sewing thread), whittling one end of the spool into a cone, and filing the nail point emerging from the cone's apex into a spindle. His was a poor substitute for one made by his father: it lacked weight and balance because of the lightweight wood of the spool; and it wobbled from an off-center spindle, careening uncontrollably into bushes or veering crazily to a standstill.

TRICKS

April Fool tricks—tricks by lying—were allowed on one day of the year only. Children tricked their parents and each other and parents tricked children. Some favorite tricks in varying disguises were played again and again.

1. A trickster told a victim he had a spot of soot or dirt on his face. The unsuspecting victim looked in a mirror and the trickster called, "April Fool!"

2. A trickster told his victim his shoelace was untied. When the victim leaned forward to look, the trickster slapped him on the buttocks and shouted, "April Fool!"

3. A trickster, looking from the kitchen window, shouted excitedly, "The cows are in the yard." All hands rushed into the empty yard trailed by the trickster's laughter and "April Fool!"

4. One child told his brother or sister, "Mama said to tell you to go bring her a load of stovewood." After the victim lugged the wood and dumped it in the wood box, the trickster called "April Fool!" from a distance and ran.

5. Mama and Papa had an annual April Fool dialogue based on Mama's birthday, March 31, and her wedding day, April 2. At breakfast on April 1, Papa said to Mama, "Well, well, Lou, so far you've missed being a fool twice." "I missed the first time but I'm not yet sure about the second time," was her reply.

6.   An intended victim, suspecting trickery, would answer a trickster's invitation with "April Fool yourself."

7.   Small children, attempting to prolong April Fool tricks into April 2, 3, and beyond, were told:

> *April Fool has come and passed*
> *And you're the biggest fool at last.*

Favorite tricks were played throughout the year:

8.   A child stealthily approached a playmate from the rear, clapped his hands over his unsuspecting friend's eyes, and stood silent while the blinded child tried to guess his name. The victim was allowed to feel the clothing of his attacker but was not allowed to turn around.

   If the blinded child failed to guess with three guesses, he tried to free himself by twisting his body and tripping the prankster; and the two fell to the ground in a laughing wrestling match.

9.   A child aware of an unsuspecting playmate approaching hid behind a tree, a building, a stump, or a barrel; waited; jumped into the friend's path shouting, "Boo!"

10.   Men and older boys played rowdier tricks. During the height of the watermelon season, late July and August, crowds of big neighborhood boys stole watermelons for the fun of it. Watermelons were plentiful and no farmer begrudged their thievery. Custom did not permit the robbed farmer a passive role, however. In this favored Sunday afternoon game, his role was to sit just inside the kitchen door with loaded shotgun at hand, watching for signs of boys crawling through the fence into the watermelon patch beyond the orchard. At the first sure sign, he left the house by the front door and crept toward the orchard, hiding behind hedge rows and fence weeds. Approaching the thieves as near as possible without danger of discovery, he waited until every boy had picked and was carrying a melon and was headed toward the fence.

    The blast of the shotgun as he shot high into the air (to allow the pellets to drop harmlessly ahead of the boys) blasted the boys into a run as the watermelons jumped out of their arms to splash open on the ground.

Watching the boys stumble over the melons or through the broken ones and crawl through the fence or roll under it leaving pieces of clothing caught on the bobwire, so shook the farmer with laughter that he seldom could steady his trigger finger for a second shot.

When the boys disappeared into the woods on the next farm, the farmer retrieved any patches of clothing, a dropped pocketknife, or any evidence useful in the next phase of the game. For the game was not over with the Sunday afternoon raid, pursuit, and flight. The weeks that followed were weeks of silence on both sides. The farmer waited for a patch to appear on a boy's pants or shirt, then pulled from his pocket the piece left on the wire fence and silently matched it with the patch on the clothing. Man and boy both laughed. Everybody there laughed in wordless glee. And the game was over.

Or at a neighborhood gathering the robbed farmer brought out the pocket knife dropped in the watermelon patch, began whittling on a stick, whittled in silence until he was sure the owner saw and recognized his property. His continued silence was a signal to the older men, one of whom responded by asking:

"You got a new pocketknife there?"
"Nope."
"I seen that knife before somewhere. Lon Hughey, have you seen that knife before?"
"Yep, seen it somewhere. Don't recollect where. Ace, you seen that knife before?"
"Yep. Seen it somewhere. Don't recollect where, though. Sam, you seen that knife before?"
"Yep. Seen it somewhere. Don't recollect where, though."

The ritual was continued from man to man and boy to boy in stern seriousness until the last boy—Cob, the owner of the knife—was asked:

"Cob, you seen that knife before?"

Cob blushed, grinned; the men slapped their legs and whooped their laughter while the knife was handed to its owner.

11.   When men rode to Wills Point in Van Zandt County on horseback, mule, or donkey, and tied their steeds to the

hitching rack in front of the saloon and later got drunk inside, their more sober friends played tricks on them by rearranging their steeds so that the owners rode home on the wrong mounts.

Or the tricksters turned the animals around, tied their tails to the hitching rack, put their saddles on backward, and waited for the fun when the stupified owners tried to mount and ride away. One victim, Orphus Trailer, was said to have mounted his donkey backward and, seeing no head, wept aloud, "Somebody cut my ass's head off."

12. Circuit-riding preachers were favorite victims of the tricks of big boys whose fear of hell and hopes of heaven were eclipsed by their delight in the preacher's discomfort. Stories of these tricks were retold again and again.

The preacher always rode in on Saturday night, spent the night in the home of a member of his congregation, preached the Sunday morning sermon, and went his way. His steed was stabled and fed in his host's barn. On one occasion, the farmer's stalls were all occupied with his own stock so the preacher's mule was stabled in a log corncrib which had a wooden floor.

During the night, the big boys, by removing the logs one at a time from the top of the crib and inserting them one at a time under the bottom of the crib, gradually built the crib floor higher and higher until, by morning, the mule was stabled in a second floor crib.

Reckoning the time the preacher would be saddling his horse to ride to church, one of the big boys arranged to happen by on his way to church in time to watch and listen to the perplexed preacher and farmer devising schemes to get the mule down. He offered help but no advice.

Later, a second boy appeared, on his way to church, to offer help but no advice; then a third and a fourth until all the tricksters were on the scene and the farmer had decided the only workable scheme was to lift the mule down with block and tackle.

One of the boys then spoke up and suggested a simpler method: removing one log at a time from the bottom until the crib floor was in its original place. That was soon done and the preacher—none the wiser but three hours too late for church—loped off down the road out of hearing of their laughter.

TUG OF WAR

Tug of War was a team game played at neighborhood gatherings. Grown men and women and children as young as five years old played together. To divide the group into teams, two well-matched men challenged each other, then taking turns, chose their teams, one player at a time. The strongest players were chosen first, the children last.

A heavy hemp rope some forty feet long was grasped by both hands by the players lined up along the rope in facing teams. Little children were always placed toward the ends of the lines for protection.

A line at right angles to the rope was scratched on the ground and the lead man of each team stood back about four feet from the line as the Tug of War began. The teammates along the rope spaced themselves so that each could brace himself with spread feet when the pull came.

The teams readied for a signal to pull, and each team tried to pull the other over the line. The victory could come from strength and weight or from teamwork. A leader who knew how to get his team to heave in rhythm could win against a heavier, stronger team disorganized by extraneous interests as when courting boys and girls were more interested in courting than in pulling.

Once a leader was pulled over the line, the losing team often let the rope go, sending the winners stumbling backward into a pile of bodies.

WILLIAM TREMBLE TOE

Players sat in a circle on chairs, on the floor, or on the ground. Each placed two or more fingers (as agreed on) before him on the floor, ground, or table with fingertips converging. One player, the counter, tapped each finger in turn in rhythm with the chant:

William, William, Tremble Toe
He's a good fisherman
Catches hens

Puts them in pens
Some lay eggs
Some none
Wire briar limberlock
Three geese in a flock
One flew east
One flew west
And one flew over the cuckoo's nest.
O–U–T spells out
You old dirty dishrag you.

The finger touched on "you" was turned down into the palm and eliminated from the counting, which started again and was repeated until all fingers but one were eliminated. That one was "It."

"It" then left the room or went away from the group out of hearing distance—some fifty feet—and waited to be called. The other players, whispering together, each chose to be a camel, an elephant, a goat, a giraffe, or a bear and also assigned an animal to "It." A spokesman for the group then called to "It":

"When you comin' home?"

"Tomorrow noon." ("It" replied)

"What you gonna bring with you?"

"A dish and a spoon and an old raccoon."

"Which had you rather come home on: a camel, elephant, goat, giraffe, bear?"

When "It" chose the animal assigned himself, he was told:

"Then come home on your own two feet."

But when he chose a name assigned to another player, that player was required to bring him home piggyback. (When the child-beast was one of the smaller children, the rider pretended to ride his back but walked leaning on his mount). When the two arrived before the group, the group leader asked the mount:

"What you got there?"

"Bag of nits" (mount answered)

"Shake him till he spits."

The mount shook, twisted, jumped, and turned until the laughing rider chose to spit. The leader asked the rider:

"Which had you rather lie down on,
a feather bed or a thorn bed?"

If the answer was "thorn bed" the order was, "Lay him down

easy," but if the answer was "feather bed" the order was "Lay him down hard." A scuffle followed while the mount tried to dislodge the rider and dump him.

The hackberry grove across the road was a favored place to play "William Tremble Toe" when neighbor families came visiting. Boys and girls from five to fourteen played the game together; and the game grew rough when, by chance, two well-matched big boys were mount and rider. The wrestling match ending the game could go on and on and stop only when the audience, tired of watching, wandered away or started another game, or when the scuffle grew into a fight and the group piled on to pull them apart before parents could discover the fight and send the fighting boys home.

By unspoken rules each child knew what to do to stop a fight. A younger child watched for a chance to grab a fighter's leg (above the knee if possible), wrap himself around that leg with his arms and legs, and cling like a leech as the fighter lurched and flung him about. Simultaneously, older players attacked the fighter from the rear and pinned his arms down. A fighter with arms pinned down and with a child wrapped around each leg as ballast was held immobilized until his anger and the anger of his opponent, similarly trussed, cooled to the point where they both said, "Nuff." That was a word of honor.

WOLF OVER THE RIDGE

Any number of players of all ages played this outdoor game. Two parallel base lines were drawn with a danger zone between. Small children, playing in their own group, scratched their lines some forty feet apart. Older players made the area fifty yards wide or more.

All players except "It" stood behind one of the base lines. "It" (the hunter) stood halfway between the base lines and called, "Wolf over the ridge." On "ridge," all players left base to dash across the hunter's ground to safety behind the opposite base line.

Any player caught joined the hunter on his hunting ground and became another catcher. The game continued until all "wolves" had become hunters.

At picnics when most of the players were big boys and young men, the game was strenuous and rough. The position of "It" was opportunity to display skill and valor. Consequently, "It" was usually a volunteer. Two, three, or four volunteers meant that straws or sticks were drawn or coins tossed to decide the matter.

Rules varied on the manner of catching and the rule was decided before the game started. Big boys and men ruled that the hunter must catch the fleeing player, throw him to the ground, and pat him on the back three times. The result was a wrestling match with a downed player maneuvering to lie on his back to prevent the three pats—usually whacks. Smaller children, especially girls, ruled that three pats on the back of an upright player caught the player.

In a group of big boys and men, the challenger customarily challenged the ablest player first for game strategy and for personal glory. The player, honored by the challenge, led the hunter on a wild chase, with the other players acting as a gallery of spectators urging the combatants on.

WRING THE DISHRAG

Two players faced, holding hands lightly, with left hand on right hand and right hand in left hand. Raising one pair of arms as an arch, the two turned their bodies to go under the arch, trailing the other pair of joined hands until they were back to back, when the second pair of arms ascended to form a second arch under which the bodies passed as the hands and arms twisted to accommodate the rotating bodies.

The movement started slowly and continued slowly until the two children established a rhythm. Then the tempo increased until the dizzy dishrag wringers fell in a heap or flung themselves apart.

Songs and Singers in Sabine Bottom

In the home or in the fields, the men and women went about their work singing or humming, except when the work was too hard (like following the turning plow or pulling stumps in bottom land; or for Mama, rendering lard or hoeing weeds in the garden). But following the harrow or sitting on the cultivator seat, Papa and the hired hands could sing, keeping time with the horses' feet. And Grandma churning or Mama ironing sang or hummed in time with the churn-dasher and the flatiron moving back and forth across Papa's white Sunday shirt.

When the noonday meal was over and Mama and Grandma had time to sit and rest, they sang to the rhythm of their rocking chairs. And when the day's work was done, the men sat on the back steps or the edge of the back gallery, plucking and strumming guitars, mandolins, or banjos and singing.

Neighbors sang together when they visited on Sunday afternoons and evenings, when they attended camp meeting at Flats, at Sunday school and church at Woosley, in singing school (where they learned to sing from shaped notes), and at funerals held in farmhouse parlors.

The McKeithens had a reed organ; they had no children, but

had a Grandma McKeithen who let Dorothy play the organ whenever Mama allowed her to go for a visit. Dorothy had to stand to pump the organ, but sometimes, when Grandma McKeithen was not too busy, she held Dorothy on her lap and pumped for her. It was there that Dorothy learned to play (on the black notes) and sing:

I dropped the baby in the dirt
I asked the baby did it hurt
And all the little thing could say
Was "Wanh! Wanh! Wanh!

Later she learned to play (with one finger) on the white notes: "My country 'tis of thee/Sweet land of liver tea." Very soon she taught herself to use both forefingers to play a harmony, but she found she sometimes had to match a black note with a white note to make the harmony sound right.

The Lon Hugheys, who lived on the far side of Shuffle Creek on the Emory road, had stringed instruments hanging on their parlor wall, and when Dorothy visited the Hugheys, Monty—one of their two grown daughters—took down the instruments to play and sing and gave Dorothy one to strum with them. Mrs. Hughey allowed Dorothy to feed her guinea hens and it was there that she learned to imitate their call "pot-track, pot-track, pot-track" and lead them through the woods toward the sawmill, answering her, as she had led the bobwhites through tall grass.

Other neighbors owned stringed instruments the sound of which Dorothy could never forget, though she could not remember the look of the instruments. It was Sid Turner, the hired hand, who taught her to finger and pluck his guitar. From Sid, Orphus Trailer, and other hired hands and neighbors, she learned to sing:

THE LITTLE MOHEE

As I was out walking I happened to see
A fair Indian maiden: the little Mohee

Come sit down beside me and take hold my hand
I see you're a stranger in this strange land.

Oh, no, you're the stranger and I own the land
But you are most welcome to dwell in my home.

Oh, no, pretty maiden, that never can be
For I have a true love in my own countree.

So now, pretty maiden, it's time that I go
For this is your country and I am your foe.

RED WING

Oh, the moon shines tonight on pretty Red Wing
The breeze is sighing and night birds crying
Far, far beneath the stars my love is sleeping
And Red Wing's weeping her life away.

SHOOT THE BUFFALO

Shoot the buffalo; shoot the buffalo
Ramble in the canebrake
And shoot the buffalo.

The monkey shot the buzzard
And the buzzard shot the crow
Ramble in the canebrake
And shoot the buffalo.

OVER THE HILL TO THE POORHOUSE

I am old and helpless and feeble
And the days of my youth have gone by
And it's over the hill to the poorhouse
I wander alone to die.

Oh see on that old doorstep yonder
I sat with my babes on my knee
No father was happier or fonder
Than I with my little ones three.

For I'm old and helpless and feeble
And the days of my youth have gone by
And it's over the hill to the poorhouse
I wander alone to die.

The boys both so rosy and chubby
And Lillie with prattle so sweet
God knows how their father has loved them
But they've driven him out in the street.

For I'm old and helpless and feeble
And the days of my youth have gone by
And it's over the hill to the poorhouse
I wander alone to die.

Papa seldom sang words except when he was sitting down with a child on his lap, or walking along with a child by his side or riding on his back or shoulders, or when he was riding along in the buggy with a child beside him. Sitting, with Little Brother on his knee, he kept time by tapping his heel and bouncing Little Brother or patting him on the back. He sang happy songs when Dorothy was crying from a fall, a wasp sting, or a stumped, bleeding toe.

SALLY GOODIN

I had a piece of pie
And I had a piece of puddin'
I give it all away
To see my Sally Goodin
I looked down the road
And I saw her comin'
I thought to my soul
That I'd kill myself a runnin'.

Hey dey diddle, the cat and the fiddle
The cow jumped over the moon, moon, moon, moon,
The little dog laughed to see such sport
That the dish ran away with the spoon, spoon, spoon, spoon.

LITTLE BOY

Little boy, little boy, who made your britches?
Mammie cut 'em out and pappy sewed the stitches.

LAMBIE

Po little black sheep
Po little lambie
Po little black sheep
Got no mammie.

FIDDLE DE FEE

Had me a cat and my cat pleased me
Fed my cat under yonder tree
Cat went fiddle de fee.

Had me a horse and my horse pleased me
Fed my horse under yonder tree
Horse went neigh, neigh
Cat went fiddle de fee.

Had me a pig and my pig pleased me
Fed my pig under yonder tree
Pig went griffy, graffy
Horse went neigh, neigh
Cat went fiddle de fee.

Had me a cow and my cow pleased me
Fed my cow under yonder tree
Cow went moo, moo
Pig went griffy, graffy
Horse went neigh, neigh
Cat went fiddle de fee.

Had me a duck and my duck pleased me
Fed my duck under yonder tree
Duck went quack, quack
Cow went moo, moo
Pig went griffy, graffy
Horse went neigh, neigh
Cat went fiddle de fee.

Had me a guinea and my guinea pleased me
Fed my guinea under yonder tree
Guinea went put-rack, put-rack
Duck went quack, quack
Cow went moo, moo
Pig went griffy, graffy
Horse went neigh, neigh
Cat went fiddle de fee.

Had me a donkey and my donkey pleased me
Fed my donkey under yonder tree
Donkey went honkkee, honkkee
Guinea went put-rack, put-rack
Duck went quack, quack
Cow went moo, moo
Pig went griffy, graffy
Horse went neigh, neigh
Cat went fiddle de fee.

KIRO, KARO

Kiro, Karo, daro war
Ma-hi, ma-ho, ma hum-sti-pum-sti-diddle
Sing song Polly, won't you ki-me-o.

THE OLD HEN CACKLED

The old hen cackled, cackled, cackled
The old hen cackled
And the rooster laid the egg

CHIC-A-BOOM BOOM

Chic-a-boom boom boom
Chic-a-boom boom
Chic-a-boom boom boom
Chic-a-boom boom
See the little girl ariding by
Oh little girl don't you cry
If you cry the horse will die
Chic-a-boom boom boom BOOM
If you don't you can ride him again
Chic-a-boom boom boom BOOM.

HUSH, LITTLE BABY

Hush little baby, don't say a word
Papa's gonna buy you a mockin' bird
If that mockin' bird don't sing
Papa's gonna buy you a diamond ring
If that diamond ring turns brass
Papa's gonna buy you a lookin' glass
If that lookin' glass gets broke
Papa's gonna buy you a billy goat
If that billy goat runs away
Tar ree rar ree boom de aye.

As Papa walked along a road, a path, or in a furrow across the field, with Little Brother and Dorothy tagging along behind him, he kept time by singing:

CAPTAIN JINKS OF THE HORSE MARINES

I'm Captain Jinks of the horse marines
I feed my horse on corn and beans
I'm Captain Jinks of the horse marines
I'm a captain in the army.

I teach the ladies how to dance
How to dance, how to dance
I teach the ladies how to dance
Yes, how to dance in the army.

THE GIRL I LEFT BEHIND ME

I struck the trail in sixty-nine
With the herd strung out behind me
I jogged along but my mind went back
To the girl I left behind me.

That girl, that girl, that pretty little girl
That girl I left behind me
I jogged along but my mind went back
To the girl I left behind me.

I'll cross Red River once again
Hope the Indians they can't find me
Then I'll go back to Tennessee
To the girl I left behind me.

LITTLE BROWN JUG

Me and my wife and my bobbed tailed dog
Crossed the creek on a hickory log
Wife fell in and my dog did too
And left me wondering what to do.

Ha, ha, ha, you and me
Little brown jug don't I love thee
Ha, ha, ha, you and me
Little brown jug don't I love thee.

When Papa was riding along in the buggy or wagon (with a child beside him) feeling sad, he sang:

THE LITTLE OLD LOG CABIN IN THE LANE

Oh, the only friend that's left me
Is that little old dog of mine
In my little old log cabin in the lane.

Oh, the hinges they are rusty
And the windows have no glass
And the board roof lets the howling blizzards in
And the only friend that's left me
Is that little old dog of mine
In my little old log cabin in the lane.

THE LONE PRAIRIE

Oh bury me not on the lone prairie
Where the wild coyotes will howl o'er me
And the north wind sweeps and the grasses wave
Oh bury me not in a prairie grave.

But they paid no heed to his dying prayer
On the lone prairie they buried him there
In a narrow grave six feet by three
They buried him there on the lone prairie.

Oh bury me not on the lone prairie
Where the wild coyotes will howl o'er me
Where the rattlesnakes hiss and the wind blows free
Oh bury me not on the lone prairie.

And the cowboys now as they roam the plain
They have marked the spot where his bones are lain.
Fling a handful of roses o'er his grave
With a prayer to Him for his soul to save.

And when the child beside him grew sleepy, he sang:

SLEEP, MY LITTLE BABY, SLEEP

Sleep, my little baby, sleep
Sleep, my little baby, sleep

Oh the possum and the coon they both mighty fine
But where is the watermelon smilin' on the vine [spoken]

Woo-oo-oo-oo the wild wind-oo-oo
Sleep, my little baby sleep.

Mama hummed little tuneless hums as she walked about the house, punctuating the hum with a grunt now and then when she lifted a stove cap to push a stick of wood into the kitchen stove. If she thought about what she was humming, she stopped and began to recite or sing poems. Two of her favorite singing poems were written by Henry Wadsworth Longfellow, who died when she was a little girl (she said):

THE BRIDGE

I stood on the bridge at midnight
As the clock was striking the hour
And the moon rose over the city
Behind the old church tower.

How often, oh, how often
In the days that have gone by
I've stood on that bridge at midnight
And gazed at that wavering sky.

How often, oh, how often
I've wished that the ebbing tide
Would bear me away on its bosom
To the ocean wild and wide.

For my heart was hot and restless
And my life seemed full of care
And the burden laid upon me
Seemed greater than I could bear.
But now it has fallen from me
Lies buried in the sea
And only the sorrow of others
Casts a shadow over me.

The moon in its broken reflection
And its shadow shall appear
As a symbol of love from heaven
And its wavering image here.

THE CHILDREN'S HOUR

From my study I see in the lamplight
Descending the broad hall stair
Grave Alice and laughing Allegra
And Edith with golden hair.

They climb up into my turret
O'er the arms and back of my chair
If I try to escape they surround me
Coming at me from everywhere.

But now with you fast in my fortress
I will not let you depart
I'll put you down in my dungeon
In the secret cell of my heart.

And there I will keep you forever
Yes, forever and a long day
Till the dungeon walls shall all crumble
And moulder in dust away.

Another of Mama's singing poems was written by Sir Thomas

Campbell, a Scotch poet (Mama said) who died a long time ago:

LORD ULLIN'S DAUGHTER

A chieftain to the highlands bound
Cried, Boatman, do not tarry
And I'll give thee a silver pound
To row us o'er the ferry.

Now who be ye would cross Loch Isle
This dark and stormy water
O I'm the chief of Ulva's Isle
And this Lord Ullin's daughter.

And fast before her father's men
Three days we've fled together
For should he find us in the glen
My blood would stain the heather.

His horsemen hard behind us ride
Should they our steps discover
Then who would cheer the bonny bride
When they have slain her lover.

Outspoke the hardy highland wight
I'll go my chief, I'm ready
It is not for your silver bright
But for your winsome lady.

And then as louder blew the wind
And as the night grew drearer
Adown the glen rode armed men
Their trampling sounded nearer.

The boat had left the stormy land
The stormy sea before her

When O, too strong for human hand
The tempest gathered o'er her.

Lord Ullin reached that fatal shore
His daughter did discover
One lovely hand was stretched for aid
And one was round her lover.

Come back, come back, he cried in grief
Across the stormy water
And I'll forgive your highland chief
My daughter, O, my daughter.

In vain the loud waves lashed the shore
Return or aid preventing
The waters wild went o'er his child
And he was left lamenting.

When Mama sang "Lord Ullin's Daughter," Dorothy saw Lord Ullin's daughter sitting in a buggy beside her young husband that rainy April Sunday afternoon, at the front gate with Papa holding the umbrella over the preacher while he performed the marriage ceremony. She saw Lord Ullin's daughter and her chieftain putting the horse to a gallop as they headed the buggy toward Red River. And the bride's father (who galloped up to the front gate later, in hot pursuit) was a tobacco-spitting swearing Lord Ullin.

Another of Mama's songs which told a story was:

BARBARA ALLEN

In Scarlet town where I was born
There was a fair maid adwellin'

Made every youth cry well a day
Her name was Barbara Allen.

'Twas in the merry month of May
When green buds they was aswellin'
Sweet William on his death bed lay
For love of Barbara Allen.

He sent his servant to the town
To the town where she was adwellin'
O haste and come to my master dear
If your name be Barbara Allen.

Then slowly, slowly got she up
And slowly drew she anigh him
And this is all she had to say
Young man I think you're dyin'.

O yes, I'm sick, I'm very, very sick
O yes, I'm nigh to adyin'
And all because I love you so
Hard-hearted Barbara Allen.

O don't you mind the time said she
O don't you mind the dwellin'
You drank a toast to the ladies round
But you slighted Barbara Allen.

O yes I mind the time said he
O yes I mind the dwellin'
I gave a toast to the ladies round
But my heart to Barbara Allen.

He turned his face unto the wall
And death was with him adwellin'
Be kind my friends and neighbors all
Be kind to Barbara Allen.

As she was walking o'er the hill
She heard the death bell aknellin'
And every note it seemed to say
Hard-hearted Barbara Allen.

O father, father dig my grave
O dig it deep and anarrow

Sweet William died for me today
I'll die for him tomorrow.

They buried them there in the old church yard
In death he was beside her
Out of his grave grew a red, red rose
And out of hers, a briar.

They grew and grew round the old church tower
Till they could grow no ahigher
And at the top twined a true love knot
The red rose round the briar.

When Mama rocked Little Brother to sleep, Dorothy stood behind Mama (one foot on each rocker) and rocked back and forth and sang with Mama:

BABES IN THE WOODS

Oh don't you remember a long time ago
Two little babes whose names I don't know

Were stolen away on a bright summer day
And lost in the woods I've heard people say.

And when it was night, so sad was their plight
The moon had gone down and the stars gave no light
They sobbed and they sighed and they bitterly cried
And the poor little things they lay down and died.

And when they were dead, the robin so red
Brought strawberry leaves and over them spread
And all the day long they sang them this song
Poor babes in the woods, poor babes in the woods
Oh, don't you remember the babes in the woods.

Sitting, quietly resting, Mama sang songs like:

THE SHIP THAT NEVER RETURNED

On a sunny day when the waves were rippled
By the softest, gentlest breeze
Did a ship set sail with a cargo laden
For a port beyond the seas.

Oh she never returned, no she never returned
And her fate is yet unlearned
For many years, long years, there are loved ones waiting
For the ship that never returned.

Said a feeble lad to his anxious mother
I must cross the wide, wide sea
For they say, perchance, in a far-off country
There is health and strength for me.

Oh she never returned, no she never returned
And her fate is yet unlearned
For many years, long years, there are loved ones waiting
For the ship that never returned.

NELLIE GRAY

There's a low, green valley on the old Kentucky shore
Where I whiled many happy hours away
Asitting and asinging by a little cabin door
Where lived my darling Nellie Gray.

Oh my darling Nellie Gray, they have taken her away
And I'll never see my darling any more
They have taken her to Georgia for to wear her life away
For to toil in the cotton and the cane.

My canoe is on the river and my song is left unsung
And I'll seek my darling Nellie Gray
And I'll float down the river in my little bark canoe
And my banjo sweetly I will play.

Oh my darling Nellie Gray, up in heaven so they say
And I'll live to see my darling evermore
Though they've taken her to Georgia for to wear her life away
For to toil in the cotton and the cane.

LISTEN TO THE MOCKINGBIRD

Listen to the mockingbird
Listen to the mockingbird
The mocking bird is singing o'er her grave
Listen to the mockingbird
Listen to the mockingbird
The mockingbird is singing o'er her grave.

I'm dreaming now of Hallie
Sweet Hallie, sweet Hallie
I'm dreaming now of Hallie
While the mockingbird is singing o'er her grave.

SWEET MARIE

Sweet Marie, come to me
Come to me, sweet Marie
For I know your face is fair
Love, to see
And because your soul is pure
I now linger at your feet
I now linger at your feet
Sweet Marie.

I'M GOING BACK TO DIXIE

I'm going back to Dixie
No more I'm going to wander
I'm going where the orange blossoms grow
I see sad tears afalling
I hear sad voices calling
My heart turns back to Dixie
And I must go.

After that song, she sang, over and over again:

HOME, SWEET HOME

Mid pleasures and palaces though far we may roam
Be it ever so humble, there's no place like home.

The stars in the skies seem to hallow us there
Which seek through the world are ne'er met with elsewhere

Home, ho-ome, sweet, sweet home
There's no place like home, no there's no place like home.

On Sunday afternoons when Mama and the children visited the McKeithens', Mama played chords on the reed organ as she sang. And when they visited the Ace Hugheys', she and the Hughey girls played stringed instruments and sang together.

Grandma sang more often than she hummed. Usually, she sang sitting in her rocking chair, knitting lace, darning socks, or piecing quilt squares. Sometimes she sang as she sat resting, her tired hands folded in her lap, rocking gently, her voice accompanied by the "clock-clock" of her rocking chair and the "click-click" of the heels of her high-laced shoes or summer slippers. When she rocked Little Brother to sleep, she sang:

GO TO SLEEP, LITTLE BABY

Go to sleep, go to sleep
Go to sleep, little baby
When you wake you shall have
A coach and six little horses

Five little mice and three little rats
A coach and six little horses
Four little dogs and two little cats
A coach and six little horses
Go to sleep, go to sleep
Go to sleep, little baby.

GO TELL AUNT ABBIE

Go tell Aunt Abbie; go tell Aunt Abbie
Go tell Aunt Abbie her old gray goose is dead.

The one she's been saving; the one she's been saving
The one she's been saving to make a feather bed.

But her songs about rivers were her favorites. Besides "On the Other Side of Jordan," "On Jordan's Stormy Banks," and "Let Us Pass Over the River," she sang:

SHALL WE GATHER AT THE RIVER

Shall we gather at the river
The beautiful, the beautiful river
Gather with the saints at the river
That flows by the throne of God.

On the margin of the river
Where bright angel feet have trod
We will walk and worship ever
By the golden throne of God.

Yes, we'll gather at the river, etc.

When Grandma sang "Tenting on the Old Camp Ground," that too became a river song in Dorothy's mind for she saw the tents pitched on the banks of the Sabine River.

TENTING ON THE OLD CAMP GROUND

We're tenting tonight on the old camp ground
Give us a song to cheer
Our weary hearts a song of home
And friends we love so dear.

Many are the hearts that are weary tonight
Wishing for the war to cease
Many are the hearts that are looking for the right
To see the dawn of peace.

Tenting tonight, tenting tonight
Tenting on the old camp ground.

We're tired of war on the old camp ground
Many are lying near
Some are dead and some are dying
Many lost in tears.

Many are the hearts that are weary tonight
Wishing for the war to cease
Many are the hearts that are looking for the right
To see the dawn of peace.

Dying tonight, dying tonight
Dying on the old camp ground

Grandma sometimes sang to herself as if nobody were listening —
slowly, sadly. And Dorothy knew she was thinking about the War
and all the dead people she loved. She sang:

DRUMMER BOY OF SHILOH

On Shiloh's dark and bloody field
The dying soldiers lay
One was a lonely drummer boy
Who beat the drum that day.

Angels round the drummer sang
They knew that he was brave
As any soldier of the field
Who lay in a Shiloh grave.

LORENA

The years go slowly by, Lorena
And snow lies on the ground again
The sun sets in the sky, Lorena
The moon beams where the flowers have been.

My heart still beats with love, Lorena
As when the summer sun shone here
But now the sun has set, Lorena
And the moon is clouded with despair.

"Contraband" was another War song she sang, after which she sang:

MY FAITH LOOKS UP TO THEE

My faith looks up to Thee
Thou Lamb of Calvary
Savior, divine
Now hear me while I pray
Take all my sins away
Oh, let me from this day
Be wholly Thine.

May Thy rich grace impart
Strength to my fainting heart
My zeal inspire
As Thou hast died for me
Oh may my love for Thee
Pure, warm and changeless be
A living fire.

This song which was a favorite with Grandma, Papa, and Mama; but each had favorite verses.

BILLY BOY

O where have you been, Billy boy, Billy boy
O where have you been, charming Billy?
I've been down the lane to see my Sarah Jane
She's a young thing and cannot leave her mammy.

How old is she, Billy boy, Billy boy,
How old is she, charming Billy?
Twice six, twice seven, twice twenty and eleven
She's a young thing and cannot leave her mammy.

How tall is she, Billy boy, Billy boy
How tall is she, charming Billy?

She's as tall as any pine and as straight as a pumpkin vine
She's a young thing and cannot leave her mammy.

Did she ask you in, Billy boy, Billy boy
Did she ask you in, charming Billy?
Yes, she asked me in with a dimple in her chin
She's a young thing and cannot leave her mammy.

Did she set for you a chair, Billy boy, Billy boy
Did she set for you a chair, charming Billie?
Yes, she set for me a chair but the bottom wasn't there
She's a young thing and cannot leave her mammy.

Can she bake a cherry pie, Billy boy, Billy boy
Can she bake a cherry pie, charming Billy?
She can bake a cherry pie as quick as a cat can wink his eye
She's a young thing and cannot leave her mammy.

O can she sweep a floor, Billy boy, Billy boy
O can she sweep a floor, charming Billy?
Yes, she can sweep a floor and never look behind the door
She's a young thing and cannot leave her mammy.

Camp meeting time in Sabine Bottom was mid or late summer when crops had been planted and cultivated and were waiting to be harvested. The neighbors in the Woosley-Flats community traveled to the Flats Schoolhouse in wagons, buggies, surreys, and on horseback at sundown, arriving as darkness fell and the pine knot torches were being lighted to make a flaming fringe of light around the brush arbor beside the schoolhouse, where the meetings were held. The people sat on backless wooden benches facing the preacher, who was standing on a platform waving his hands as he lined out the songs for the congregation:

THE OLD TIME RELIGION

'Tis the old time religion
'Tis the old time religion
'Tis the old time religion
It's good enough for me.

It was good for our fathers
It was good for our fathers
It was good for our fathers
It's good enough for me.

It was good for our mothers
It was good for our mothers
It was good for our mothers
It's good enough for me.

It was good for Paul and Silas
It was good for Paul and Silas
It was good for Paul and Silas
It's good enough for me.

It was good for the Hebrew children
It was good for the Hebrew children
It was good for the Hebrew children
It's good enough for me.

It was good for the Prophet Daniel
It was good for the Prophet Daniel
It was good for the Prophet Daniel
It's good enough for me.

After the sermon, before calling for sinners to the mourner's bench, the preacher called for the song:

THE JUDGMENT DAY

There's a great day coming, a great day coming
There's a great day coming by and by
When the saints and the sinners will be parted right and left
Are you ready for that day to come?

Are you ready? Are you ready?
Are you ready for the judgment day?
Are you ready? Are you ready?
Are you ready for the judgment day?

One by one the sinners marched down the aisles to kneel in a long line before the preacher, who prayed aloud, his voice rising above a gathering "Amen" from the congregation, until finally, a sinner arose to shout "Praise God" or "Hallelujah" above the voices of the preacher and the congregation. Other saved sinners arose, one by one, to join him, and the families of the shouters went forward to hug and kiss their repentent kin while the preacher lined out the song:

AMAZING GRACE

Amazing grace, how sweet the sound
That saved a wretch like me
I once was lost but now I'm found
Was blind but now I see.

'Twas grace that taught my heart to fear
And grace my fears relieved
How precious did that grace appear
The hour I first believed.

Through many dangers, toils, and snares
I have already come
'Tis grace has brought me safe thus far
And grace will lead me home.

When we've been there ten thousand years
Bright shining as the sun
We've no less days to sing God's praise
Than when we first begun.

Religious songs sung at funerals were "Nearer My God to Thee" and "Rock of Ages." And in Sunday school at Woosley (after the Sunday school teacher had required each child to stand and recite the golden text on the Sunday school card) they all sang:

JESUS LOVES ME

Jesus loves me this I know
For the Bible tells me so
Little ones to Him belong
We are weak but He is strong.

Yes, Jesus loves me
The Bible tells me so.

BRINGING IN THE SHEAVES

Bringing in the sheaves
Bringing in the sheaves
We shall come rejoicing
Bringing in the sheaves.

On the way home from Sunday school and all week long, Dorothy and Little Brother liked to sing "Bringing in the Sheaves" in the Chinese words Aunt Eddie had taught them:

Durn upe tink wah chee
Durn upe tink wah chee
Wash a winken shiloh
Durn upe tink wah chee.

"Durn," in the song, was a Chinese word (Aunt Eddie said) and not the swear word the Driggers boys used.

Epilogue

The genesis of this book, like the Biblical Genesis, includes many chapters of "begats." One idea begat another over the years. In the beginning, long before Dorothy started to school, her Grandma Gray taught her to write her name: Dorothy Gray Mills. Then Dorothy taught herself to write it backwards.

In the first grade in Lone Oak the children had notebooks in which to write only what the teacher, Mrs. English, instructed. The first assignment was the child's name, written on the top line of the first page by Mrs. English, who walked up and down the aisles inspecting handwriting as each child slowly copied the name, line under line until the page was filled. Dorothy carefully copied Mrs. English's handwriting to the middle line; decided to fill the rest of the page with her name written backward: Sllim Yarg Ythorod; then sat waiting for inspection. Mrs. English walked down the aisle, her white shirt-waisted bosom leading, paused at each desk, peered over her bosom through spectacles pinching her nose, approved or scolded, and then moved on.

When she reached Dorothy, she leaned far over, clipped her glasses more firmly on her nose to see better, and frowned. Dorothy had disobeyed; Mrs. English took her notebook and sent her to stand in the corner, face to the wall, for the rest of the morning. Why writing her name backward was a sin in school, she did not know. At home it was not. But as the long morning grew longer and longer, her sagging, weary body taught her never to commit that school-sin again. And for threescore and seven years, she never did. So ends chapter one of this genesis.

One school day begat another until, eventually in college in the early 1920's, in Denton, Texas, she not only learned more about Grandma's eunuchs but also, and more important, became acquainted with the study of psychology (G. Stanley Hall — or was it Thorndyke) and with Emerson's essays in the required course in American Literature.

Her memory of the psychology course includes the name of the textbook author (maybe), the droning voice of the professor (but not his face, name, nor what he said) standing on a platform looking down at the class, and a pickled human brain floating gently in a huge glass jar on the teacher's desk. She also remembers struggling to stay awake by doodling the convolutions of the pickled brain. That is all. She passed the course by memorizing meaningless words and sentences from the textbook.

It was Emerson (that is, Emerson, Dr. Brown — the professor — and a group of Denton ministers of the Gospel) who started a long chain of experiences that immediately inspired an interest in philosophy which in turn, years later, led her back to psychology. The ministers demanded that the college president fire Dr. Brown, charging him with atheism because of Emerson's "Divinity School Address." The entire class, loyal to Dr. Brown and Emerson, caucused under the oak trees on campus and planned the defense: representatives were elected and sent to the college president to protest the ministers' demands; and the rest of the class went to the library to read everything the library offered of Emerson's works in preparation for debate with the ministers, and, if necessary, with the president. The representatives soon returned with presidential assurance that neither Dr. Brown nor Emerson was in any danger. For Dorothy, however, that was not the end of the story but the beginning of a long, cumulative tale like "The House that Jack Built."

Emerson's "Self-Reliance" (together with Thoreau's "Civil Disobedience") had produced the courage and zeal to defend Emerson and Dr. Brown. But "Over-Soul" sent her to Plato's "Symposium on Love" and "Experience" sent her to Emmanuel Kant's *Critique of Practical Reason* (both unassigned).

Plato led her to Socrates. And the two taught her the meaning of something she had perceived long ago in Sabine Bottom and had been perceiving ever since: her Grandma Gray, who had grown up in a culture and period of history where she was not allowed to study the Greek philosophers, nevertheless knew what Plato knew about Love — Love is a binding force binding men together, and hate is a divisive force driving men apart; Love ennobles the lover and hate destroys the hater. Grandma also knew what Socrates knew about teaching and learning: she never gave advice to man or child until it was sought; then she helped the seeker analyze the problem and find the answer through her wise, gentle questions. She never argued. "A man convinced against his will is of the same opinion still," she often said.

Emerson and Dr. Brown could not know what they were teaching Dorothy nor could she know what she was learning. But if this book should include a page of acknowledgements, perhaps the list should begin with the ministers of the Gospel in Denton, Texas, who stimulated the surge of adrenaline to initiate her long pursuit of knowledge about human behavior.

Dorothy has never pretended to be a professional philosopher, psychologist, or anthropologist. She insists that, if she must be labeled, she be called an eclectic school teacher. She has always sought, selected, and used what seemed to her the most useful elements in all systems or schools of thought. Perhaps "the genesis" of this book should be called "The Odyssey of a Country School Teacher."

As a wandering school teacher, Dorothy in 1930 became a teaching principal in a consolidated rural school in New York State. One problem that soon became her great concern was the fact that most of the children, especially the boys, reached the junior high school grades "hating" poetry. Looking for the causes, she learned that their elementary classroom experiences with poetry had included: (1) homework memory assignments of (2) poems chosen by the teacher (a woman) for (3) didactic purposes and (4) memorized as a chore to escape punishment.

Then one spring day at noon she stood at an open classroom window pondering that problem, casually watching the children play on an unsupervised playground. Skip ropes were turning; marbles, rolling; balls, bouncing. Gradually she became aware of metaphoric, rhythmic language accompanying the body movements of the children. She heard

> One, two, three, aleery
> Four, five, six, aleery
> Seven, eight, nine, aleery
> Ten, aleery, postman.   (for ball bouncing)

and

> All in together, girls
> Never mind the weather, girls.   (for rope skipping)

and

> Roll, roll, Tootsie, roll
> Roll, marble, in the hole.   (charm for marbles)

and

> House to let, inquire within
> Lady put out for drinking gin
> If she promises to drink no more
> Here's the key to her back door.   (shouted for rebellious fun)

By the time the bell rang calling the children in, she had counted on her fingers more than a dozen rhymes and formulae; and when the children came to class, rhymes, rhythms, and metaphors of the playground language were discussed. The next day, self-assigned homework was brought in, and by week's end, the class had a collection of more than two hundred playground rhymes.

It soon became clear to Dorothy that their joy in poetry came from orchestrated body movements, including the voice. One class discussion led to another: metric and cadenced rhythms; kinds of rhymes and sound-meaning (rollicking and frolicking as opposed to cold and bold). Discussions led to dramatic choral reading activities, to group creative verse writing, to individual creative writing, and to reading poetry in books, first to limericks, then to "Jabberwocky," and gradually to serious poems.

In group compositions all members of the class participated, contributing lines and voting for the best. For example, starting with the line, "John had a girl friend, Louise" (written on the blackboard), twelve-year-old children composed the following limerick:

John had a girl friend, Louise
Who owned a great many fleas
When she started to shakin'
Every flee would awaken
And Louise had to scratch all her fleas.

By year's end the children were writing in small groups of two or three, and alone.

One twelve-year-old boy, after a Sunday visit to a "shell-shocked" uncle in a veteran's hospital, wrote:

SHELL SHOCK

Doc, I ain't crazy
Don't tell me I'm crazy
That ain't confetti
Them are bombs
Bombs dropping
Rifles shooting bullets over my head
I hear machine guns rattling
Still we wait in the trenches

I do not scream
I do not hit my head against the wall
You got me wrong, Doc
We're going over the top!
I AIN'T CRAZY!

Dorothy's pedagogical purpose was to open doors for children to the joys of literature in books, and to self-confidence and pleasure in developing their own power over language, manipulating and playing with words.

Having learned so much from so little exploration of the playground, she was curious to learn more. Going to the library for help, she soon found, to her surprise, that "House to let, inquire within..." was not a current response to the "Bathtub full of gin" days of the 1920's, as she had ignorantly assumed, but had been recorded in a similar version by Sir James Orchard Halliwell in the 1840's as a rhyme used by naughty boys in Dorsetshire, England, as they stood across the street from a house with a "To let" sign on it and shouted the rhyme when a prospective tenant appeared.

The first record of "Roses red and violets blue..." (the ancestor of thousands of autograph album rhymes), she found, was written by Edmund Spenser in "The Faerie Queen" addressing Queen Elizabeth I. The line, she knew, could be much older, since Spenser borrowed heavily from folklore and other sources.

In the mid and late 1930's, in a public school in New Jersey, Dorothy taught first generation and immigrant children who had learned to be ashamed of their homes and their parents who spoke another language and followed foreign customs. They lacked self-respect and were therefore reluctant to write or talk about themselves, their lives, their interests, their neighborhoods, or their families. She suggested that they each choose a pen name (she told them about Mark Twain) and then write about a dream, a daydream, an early memory, or an adventure, after which they could change all first person pronouns to third and thus create a biography. (Who knows? Sllim Yarg Ythorod may have whispered the suggestion.) The strategy worked. The children began to view themselves more objectively and wrote more freely. Among titles of compositions were: "Sleeping Three in a Bed," "The Girl Who Swallowed Her Tooth," "Making Ravioli," "Doing Dishes," "Near the Waters of Spain," "My Voyage to America." Among their pseudonyms were: Pee Wee, Joe Blow, Veronica Lake, Joe Louis, and Scarlett O'Hara.

Meanwhile the children (seventh and eighth graders) collected, compiled, and bound a book of playground verses which included, among other categories: (1) counting-out formulae; (2) ball-bouncing rhymes; (3) rope-skipping rhymes; (4) fortune telling rhymes; (5) charms; (6) riddles; (7) tongue twisters; (8) taunts; and (9) satires on adult pomposity and elegance. Examples follow:

> *Ancy, Nancy, tootsie lolla*
> *Follow madinky, dinky dolla*
> *Follow maloa, follow maloo*
> *Out goes Y-O-U.* (counting out)

> *I won't go to Macy's any more, more, more*
> *There's a big, fat policeman at the door, door, door*
> *He grab me by the collar and he make me pay a dollar*
> *So I won't go to Macy's any more, more, more.* (ball-bouncing)

Blue bell, cockle shell
Ivy, ivy, over
Blue bell, cockle shell
Evy, ivy under. (chant for skipping rope)

Strawberry jam, Queen of tarts
Tell me the initials of your sweetheart
A, B, C, etc. (fortune telling by skipping rope)

Pin, pin, give me good luck
For I am the one who picked you up. (charm)

Down in the meadow stands an old horse
All saddled, all bridled, all ready to go
I've told you his name three times in a row
And still you don't know. (riddle: answer — All)

The skunk sat on a stump
The skunk thunk the stump stunk
The stump thunk the skunk stunk. (tongue twister)

Mary bom bary
Tillie ary, go sary
Tee legged, tie legged
Bow legged Mary. (taunt)

Ladies and jellyspoons
I come before you
To stand behind you
To tell you something
I know nothing about.

The next Thursday
Which is Good Friday
There will be a mother's meeting
For fathers only.

Admission free, pay at the door
Take a seat and sit on the floor
It makes no difference where you sit
The man in the gallery's sure to spit.

The next number on the program
Will be the fourth corner of the round table.

We thank you for your unkind attention.

In the classroom the children were encouraged to analyze and write about their play life. They were also encouraged to analyze and write about the comic books they were reading, the movies they attended, and the radio programs they listened to. Dorothy became increasingly convinced that a child's education took place, willy-nilly, in school and out of school. And she believed that if the school functions in a democratic society (which can survive only by individual decision making), then children need to learn to examine their own lives and, in the process, learn to make decisions by making decisions, in school and out: decisions related to the lives they actually live since they can not make decisions about superimposed abstract lives existing only in the mind of a teacher or in a textbook. With a holistic view of the educational process, she went back to the playgrounds.

On the playground, Dorothy was learning more about the complexity of play activities. She began to understand: (1) that meaning in play words and sounds had to be sought in the context in which sound operated as an integral part of a ritual or orchestrated movement; (2) that not only was a child's entire body involved in a coordinated movement (including voice), but (3) that bodies moved together in rhythm with inanimate objects (the rope smacking the ground, heard, and reaching its highest point in the sky, seen, told one child when to run into the turning rope and another when to run out).

The meaning of "context" expanded as Dorothy learned more about the impact of play environment (home, school, and community limitations on play). For example, neighborhood gangs or play groups (children living within two or three city blocks) adapted games to fit the circumstances: (1) size of players; (2) sex of players: all boys, all girls, or mixed group; (3) number of players in the group; (4) places available for play; (5) roles assigned or assumed within the group structure and why; and (6) approval or disapproval of a game or activity by parents or teachers. Within one community, a traditional game, so adapted, produced several offspring. Once a set of rules was adopted, however, those rules were sacrosanct. The group, as Dorothy came to view it, behaved as a society in microcosm, establishing its own system of law and order and acting together against outside interference from adults and other gangs or play groups.

It became clear that those children were no ancestor-worshipers; their process of transmission of lore included creation as well as interpretation. They retained what was useful, discarded what was not, and created what circumstances required. Dorothy thought of folklore as moving, like a glacier, over space and time, picking up and depositing, and gradually disappearing in a terminal moraine that might or might not contain elements of its beginnings.

The libraries Dorothy explored produced no evidence of research in the folklore of English-speaking children since the 1890's: W. W. Newell's *Games and Songs of American Children* appeared in 1883 and Alice Bertha Gomme's two-volume *The Traditional Games of England, Scotland and Ireland* was published in 1894 and 1898. Those nineteenth-century scholars had been disciples of Darwin, and agreeing with his theory of unilinear evolution, had interpreted folkloristic materials as valuable only as relics to explain the past. Their collections were based on written reports of adults' memories of their own childhood play and not upon first-hand observation of children. No attention was given to the process of transmission and very little to the context of the verbal lore. For nineteenth-century folklore scholars, the total value of traditional play lore was found in the words.

Dorothy's use of the playground as laboratory distinguished her method of study and would, she saw, determine the character of the results. Her purpose was not that of an antiquarian making a pack rat, museum collection of fossils but that of a school teacher trying to find out what and how children learn and teach each other and why.

With the aid of fellow teachers in other states, Dorothy's research expanded from 1931 through 1936 until the project grew, by chance, into a doctoral dissertation, "Folk Jingles of American Children," 1938, New York University. By decree of the doctoral-sponsoring committee (and in spite of Dorothy's protests) the dissertation was limited to literary, verbal, and historic aspects of traditional play lore. Notwithstanding its limitation, the study was in many aspects a departure from nineteenth-century collections and was dubbed "pioneer" in some academic circles.

Dorothy wanted the dissertation to include other hitherto unexplored areas of research. For examples: paralinguistic channels of playground communication; the teacher-learner relationship on the playground compared to the teacher-pupil adversary relationship in the classroom; and other vaguely perceived and unarticulated questions emerging with every visit she made to a playground. Children would be her teachers, that she knew.

With the dissertation officially accepted, Dorothy bought a gold tassel for her mortarboard and went her own solitary way, which led her into wider and wider fields both geographically and philosophically. The nineteenth-century scholars led her into long thinking about the changing position of children in human society throughout history (as revealed in such diverse sources as Charles Dickens' novel *Hard Times* (1854), French historian Philippe Aries' *Centuries of Childhood* (1960), Claude Levi-Strauss's studies of primitive and modern societies, and *The Organizer's Manual* by the O. M. Collective, for campus dissidents (1971). Seeking to understand the reason for change, she sought the psychologists.

Although her pursuit of Gestalt began in the 1930's and contributed to her method of studying children's play, it was not until the middle and late 1940's that Dorothy had an opportunity to observe and participate in a child-study program based on the Gestalt theory (learning takes place by a complex process involving mental organization). Therefore, to understand a child's behavior, a Gestalt researcher keeps anecdotal notes on a child's behavior over a long period of time (two or three years), objectively recording behavior in as many different relationships and situations as possible; then examines the accumulated data, looking for patterns (configurations) of behavior that reveal motivation and answer the question, "Why does this child behave as he or she behaves?"

The Maryland college in which Dorothy taught in the 1940's became a center for an in-service program of child study for public school teachers in the area. From 1946 to 1948, with permission of the program director, Dr. Daniel Prescott, Dorothy participated unofficially in the program by attending seminars when her schedule permitted and by carrying out a two-year study of two college students (G.I. veterans of World War II).

In the late 1950's and 1960's Jean Piaget's research aroused her interest. His clinical method of research that led to his theories of cognitive development appeared to coincide with John Dewey's view that learning takes place through experience, and that experience depends on the stage of a child's cognitive development. "You can begin teaching a child *only* where he *is*," said John Dewey (as best Dorothy remembers). Piaget's *Play, Dreams and Imitation in Childhood* (1962, Morton Library edition) together with Johan Huizinga's *Homo Ludens* (1955, Beacon Press edition) and Roger Caillois's

Man, Play, and Games (1962), contributed to Dorothy's expanding view of the nature and function of play in human society, and intensified her long-held wish to study one child's life in depth.

In 1954, awarded a Fulbright research grant to study Australian children's folklore, she proposed a study limited to a small area (one school, one class, or one child), but the committee evaluating her proposed project decreed that she make a "survey" of the traditional play customs of all Anglo-Australian children. Again she capitulated, remembering old Omar Khayyam's words, "Better a spark within the tavern caught than in the temple lost outright."

In 1962–1963, on sabbatical leave in Tonalá, Jalisco, Mexico, she undertook a study of one child, "Pedro Was His Name." The study included Pedro (twelve years old), his work and play relationship in the family, neighborhood, and school. When Dorothy had to leave to return to her academic duties, the study was incomplete. She left, hoping to return, but circumstances thereafter prevented and "Pedro Was His Name" remains unpublished.

From 1967 to 1969 at the University of Nebraska Dorothy was consultant to graduate student-participants (all teachers on leave of absence from schools and colleges throughout the United States) in a special in-service program. Seven participants each chose to study the play life of one child for one year. A group of twenty chose to study one game, rope-skipping, in all its variations on one playground and later on twenty different playgrounds.

In Lincoln, Dorothy also met and became playmates with Ingrid, then three years old. Playing the roles Ingrid assigned her, she began recalling other three, four, and five year olds with whom she had been playmates and she began making anecdotal notes on the play sessions with Ingrid. The notes were too few and fragmentary to constitute a one-child study but Ingrid led Dorothy back to Sllim Yarg Ythorod, who eventually wrote this book.

Upon retirement from teaching in 1969, the accumulation of unpublished data on children's playlore in the United States, Australia, and Mexico faced Dorothy. At the same time her children, grandchildren, sisters, brother, nieces, and nephews formed a conspiracy to inveigle her to write a family history to include the old family letters, genealogical data, and family legends and stories recorded in notes since the 1930's.

As she ferreted out all the notes squirreled away and began to examine and organize them, she found that they composed themselves into an anecdotal record of preschool and early school days. She found that she had recorded not only observable behavior but also her subjective, emotional, and cognitive responses as well.

Over the years she had developed a method of eliciting from children their subjective reactions to observable actions. Consequently when the time came to write a report on "Childhood in Sabine Bottom, 1902–1910," conditioned by her own training, Dorothy consulted Sllim Yarg Ythorod who agreed to carry out the task. Sllim (the existential Dorothy) has been—since her school days in Lone Oak—a maverick in the academic corral.

Dorothy knows that some of her academic colleagues will decry her failure to subscribe to their pet theories and academic formulae (footnotes, bibliography, index, etc.) meant to display gargantuan scholarship. Sllim deliberately shunned those trappings as irrelevant to her purposes. The word "footnote" was not in Dorothy's preschool vocabulary. The word "note," she knew, meant a piece of paper on which a schoolboy wrote "I love you" and sneaked across the room to the girl of his choice. (Her sisters had told her that.) Writing notes was a sin for which the writer, if caught, would be whipped. Had Dorothy heard the word "footnote," the word would have meant a love note written with the toes instead of the fingers. And she and Little Brother would have practiced, he with his left foot and she with her right.

Footnotes for every traditional game and play custom in "Catalogue III, Play Life" have been published in many studies which follow the formulae of nineteenth-century scholarship. Any pedant who wants footnotes must do his own drudgery.

Many collections and studies of children's play have appeared since 1938, some still reflecting the nineteenth-century preoccupation with origins and history. However, as academic attention to children's play (including traditional lore) has gradually increased, playgrounds have received more attention. The subject "Play" is now a respected "in" thing in Academia. Not so in the 1930's, when Dorothy's doctoral dissertation was publicized in a leading weekly news magazine as the work of a pixilated female school teacher who sat on a curb encouraging naughty children to whisper naughty rhymes to her when she should have been in the classroom teaching them their three R's.

What Dr. Brian Sutton-Smith (psychologist, Columbia University) has called "the triviality barrier"—the prevailing adult view that children's play and, indeed, children's behavior, is trivial and inconsequential—appears to be breaking down.

Consequently, the scholars are putting their heads together to listen to children with tape recorders and to feed the tapes into computers which disgorge answers to be fed into teaching machines. Recently a three-day conference was convened in Atlanta, devoted entirely to the discussion of "Play"; attended by the sages of the land (psychologists, educationists, sociologists, anthropologists, philosophers, folklorists) and other worried academicians and laymen. Dorothy hopes her book can be useful to scholars as well as to laymen.

She hopes her book will not be read as a nostalgic lament for a world gone by. Instead, she hopes it can lead each reader back to a child buried and half, but not wholly, forgotten—a child who can lead the reader to the children of today and go with them into a safe future before the war lords of the world solve the overpopulation problem with a computerized bang.

Dorothy said goodbye to the schoolroom in 1969. Then she and the author revisited the farm in Sabine Bottom. Stopping first in Point to visit with Sallie (Calloway) Tipton, they took the road south to Woosley and Flats. The road had not changed except to acquire a paved surface. It passed east of the Woosley Schoolhouse (since replaced by a little white church and parsonage). The grove of large oak trees was still there. The same three-strand barbed-wire fence followed the east side of the road. And beyond the fence, the same thicket of scrub oak straggled to the corner where the Williams' gin once stood. Next came the Sam Calloway farm, since owned by Charlie Calloway, youngest of the Sam Calloway boys. The old house had been replaced by a handsome ranch-style house surrounded by modern barns, all enclosed in white board fences. Further south they stopped at the Driggers place. The old boxed-and-stripped, unpainted house had been replaced by a neat white house, and south of the house were cattle chutes for loading cattle for market.

There they stopped the car and sat a while to get their bearings, for the old road had changed. The new road ran straight south toward Sabine River. The old road, which had turned east to the Mills farm, then south to the river, had been closed and was used as a cattle lane to bring cattle up from bottom pasturelands to the chute. They could see a white barn standing about where the old barn had stood. The house was gone. Calloway land, Sallie had told them, now included the old Driggers place, Mills and Malloy farms, and extended almost to the river.

The same blue dome above, however, was anchored to the earth by the same circle of trees. That had not changed. The same autumn sun, halfway up the sky, cast the same angled shadows as small white clouds changed from sheep to elephants to giraffes drifting across the blue sky. And behind the drifting clouds the same eavesdropping Presbyterian God lurked, knowing all their childhood sins. The invisible presence of God, Santa Claus, and Mr. Searsanroebuck belonged to the ultimate reality of that childhood as well as the corn bread and buttermilk on the supper table.

The journey back to Sabine Bottom was a long one. It took Dorothy around the "Round, Round World." Thousands of children traveled with her on the crusade in search of the child-she-was. They recollected the way for her when she got lost and explained the meanings of her recollections. Without their companionship, she could never have returned to that childhood in Sabine Bottom, nor could she have found the author of this book. But the happy companionship and the end eventually became one.